I0446881

Master Candlestick Patterns for Profitable Trading

Joseph T. Miller

All rights reserved. Copyright © 2023 Joseph T. Miller

<u>Funny helpful tips:</u>

Your journey is a reflection of your spirit's resilience; embrace each step with gratitude and pride.

Stay committed to your business vision; it's the guiding light during challenges.

Master Candlestick Patterns for Profitable Trading : Unlock the Secrets of Candlestick Patterns and Boost Your Trading Profits with Expert Strategies

Life advices:

Engage with books that explore existential themes; they delve into the meaning and purpose of life.

Your journey is a reflection of your choices; navigate with intention and purpose.

Introduction

Welcome to this book, a comprehensive guide designed to empower novice traders with the essential knowledge and skills to effectively analyze price action using candlestick charts. By understanding the art of reading individual candlesticks and recognizing key candlestick patterns, you will gain valuable insights into market trends and make informed trading decisions.

In this guide, we will explore the fundamental principles of candlestick charting and how it can be utilized to enhance your trading strategies. We will dive into the world of candlestick patterns, both bullish and bearish, and unveil their significance in determining potential market reversals or continuations. Additionally, we will introduce you to various technical indicators that complement candlestick analysis, providing additional confirmation and validation of your trading decisions.

By the end of this guide, you will have a solid foundation in candlestick trading, enabling you to interpret price action charts with confidence and execute trades based on sound analysis. We emphasize the importance of risk management and the development of a trading plan to ensure long-term success in your trading journey.

Remember, trading involves risk, and it is crucial to approach the markets with discipline, patience, and a well-defined strategy. Candlestick analysis, combined with technical indicators and proper risk management, can significantly enhance your trading performance and increase your probability of success.

Whether you are a novice trader or have some experience in the markets, this book will serve as a valuable resource in your quest to become a proficient trader. So, let's embark on this journey together and unlock the potential of candlestick charting to achieve your trading goals.

Contents

Candlestick Chart Basics

What is a candlestick chart?

A candlestick chart is simply a variation of the well-known line chart that shows us the historical prices of a security. To calculate a standard candlestick chart you need the following price data:

- The Open
- The Close
- The High
- The Low

The idea behind candlestick charts is that the information provided by the difference between a candle high, low, open and close can enable us to better gauge investor sentiment during a given period.

A quick look at a line chart and a candlestick chart will highlight the difference between the two:

Reading individual candlesticks

As I mentioned above, every candlestick chart is populated by individual candlesticks that provide visual confirmation of the high, low, open and close of any given period.

For example, if you are looking at a 5 minute chart, each candlestick will tell you the high price, low price, open price and close price of each 5 minute period.

If you are looking at a daily chart, each candlestick will tell you the high price, low price, open price and close price of each daily period. And so on.

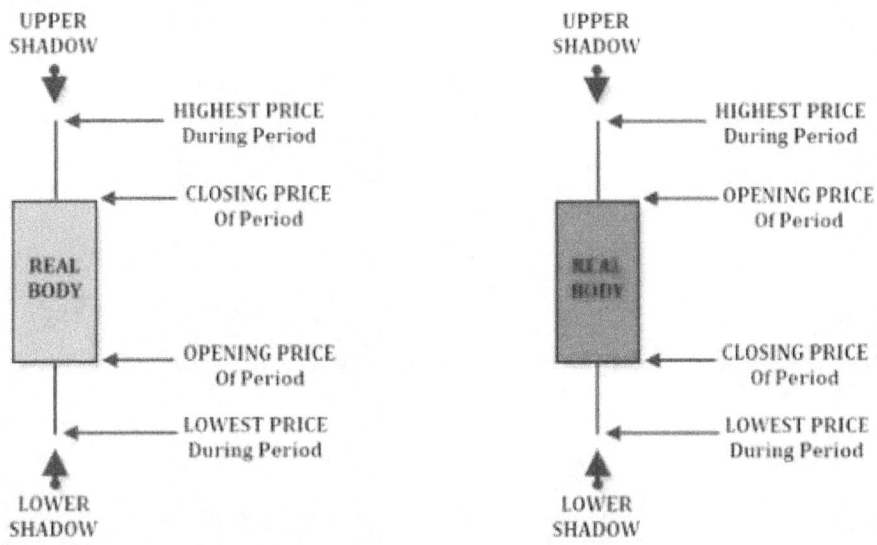

The structure of all candlesticks (irrespective of timeframe) is the same except for one difference:

Green (some charts use white) candlesticks signify that the price has closed higher than it opened during the timeframe period that you are viewing.

Red (some charts use black) candlesticks signify that the price has closed lower than it opened during the timeframe period that you are viewing.

You might reasonably be wondering how a candlestick chart helps us to gauge investor sentiment. If you take a look at the next picture of a line chart and a candlestick chart side-by-side (daily time-frame) you will see.

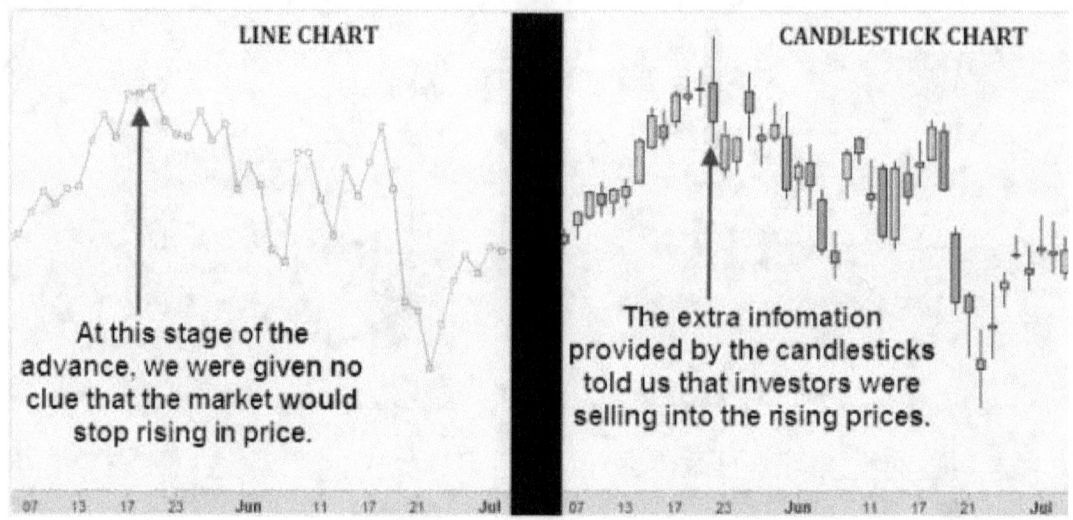

LINE CHART

At this stage of the advance, we were given no clue that the market would stop rising in price.

CANDLESTICK CHART

The extra infomation provided by the candlesticks told us that investors were selling into the rising prices.

The candlestick on the right of our example (highlighted in yellow) helps us gauge investor sentiment because it provides us with visual evidence that significant selling was occurring at the recent highs.

For example, studying the highlighted candle in the above chart we can see that the price opened higher than it closed (indicated by the red colour of the candle), but more importantly we see that even though buyers had pushed the price to new highs (indicated by the upper shadow), by the end of the day sellers had caused the market to close lower than at any other time during the past 3 days.

At its simplest, a red candlestick tells us that there are more sellers than buyers and a green candlestick tells us that there were more buyers than sellers.

The shadows are then providing us with further information because they alert us to periods when price has been controlled by the bulls and then taken back by the bears, or vice versa.

If there are no shadows, we know that either the bulls or the bears were in complete control of the market during the period.

Most importantly, it is the difference between the high and low or the open and close, as well as the lengths of the upper and lower shadows, which provide us with the different candlestick patterns that I will test.

Candlestick Patterns

There are literally hundreds of candlestick patterns and signals available to read about online, any of which can be incorporated into a complete trading strategy. While it would be interesting to test each of them, I will leave that to a more studious author!

It is not my intention to focus too long on the descriptions or psychology that lies behind each pattern either. Steve Nison's book *Japanese Candlestick Charting Techniques* has covered those topics in depth. (If you haven't already read Steve Nison's book, I would urge you to do so.)

Instead of rehashing what has already been written about so eloquently, this book will focus more on the *actual results* of trading the candlestick patterns.

For your information, the patterns which I decided to test were chosen by the popularity with which they are requested on my blog.

Following is a brief description and diagram of the 14 most commonly enquired about candlestick patterns.

Bullish Candlestick Patterns

The bullish engulfing pattern

The bullish engulfing pattern is a reversal pattern that is comprised of two candlesticks. The first day is a down day which indicates that sellers were controlling the market.

The second day opens lower than the first day close and closes higher than the first day open. The second day thus *engulfs* the first day. The precise rules are as follows:

- Price must be in a down-trend.
- The first day must be a down day.
- The second day must open lower than the first days close.

- The second day must close higher than the first days open.

As ever, a picture paints a thousand words.

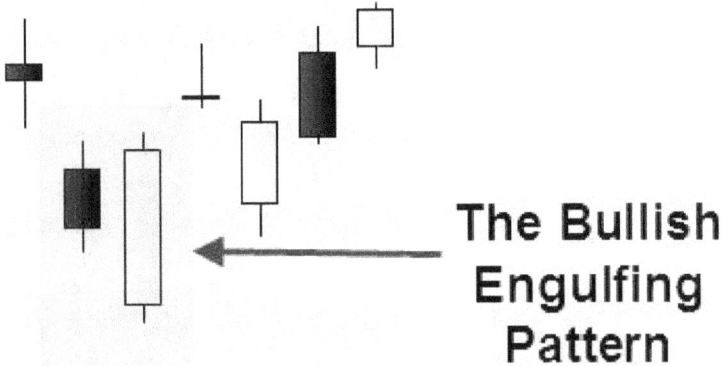

The Bullish Engulfing Pattern

The morning star pattern

The morning star pattern is a 3 day reversal pattern that is supposed to signify the bottom of a downtrend. The rules for a morning star pattern are as follows:

- Price has been in a downtrend.
- The first day of the pattern is a down day (a black or red candle).
- The second day of the pattern gaps down from the first day and creates a candle that doesn't close higher than the first day close.
- The second day is also an indecision day signified by a small real body in relation to its entire day range.
- The third day of the pattern is a large up day (a white or green candle) that closes higher than the half-way point of the first day.

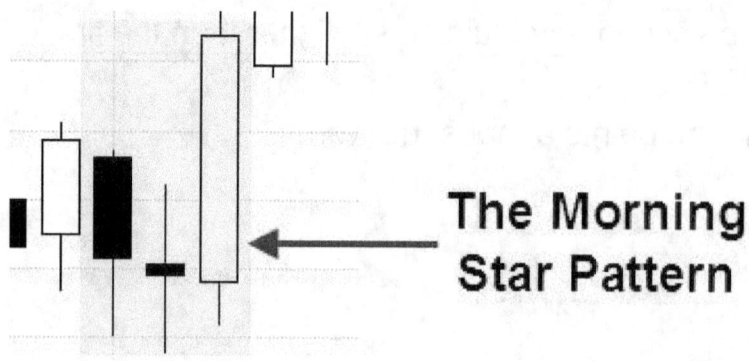

The Morning Star Pattern

The piercing pattern

The piercing pattern is a 2 day pattern that occurs during a downtrend. As with each of our bullish candlestick patterns, the piercing pattern is supposed to signify that a change in investor sentiment has occurred and a reversal is imminent.

The rules for a piercing pattern are as follows:

- Price has been in a downtrend.
- The first day of the pattern is a larger than average down-day.
- The second day of the pattern opens lower than the first day low.
- The second day closes at least halfway into the real body of the first day.
- Note that if the second day closes higher than the first day open the pattern would become a bullish engulfing pattern.

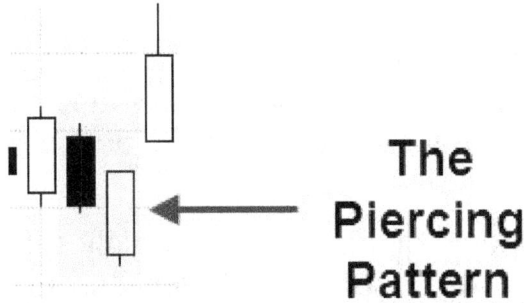

The Piercing Pattern

The hammer pattern

The hammer is a 1 day pattern that occurs during a downtrend. It is similar to the dragonfly doji pattern because the real body of the candlestick is small in relation to the lower shadow.

The difference to the dragonfly doji is that a hammer signal does not need to close at the high of the day nor at the same price as the open. The rules are as follows:

- Price must be in a downtrend.
- The hammer day must have a lower shadow at least 2 times longer than the real body.
- The upper shadow must be 10% less than the entire day range.
- The real body must close in the upper half of the entire day range.

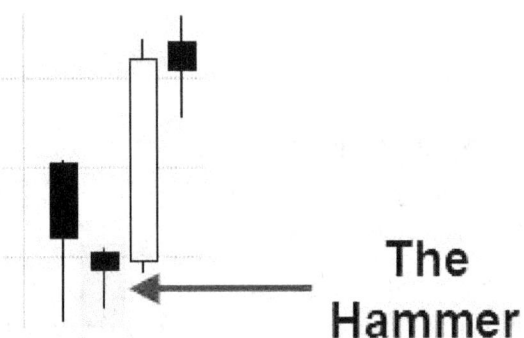

The Hammer

The bullish kicker pattern is the most powerful reversal candlestick pattern of all according to Steven Bigalow, the author of *Profitable Candlestick Trading*. Without first carrying out our own tests, I wouldn't want to vouch for that!

However, the visual aspect of the pattern certainly suggests that a significant change of investor sentiment has occurred.

The bullish kicker signal is a 2 day pattern that is supposed to signify a reversal in a downtrend. The rules of the bullish kicker pattern are as follows:

- Price has been in a downtrend.
- The first day is a down day.
- The second day opens equal to or higher than the first day's high.
- The second day low is higher than the first day high.

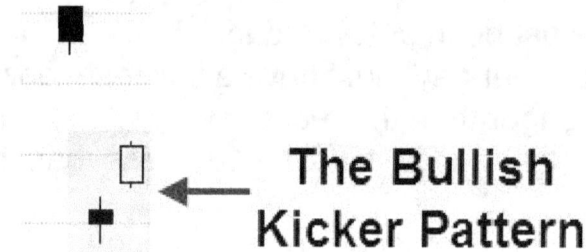

The Bullish Kicker Pattern

The bullish harami pattern

The bullish harami pattern is commonly known in the west as a bullish inside day. It is a 2 day pattern where the first day is a continuation of a downtrend and creates a large down day.

The second day creates a smaller body and the open and closing price are contained within the open and closing price of the first day. The exact criteria are as follows:

- The price must be in a downtrend.
- The first day is a down day.
- The second day opens lower than the first days open and closes higher than the first days close.
- The second day can either be an up day or a down day. (I shall test both rules to determine whether one is better than the other.)
- Some people require that the high and low of the second day are within the first day range as well. (I will also test that rule too.)

The Bullish Harami Pattern

The inverted hammer pattern

The inverted hammer is a 1 day pattern. It is created during a downtrend and is supposed to signal that reversal is imminent.

The inverted hammer shows indecision because even though selling has occurred during the day, at one stage the bulls had been able to push price higher. The exact rules for the inverted hammer pattern are as follows:

- Price has been in a downtrend.
- The upper shadow must be at least 2 times larger than the real body.
- The lower shadow must be less than 10% of the entire day range.

- The real body must be in the lower half of the entire day range.
- The real body has an open and close that are lower than the previous days open and close. (A real body gap down)
- The inverted hammer can be an up day or a down day. It is often written that the inverted hammer as an up day has more bullish implications. (Our tests will tell us of that is true.)

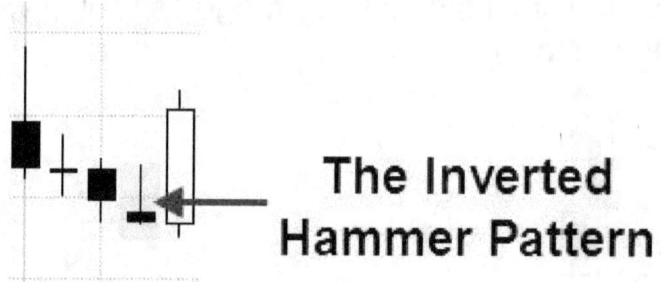

The Inverted Hammer Pattern

Bearish Candlestick Patterns

The bearish engulfing pattern

The bearish engulfing pattern is simply the reverse of a bullish engulfing pattern. The bearish engulfing pattern occurs in the context of an up-trend and is supposed to signify that sellers (bears) are taking control of the market away from the buyers (bulls).

The bearish engulfing pattern is a 2 day signal that requires the following rules:

- Price must be in an up-trend.
- The first day must be an up day.
- The second day must open higher than the first days close.
- The second day must close lower than the first days open.

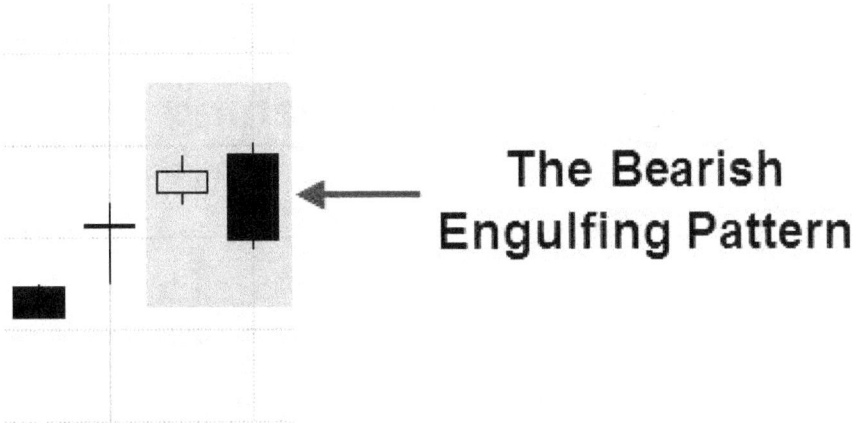

The Bearish Engulfing Pattern

The evening star pattern

The evening star pattern is a 3 day reversal pattern that is supposed to signify the bottom of a downtrend. It is the exact opposite setup to the morning star pattern. The rules for an evening star pattern are as follows:

- Price has been in an uptrend.
- The first day of the pattern is an up day.
- The second day of the pattern gaps up from the first day and creates a candle that doesn't close lower than the first day close.
- The second day is also an indecision day signified by a small real body in relation to its entire day range.
- The third day of the pattern is a large down day that closes lower than the half-way point of the first day.

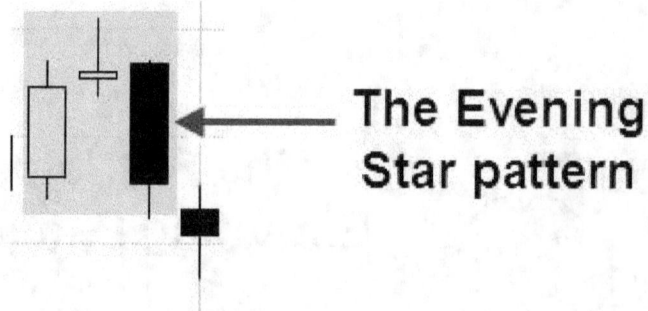

The Evening Star pattern

The dark cloud cover pattern

The dark cloud cover pattern is a 2 day pattern that occurs during an up-trend. As with each of our bearish candlestick patterns, the dark cloud cover pattern is supposed to signify that a change in investor sentiment has occurred and a reversal of the existing up-trend is imminent.

The rules for a dark cloud cover pattern are as follows:

- Price has been in an up-trend.
- The first day of the pattern is a larger than average up day.
- The second day of the pattern opens higher than the first day.
- The second day closes at least halfway into the real body of the first day.
- Note that if the second day closes lower than the first day open the pattern would become a bearish engulfing pattern.

The Dark Cloud Cover Pattern

The hanging man

The hanging man is a 1 day pattern that occurs during an up-trend. It is the exact same setup as the hammer but because it is supposed to signify a reversal of an uptrend and not a downtrend it has a different name.

The rules are as follows:

- Price must be in an up-trend.
- The hanging man day must have a lower shadow at least 2 times longer than the real body.
- The upper shadow must be 10% less than the entire day range.
- The real body must close in the upper half of the entire day range.

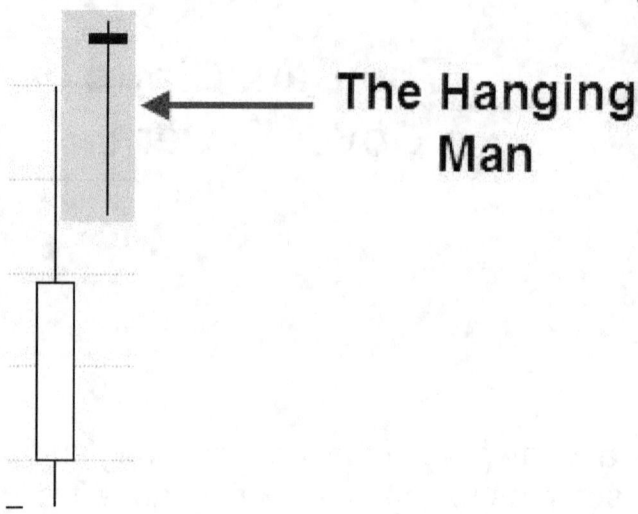

The Hanging Man

The bearish kicker pattern is a 2 day pattern that is supposed to signify a significant change of investor sentiment and precede a reversal of an uptrend.

The rules of the bearish kicker pattern are as follows:

- Price has been in an up-trend.
- The first day is an up day.
- The second day opens equal to or lower than the first day's low.
- The second day high is lower than the first day low.

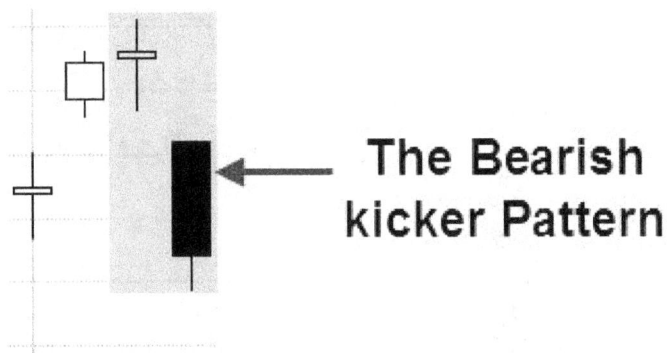

The Bearish
kicker Pattern

The bearish harami pattern

The bearish harami pattern is commonly known in the west as a bearish inside day. It is a 2 day pattern where the first day is a continuation of an up-trend and creates a large up day.

The second day creates a smaller body and the open and closing price are contained within the open and closing price of the first day. The bearish harami is exactly the same pattern as a bullish harami pattern except that it occurs during an up-trend.

The exact criteria are as follows:

- The price must be in an up-trend.
- The first day is an up day.
- The second day opens lower than the first days close and closes higher than the first days open.
- The second day can either be an up day or a down day. (I shall test both rules to determine whether one is better than the other.)
- Some people require that the high and low of the second day are within the first day range as well. (As I will with the bullish harami pattern, I will also test that rule too.)

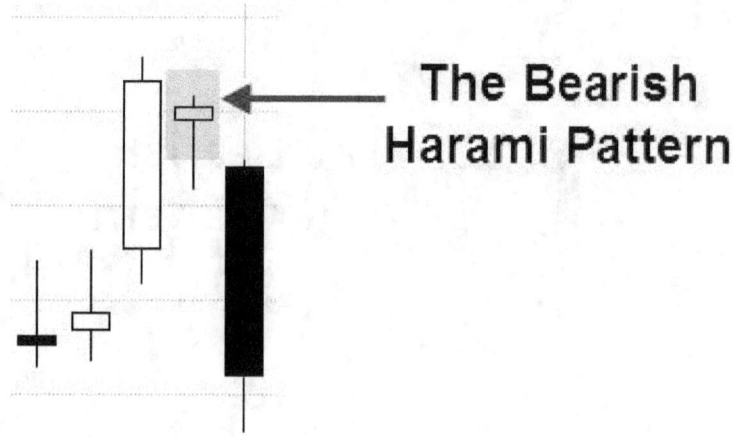

The Bearish Harami Pattern

The shooting star pattern

The shooting star pattern is a 1 day pattern that is the same as the inverted hammer except that it occurs during an up-trend.

The shooting star shows indecision because even though buying has occurred during the day, the bears have taken control of the market to close the price in the lower half of the day's range. The exact rules for the shooting star pattern are as follows:

- Price has been in an up-trend.
- The upper shadow must be at least 2 times larger than the real body.
- The lower shadow must be less than 10% of the entire day range.
- The real body must be in the lower half of the entire day range.
- The shooting star can be an up day or a down day. But it is often written that the shooting star as a down day has more bearish implications. (Our tests will tell us of that is true.)

The Shooting Star Pattern

You now know how to identify each of the major candlestick patterns that we shall be testing in later chapters.

In the next chapter I will explain the indicators that I will be using in a bid to improve the efficacy of each candlestick pattern.

As I mentioned in the introduction, I am a strong proponent of having *specific* trading rules because without them you will often find yourself taking trades based on nothing more than a gut feeling.

If you are guilty of trading on emotion instead of logic, the next chapter will lay out the tools that are guaranteed to help you better improve the regularity with which you follow a trading plan that you know to have a positive expectancy.

Technical Indicators

Technical Indicators are based upon mathematical calculations that include price, volume and momentum. There are literally 100's of technical indicators at a traders disposal, each of which offering a chance to view price from a different perspective.

It is often written that technical indicators are able to forecast price changes. I am extremely dubious whether that is true, however, I do believe that technical indicators are a vital component of a technical trading strategy and that's because without them it is very hard to quantify your rules.

To give you an example, presume that you regularly trade hammer candlestick patterns and that you have recently noticed that when a market seems to be very strong, the pattern stops working so well.

You'd like to know whether a very strong market is a bad time to trade hammer patterns, but how? That's what technical indicators are for.

In the above example, you could apply a ROC indicator to your charts and test all hammer patterns with and without a ROC filter of your choosing.

Without using technical indicators, it can be very hard to quantify anything that you might have noticed about the market and think might give you an edge.

Take another example, the following chart is a naked price chart.

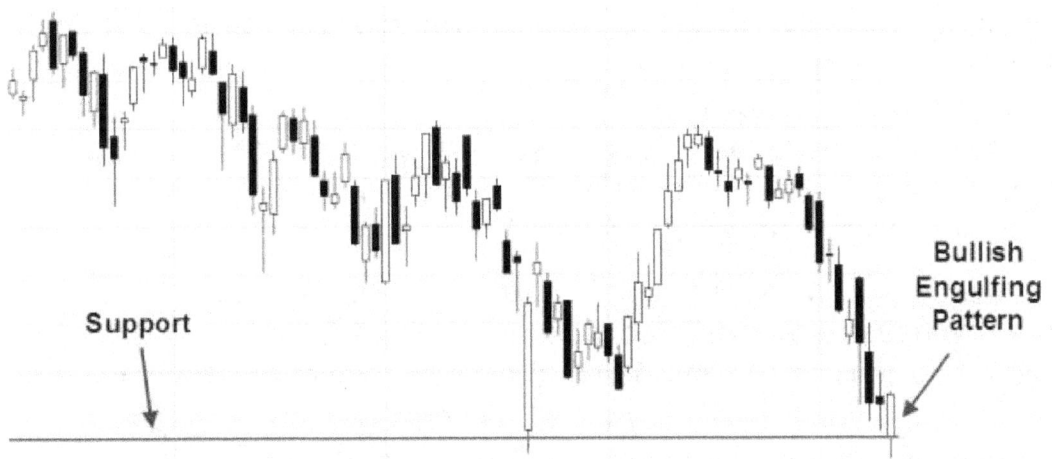

Support

Bullish
Engulfing
Pattern

A valid candlestick pattern at support is a classic buy signal, but how often will this set-up produce a winning trade?

It's hard to say because one trader might see support where I have highlighted it in the above picture, whereas another trader might see support in a slightly different place.

Slightly different
support

Over a thousand trades, the small change in where a trader sees support can have a huge impact on the profits or losses made.

My argument is that if you can't follow the rules to a strategy which involves something as simple as a binary decision (which is what you have with mechanical trading strategies), you have even less chance of following the rules to a strategy which involves multiple areas of subjectivity (which is what you have if trading from trend-lines or similarly subjective patterns).

A trader will begin to question her strategy when the last ten trades in a row have been losers because she will have no idea if it's because she is finding support in the wrong place, or whether it's because the volatility of the market has changed, or perhaps it's because the pattern only works during a broader market up-trend.

There are 100's of reasons for why a trader might have had 10 losing trades in a row, but without being able to test a strategy before taking it live, it is hard to know what those reasons might be.

Imagine that we knew only 40% of bullish engulfing patterns worked when the market was not volatile. Would you take the trade from the above chart? If you're not sure I understand.

After all, is the market from our image volatile or not?

Again, this is where technical indicators come in handy. The next chart is the same as the one above, but I have added the historical volatility indicator. We have a simple rule that says 'don't trade bullish engulfing patterns unless the market is volatile'.

We then need to define volatile. For examples sake let's say that a historical volatility indicator above 40 is telling us that the market is volatile and if the indicator is below 40 the market is not volatile.

Presume that we have tested the bullish engulfing pattern on 1000's of different stocks and we know that if the historical volatility indicator is below 40, the pattern has less than a 40% chance of producing a profitable trade – and the average losses are larger than the average gains.

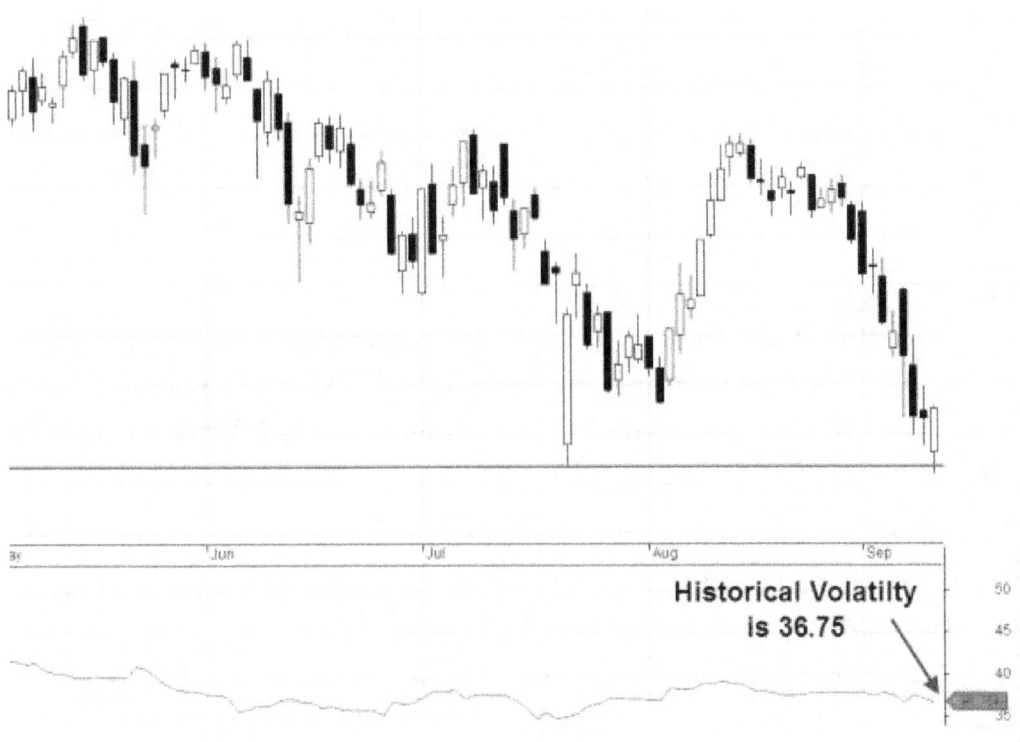

Historical Volatilty
is 36.75

My question to you now is would you buy the above stock at the current price? I hope you said no because if you didn't, it is 60% likely that you just took a trade that will lose you money over the long run.

In my other book I go to great lengths explaining a trading expectancy and why the win rate of a trading strategy is far less important than how much you win when you're right and how much you lose when you're wrong.

So if we know that trading the bullish engulfing candlestick when the market is not volatile has a negative expectancy, but trading them when the market is volatile has a positive expectancy, I think we can both agree that only trading bullish engulfing candlesticks when a market is volatile would be the best course of action.

Remember that it's only by incorporating technical indicators into our strategies that we are able to test such differences without any ambiguity creeping into our decision making process.

Technical indicators are not predictive

I think that the majority of people who shun technical indicators do so because they have had bad experiences when using them to trade, and I think that nine times out of ten, those bad experiences were a result of being taught that technical indicators have predictive powers.

They do not!

Technical indicators will not tell you what the market is going to do next. If they could, we'd all be rich by now.

But they are invaluable because they give us a means for clearly defining our trading rules and better still, they provide us the opportunity to test our strategies using the exact same rules that we can then use to trade live.

The confidence gained from knowing exactly how well a particular strategy has performed in the past should not be underestimated.

Please understand that I do not doubt that there are traders who can look at a naked price chart and know a good trade when they see one. But for the majority of people, the less uncertainty they have when making a trade, the better the outcome will be.

To provide you with a set of specific rules and filters that can be applied to each of the candlestick patterns in this book, I will be testing each pattern with a range of the most popular technical indicators and indicator parameters.

The technical indictor filters which are used during the tests.

When formulating how I would structure this book, I realised quickly that if I were to present the results of **every** pattern and **every** filter that I tested, the book would be 1000's of pages long and contain ridiculous amounts of graphs and tables – but little actionable advice.

I read books as well as write them, and seeing that I would have no interest in reading a book that contained 1000's of graphs, I figured that you wouldn't want to read one either!

Instead, the next few pages will explain each of the filters that I applied during the tests. Rest assured that if any of the following filters improved the patterns tested, I will explain so in the relevant chapter – if I don't mention the following filters during the individual pattern chapters, it simply means that they didn't improve the candlestick patterns that are tested.

Following is the description of each technical indicator filter that I will apply to the different candlestick patterns, as well as an explanation of the different parameters used in the tests.

Moving averages

Moving averages are probably one of the most widely known technical indicators. To calculate the moving average we simply decide upon the look-back period that we are going to use and calculate the average price during that period.

In testing our candlestick patterns, I wanted to know whether patterns were improved by only trading them above or below a range of different moving averages.

The parameters of the moving average tested were set between 10 and 200 days in increments of 10.

E.G, the 10 MA was tested, the 20 MA was tested, and the 30 MA was tested and so on….

For example,

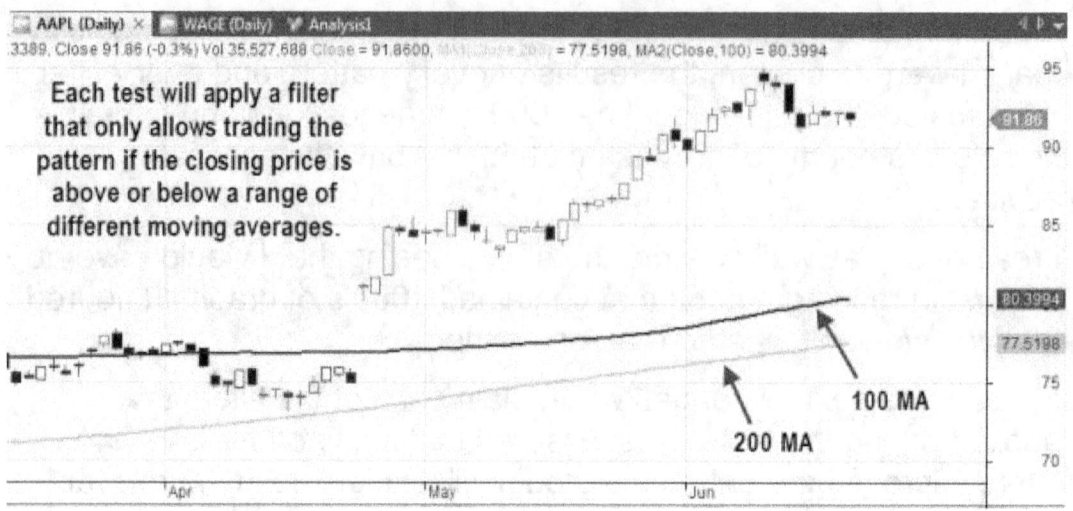

AAPL (Daily) × WAGE (Daily) Analysis1

3389, Close 91.86 (-0.3%) Vol 35,527,688 Close = 91.8600, MA(Close, 200) = 77.5198, MA2(Close, 100) = 80.3994

Each test will apply a filter that only allows trading the pattern if the closing price is above or below a range of different moving averages.

100 MA

200 MA

91.86

95
90
85
80.3994
77.5198
75
70

Apr   May   Jun

Another filter that I apply to each of the patterns is based upon the notion that patterns work better if they occur *at* a certain moving average. The idea being that the moving averages work as a 'dynamic support or resistance zone'.

To test the above filter I applied a range of moving averages set between 10 and 200 days in increments of 10. The filter that I applied would only allow trading a pattern if they occurred within 1% of each particular moving average.

For example,

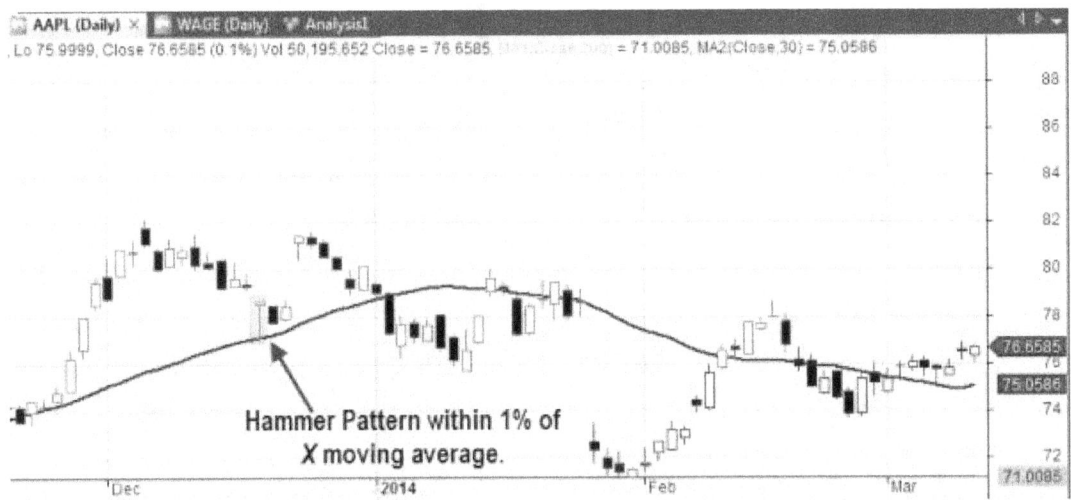

Lo 75.9999, Close 76.6585 (0.1%) Vol 50,195,652 Close = 76.6585 = 71.0085, MA2(Close,30) = 75.0586

Hammer Pattern within 1% of
X moving average.

The final way that I used the moving average was in my definition of the broader market environment.

To define a broad market up-trend I applied 2 moving averages to the SPY. The first moving average (FastMA) will be 40 periods and the second moving average (SlowMA) will be 120 periods.

Trend definition

- The market (as gauged by the SPY) is in an **up-trend when the 40 day moving average is above the 120 day moving average.**
- The market (as gauged by the SPY) is in a **down-trend when the 40 day moving average is beneath the 120 day moving average.**

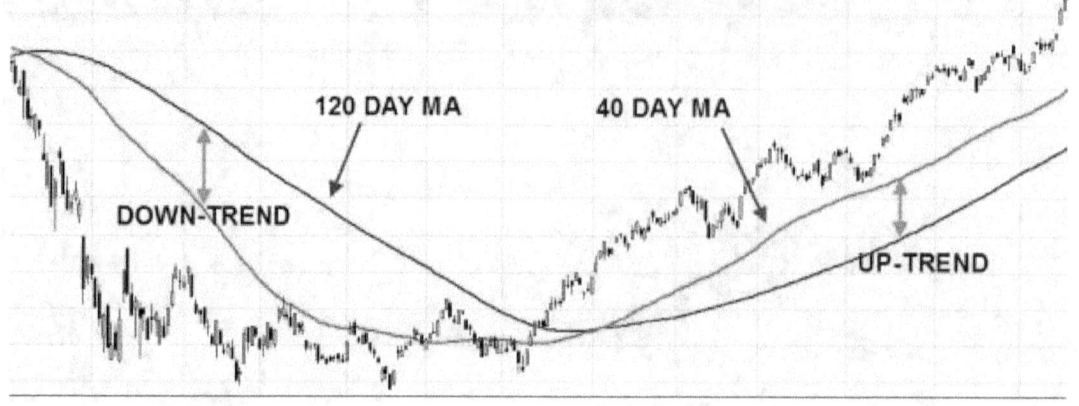

Historical volatility

The historical volatility indicator plots the annualized standard deviation of daily returns. In simpler terms, stocks that have small percentage moves have a low volatility and stocks that have larger percentage moves have higher volatility.

The more volatile a market is, the larger the daily price moves are in percentage terms.

It will be of particular interest to test whether stocks with higher volatility readings will produce better reversal signals when we test our various candlestick patterns. For your information, the look-back period that I will use for the HV indicator is 60 trading days (roughly 1 QTR).

Volatile definition

- Stocks are considered **volatile if the historical volatility indicator is over 40.**
- Stocks are considered to **not be volatile if the historical volatility indicator is under 40.**

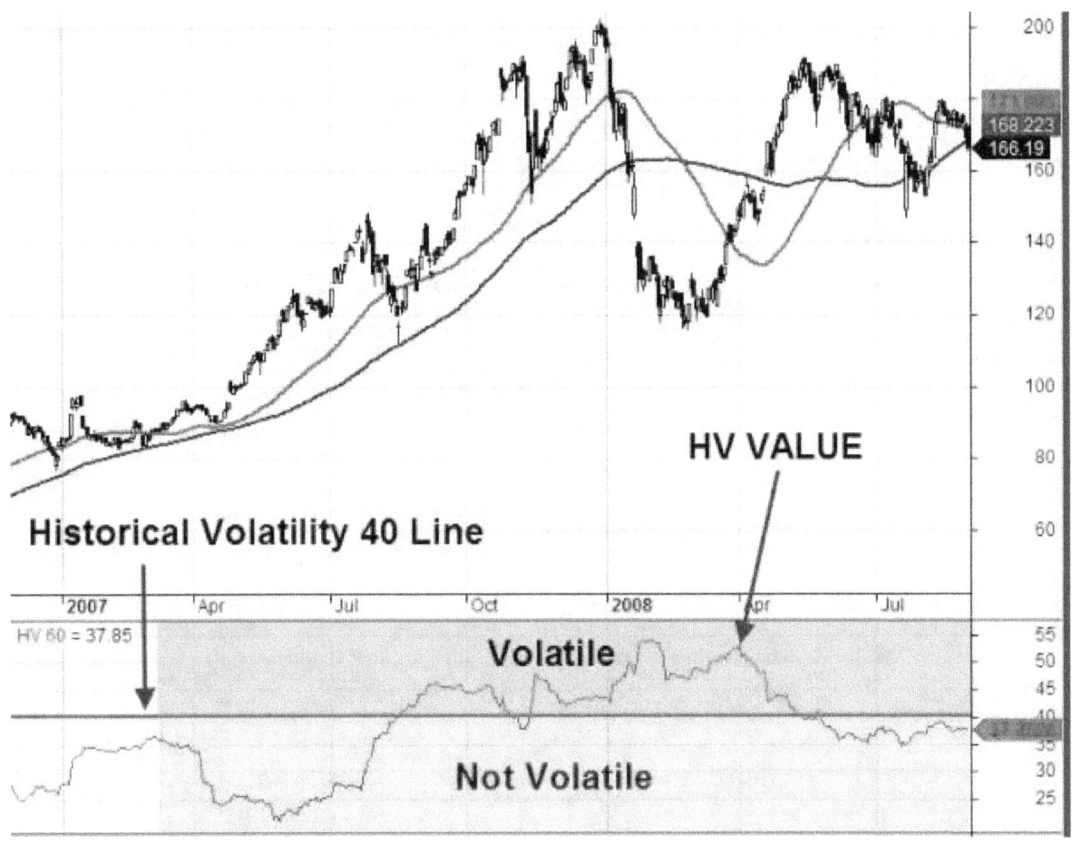

Relative Strength Index

The relative strength index (known as RSI) is an oscillating indictor that measures the strength of price moves in relation to previous price moves. There are countless websites online that explain the exact calculations so I won't bore you with detail.

The key point is that the RSI indicator can help us quantify how weak or strong a market has comparatively been during the past **x** days.

The textbook way to use the RSI indicator is to look for reversals when the RSI is overbought or oversold.

To test whether patterns perform better when a stock is overbought or oversold (depending upon whether the pattern is bearish or bullish), I applied a RSI filter (set to 8 days) to each pattern that was tested.

The filter then tested each bullish pattern when the RSI was below 30 or each bearish pattern when the RSI was above 70.

For example:

Another way that I used the RSI was in my definition of the broader market environment. It will be of particular interest to see whether each candlestick pattern performs better during very strong market trends, or weaker to sideways markets.

To define these various market conditions I apply a combination of the RSI and the 40/120 day moving averages to the SPY.

Trend strength definition for up-trends

- **Strong up-trend** when 40 day MA > 120 day MA and RSI is over 70.
- **Long-term up-trend/short-term pullback** when 40 day MA > 120 day MA and RSI is below 30.

Trend strength definition for down-trends

- **Strong down-trend** when 40 day MA < 120 day MA and RSI is below 30.
- **Long-term down-trend/short-term rally** when 40 day MA < 120 day MA and RSI is above 70.

Stochastics Oscillator

The stochastics oscillator is another indicator which is commonly used to define whether a market is either overbought or oversold. The common definition being that if the Stochastic is below 20 a market is oversold and if the stochastic is above 80 a market is overbought.

For each of the patterns tested in the book I applied a stochastic filter (set at 12,3,3) which would only permit bullish patterns when the stochastic reading was below 20 or bearish patterns if the stochastic reading was above 80.

The stochastics filter would only allow bullish patterns if they happened when the stochastic was below 20

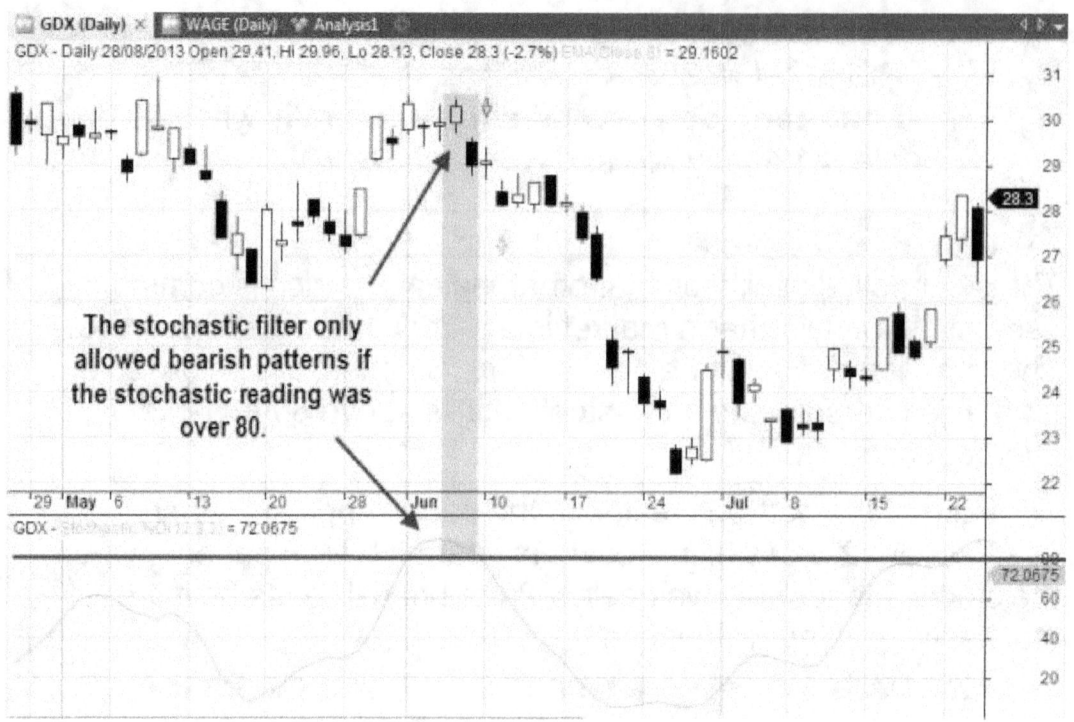

The stochastic filter only allowed bearish patterns if the stochastic reading was over 80.

Bollinger Bands and Keltner Bands

The Bollinger and Keltner bands are two well-known technical indicators which can be used to plot bands (sometimes called envelopes) above and below price. The bands are then often used to identify when a market has moved too far above or below its mean price.

In the case of the Bollinger bands, the bands are calculated by adding or subtracting 2 standard deviations from a 20 day moving average.

The Keltner channels are calculated by adding or subtracting 2 * the value of ATR(20) to a 20 day exponential moving average.

For each of the patterns tested in this book I will apply a filter that only allows bullish patterns if they occur beneath a lower band or only allows bearish patterns if they occur above an upper band.

The following 2 charts illustrate that the Bollinger bands and Keltner channels serve a similar purpose:

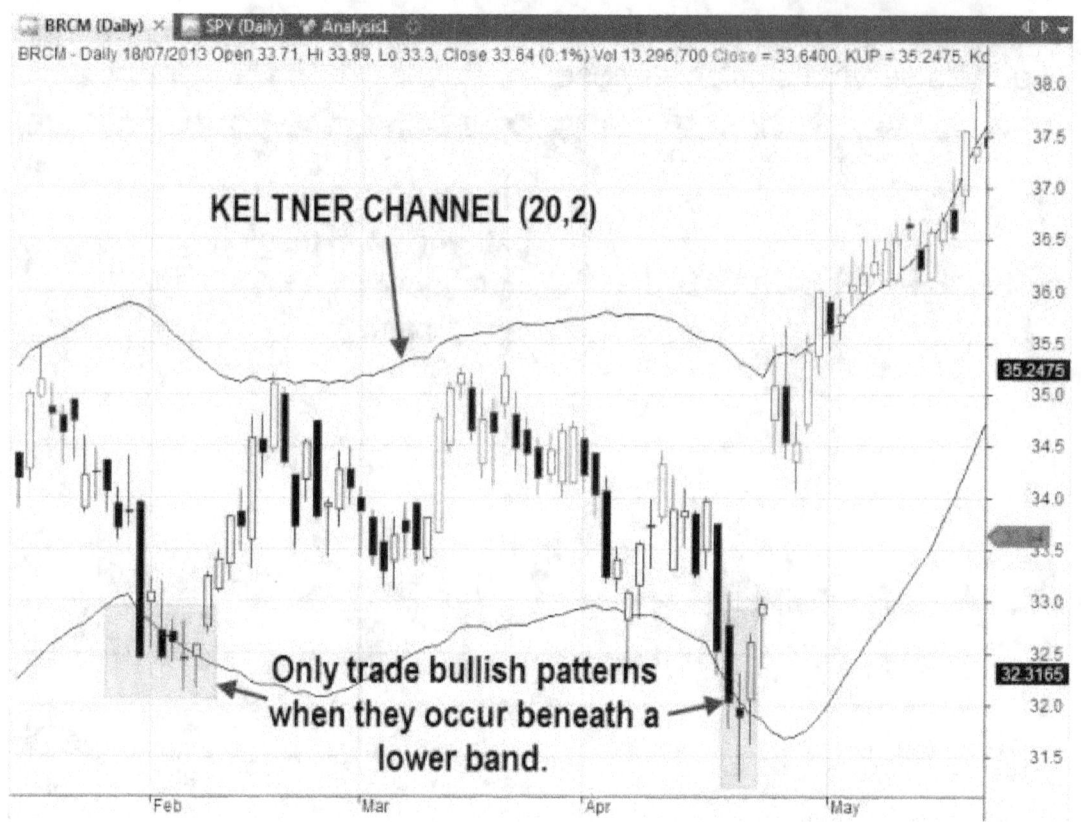

BRCM (Daily) × SPY (Daily) Analysis1

BRCM - Daily 18/07/2013 Open 33.71, Hi 33.99, Lo 33.3, Close 33.64 (0.1%) Vol 13,296,700 Close = 33.6400, KUP = 35.2475, Kd

KELTNER CHANNEL (20,2)

Only trade bullish patterns
when they occur beneath a
lower band.

Rate of Change %

The ROC % is a simple indicator which tells us how strong or weak a stock has been over a given period.

When applying the ROC filter to each of the patterns in this book, I tested a range of parameters that were set between 10 and 300 days (tested in increments of 10), and I tested a range of ROC thresholds that were set between -25% and +25% (tested in increments of 5%).

For example, a test might include a filter that would only allow a pattern if the 20 day ROC was above 5%, another filter would only allow a pattern if the 50 day ROC was below -15%, and so on.

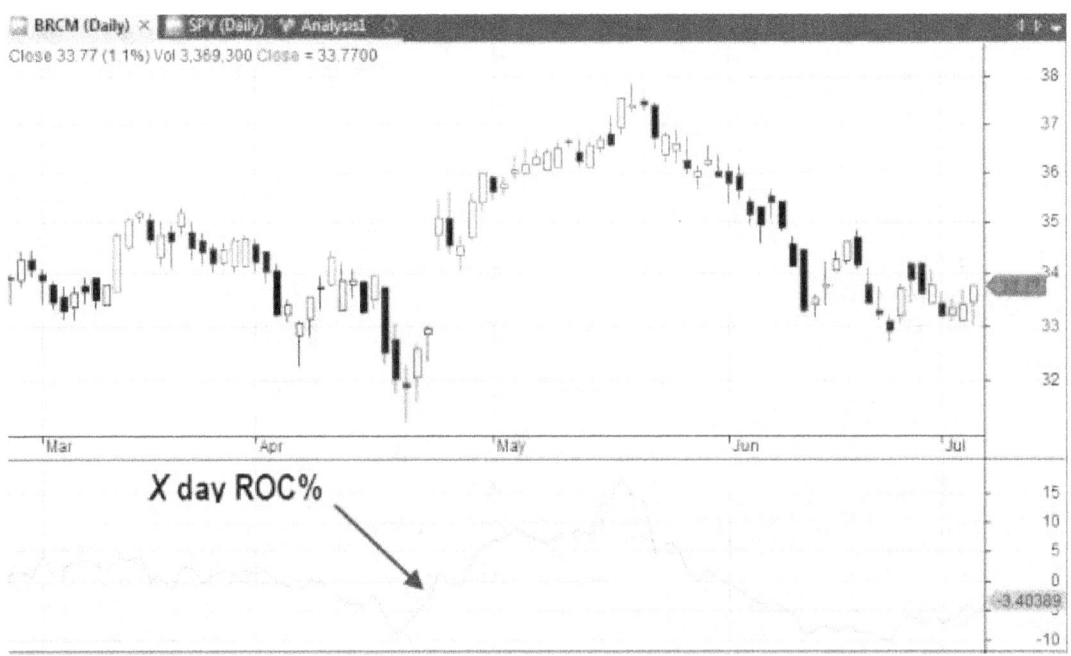

X day ROC%

ConnorsRSI

The final indicator filter that I tested was the ConnorRSI. To learn more about the ConnorsRSI, you can read this article.

To summarise, the ConnorsRSI is a momentum oscillator that is used to gauge whether a market is overbought or oversold. The neat aspect of the ConnorsRSI is that it combines the relative strength of price changes, the relative momentum of price changes and the consecutive number of up or down days into a single formula.

For each of the patterns tested in this book I will apply a filter that only allows bullish patterns if they occur when the CSRI reading is below anywhere between 50 and 5 (tested in increments of 5), or only allows bearish patterns if they occur when the CSRI reading is above anywhere between 50 and 95 (tested in increments of 5).

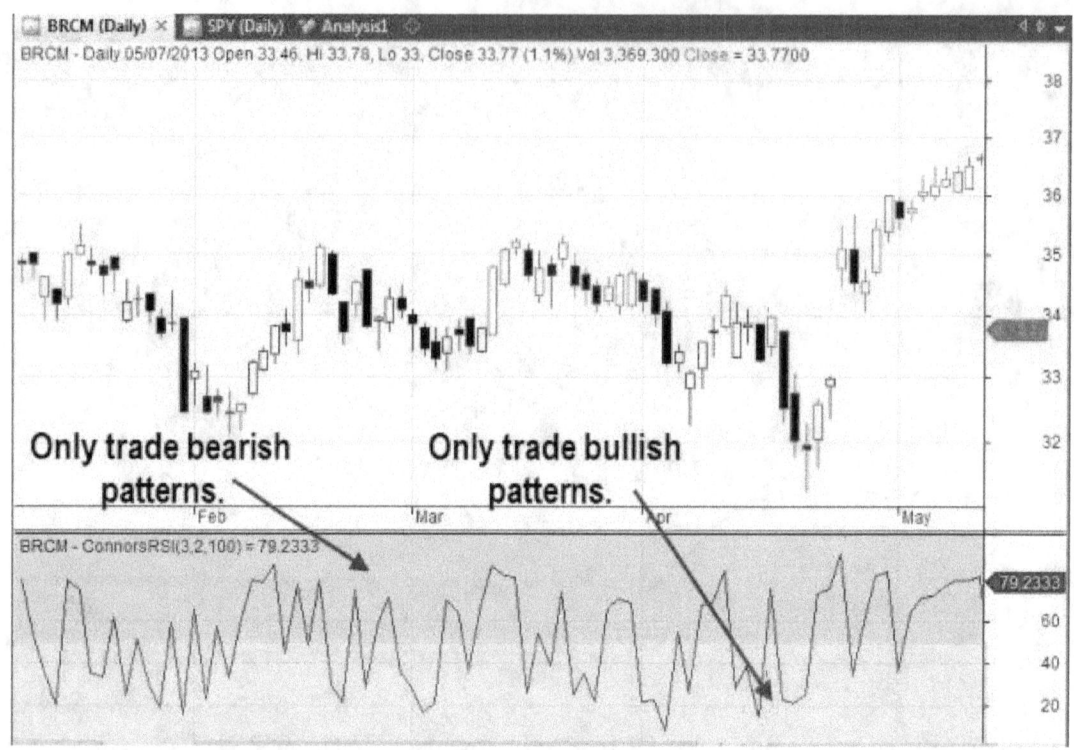

Conclusions

I should reiterate at this point that the technical indicators which I have described are not magic bullets that are going to prevent losing trades. I am testing these particular indicators and settings because they are some of the most well-known.

The decision to use these particular indicators is in no way an endorsement of their efficacy.

The purpose of this book is to test the most popular candlestick patterns and attempt to identify the market conditions where each pattern has the greatest chance of being profitable.

If the above filters help us to do that, I'll let you know…If the above filters don't improve the performance of the patterns, next time that you are on a trading forum and someone says that "so and so works better when the stochastics are oversold", you'll know that they are probably talking nonsense!

Testing the Candlestick Patterns

Candlestick patterns are presumed to offer traders an effective way to trade the markets with a high probability of finding winning trades. However, before we blindly accept that a pattern is going to help us make money, we must first see the evidence.

Universal back-test configuration:

The tests I shall carry out in the next 14 chapters will each have the following criteria:

- All patterns will be tested on a survivor-free database that includes all stocks listed on the Rusell3000 as reported by Norgate premium data services.
- Only stocks that are $5.00 and above will be tested.
- Only stocks with an average daily volume (20) of at least 100,000 shares will be tested.
- Each pattern will be tested on a sample of data between 01/01/2004 and 28/02/14.
- A buy and hold strategy during our sample period produced a 67.13% return with a maximum drawdown of 56.44%. The CAR/MDD was 0.09.
- All positions will be entered at the open of the day following the pattern unless stated otherwise.
- The default holding period for all positions will be 5 days.
- Whenever we have more signals to enter the market than are allowed by our maximum open positions rule, we rank the stocks by order of the highest volume first.

The tests in this book are intended to provide you with an honest appraisal of how each particular pattern has performed in the past and how different market environments can impact that performance.

I have intentionally avoided testing on out of sample data because my aim is to show you what has worked in the past, not what has a statistically significant likelihood of working in the future.

The final strategy rules in this book include filters and pattern rules that have been through an element of optimization. The reason being is that I wanted you to know the **best** possible results that you might achieve from trading candlestick patterns.

In reality, the final strategy rules in this book will likely perform far worse in the future than they have in the past.

A final point, while it would be interesting to test the win rate and average gain/loss of every single pattern that occurred during our sample period, I think that the results would be of little use.

In reality, you would not be able to trade every pattern in live markets because there would be too many of them.

To better replicate how one might trade the different patterns, I have tested all patterns with a hypothetical $30,000 account.

Tests include a rule which only allows 5 maximum open positions at a time, with each position being worth a maximum of $6000. No compounding is applied to the position-sizing formula.

I have also included transaction costs to be reflective of those incurred with Interactive Brokers. Slippage is not factored in the results.

Back-Testing questions

Why have I chosen the particular indicator settings?

I wanted to be sure that these tests were more about the candlestick patterns and less about the indicator settings. Although I test a variety of different indicator thresholds, the majority of indicator settings are left as default.

Furthermore, I have only included indicator filters in the final strategies when the parameters/thresholds used were relatively robust.

To give you an example of parameter robustness, the following example can be made:

Parameter robustness

> *"Practically speaking, a robust trading strategy is one that produces consistently good results across a broad set of parameter (input) values applied to many different markets tested for many years"*
>
> \- Perry J Kaufmann

When developing trading rules it can be very easy to optimize the parameters that you use and curve fit your strategy rules to the past data. To avoid this, we can check the robustness of the parameter or threshold values by making small changes to them and comparing the results produced across a number of test runs.

For example, suppose that you have a trading strategy which is improved by adding a moving average filter which only permits a trade if the closing price is above a 100 day moving average.

To check the robustness of the rule, you would run the same test again, but instead of using a 100 day moving average, you would use 60,70,80,90,110,120,130,140 and so on.

If the 100 day moving average filter is robust, you should not see a significant difference in the results produced by each test run. If you do see significant changes in the results, it is probable that the 100 day moving average filter has been curve fit to the past data.

For example, the following table shows the results of a strategy after applying a variety of moving average filters with a range of parameter values (days used in the moving average calculation) set between 10 and 190.

The *y* axis plots the net profit produced by each run and the *x* axis plots the moving average parameter that was used.

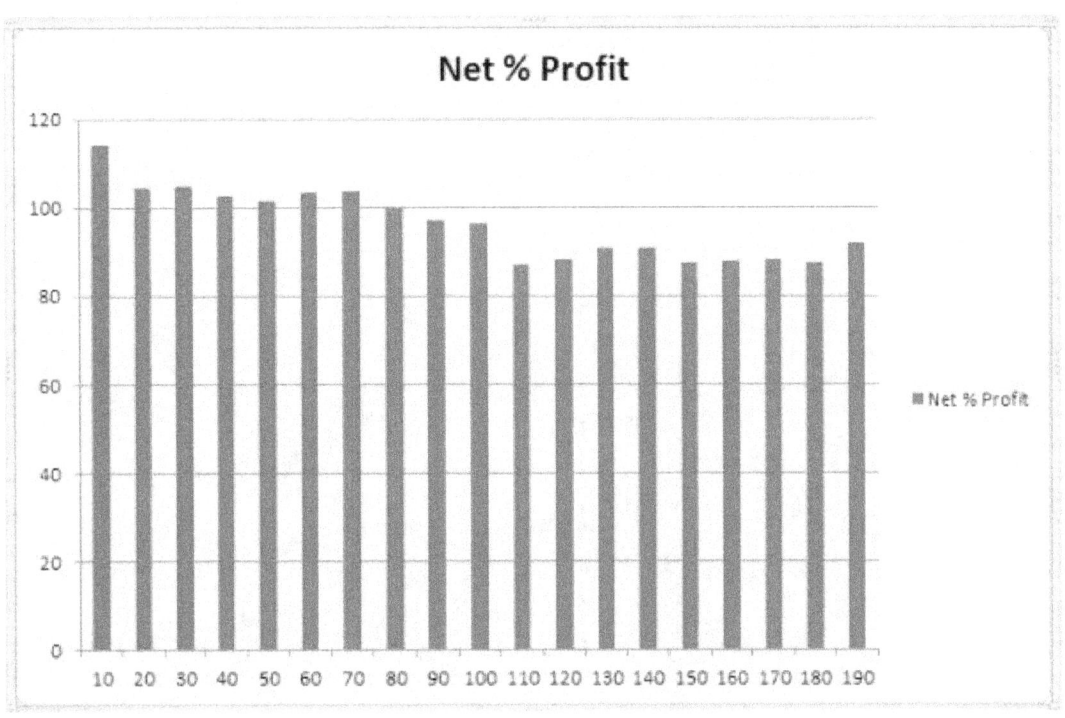

Notice that each of the test runs produced similar results, irrespective of the particular moving average that we used. In the above example, we can presume that our 100 day moving average filter is robust.

If the 100 day moving average filter were not robust, the results of our tests would be more like this:

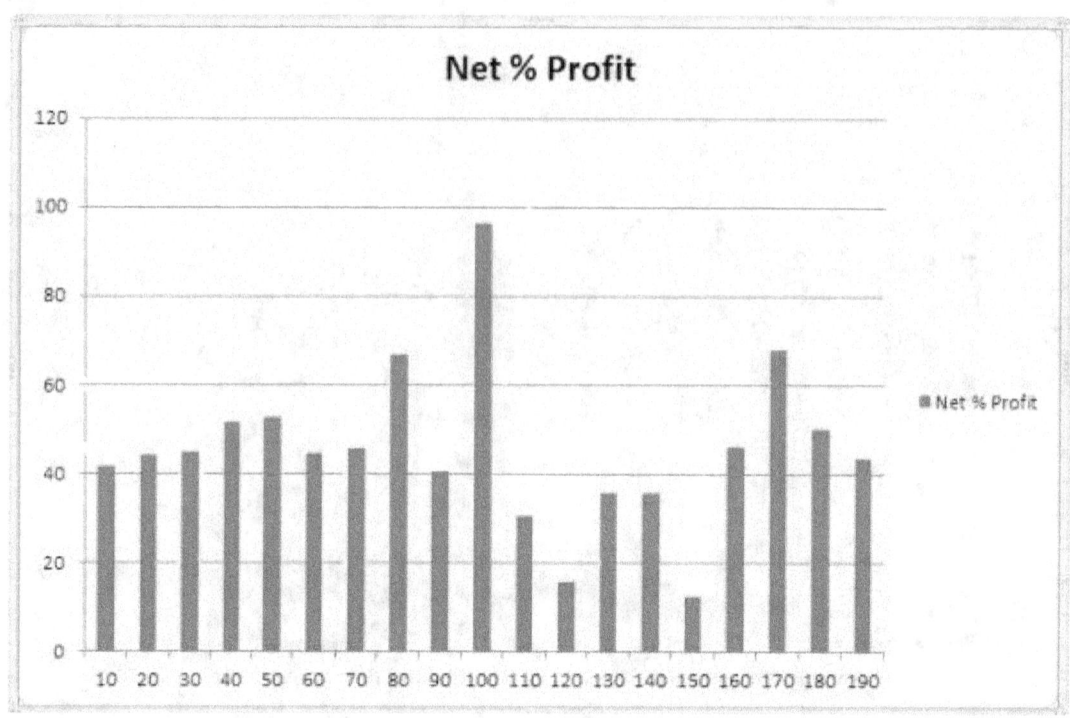

In the above example, we can see that the net profits produced by the 100 day moving average are likely to be the result of outliers in the data.

If we still wanted to use a moving average filter in our final strategy, we would instead choose the 50 day moving average because it is from a far more stable region of the parameter thresholds that were tested. (Meaning that neighbouring values produced similar returns)

Are delisted stocks included in the database?

The strategies in this book will be tested on all stocks which existed on the Russell3000 *at the moment in time of the trade*. In other words, the tests in this book do not suffer from survivorship bias and delisted stocks *are included* in the database.

Even still, I always recommend that you presume the returns produced during a test are the **absolute best** that you can expect a strategy to make if taken live.

In reality, it often pays to presume that any test results will be **significantly** worse when taken live. Only after trading a strategy on unseen data and for a long enough time to build a significant sample size, can you have true confidence in the rules and expected returns.

Why have I have only tested on stocks over $5.00 and with at least 100,000 shares daily average volume?

The basic idea behind candlestick patterns is that they provide a visual clue that market sentiment has changed. It is therefore important that the markets we look at have a fair degree of participation.

We also need the liquidity for our tests to be realistic. Stocks priced under $5.00 that are traded on light volume are more likely to have wider spreads and because we do not include slippage in our test returns, it would be wise to stick with the stocks we know to have a higher chance of getting filled at the price we'd want if taking our strategies live.

Why have I chosen the particular dates used in the sample period?

Markets are constantly evolving and adapting, strategies might work in one market environment but not in another. It would therefore be dangerous to test our patterns on a single period with a single market environment.

For example, if I tested all bullish harami candles on a sample period that was a raging bull market, the returns would probably be fantastic, simply because buying the market at any time wold have likely produced a winning trade.

We couldn't really infer that the performance was necessarily to do with the bullish harami pattern itself.

Markets move one of 3 ways. Up, down or sideways. We therefore need a sample period that includes at least some time when the market was up, down or sideways.

If we look at the period that I have chosen to test the patterns (01/01/2004 – 28/02/2014), we can see that the market (as gauged by the SPY) had multiple periods when it was trending up, moving sideways and trending down. We therefore know that each pattern that we test will have had to endure each of those different market conditions.

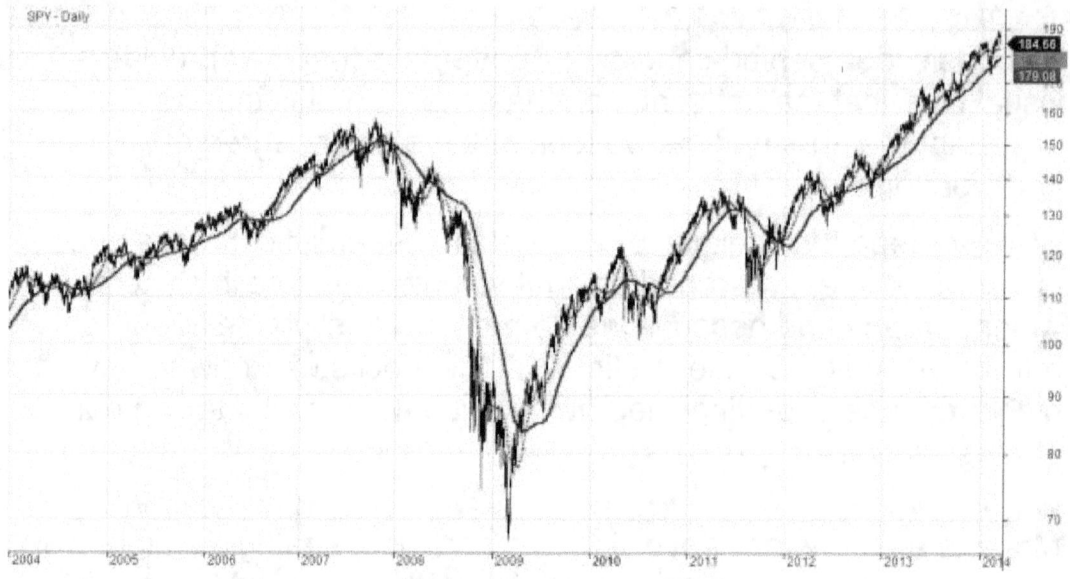

Why do entries occur on the day following a signal?

The short answer is that it's easier to execute such a system in practice. Each evening we would scan our charts for the pattern we wanted to trade in the current market environment and we would know what trades we needed to place the following morning.

It's also worth pointing out that candlestick patterns are only known at the *close* because the close price is one of the data-points that is used to create the candle.

It is therefore impractical to test a strategy that required entering on the close because we have no way of knowing what pattern has occurred, until *after* the close.

For example, if our test rules required that we bought all bullish engulfing patterns at the close, we would be simulating knowledge that in a live market we could not have. We would have to wait for the close to know whether there has been a bullish engulfing pattern or not.

Reading the future is an awesome trading strategy, but sadly it's only possible to do in testing. Make sure that you don't test a strategy that requires tea leaves and a tarot card when taken live!

What about Exits?

Depending on the strategy, open positions will be exited at a predetermined stop-loss or profit target. Some strategies will require positions to be exited at the close of a trading day, I will highlight whenever this is the case.

Why do I rank signals in order of largest volume?

From a point of curiosity, knowing how profitable every single pattern has been over a sample period would be interesting. But in reality, account size and the impracticality of trading every single pattern in a live market would make such a test useless if it were intended to provide a real strategy to eventually go live with.

To make our tests as realistic to the market conditions we will face when live, we must have a rule that determines which stocks to trade when there are more entries available than our account allows.

Using volume to sort the patterns seems a reasonable thing to do because if a pattern is supposed to be gauging market sentiment, greater volume suggests a greater gauge of sentiment.

For example, if you look at a penny stock chart you'll often see multiple doji patterns.

However, it would not be wise to decipher the patterns as a clue regarding investor sentiment because they are simply reflective of a market that is so thinly traded that the open and close will often be at the exact same price.

Stocks with very little volume will sometimes only trade for 2 or 3 different prices in a single day.

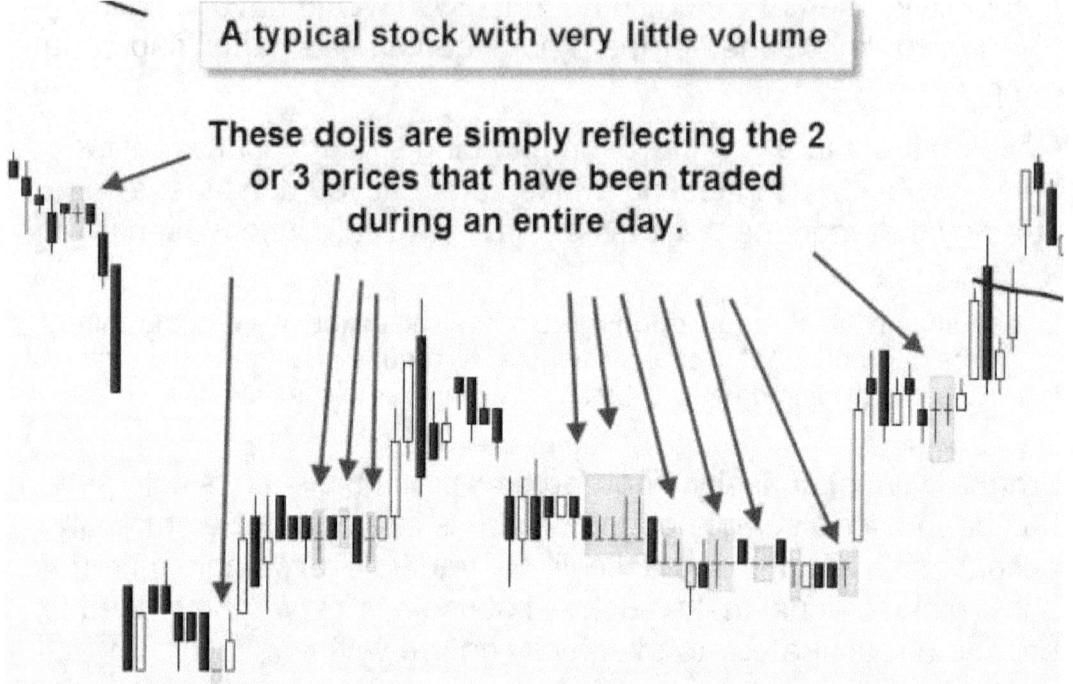

A typical stock with very little volume

These dojis are simply reflecting the 2 or 3 prices that have been traded during an entire day.

What are your tests looking for?

Profitable strategies obviously! It's a good question though because there is more to strategy development than simply optimizing the parameters to find the largest profit.

After all, profitability can be changed with simple position sizing modifications.

It is imperative when you do your testing that you consider how well you would be able to stick to the rules of a strategy in a live market.

For example, we could optimize our bullish engulfing pattern to the point where it outperformed the market by 300%, but to do so the test showed a max drawdown of 79%.

I don't know about you, but however much I would love to say that I could live through that drawdown and stick to my rules… I'd be lying through my teeth if I told you that I could!

Be conscious that profit isn't everything. It is a better approach to compare profit with the risk taken to achieve that profit.

It's also important that you have multiple trading strategies that are uncorrelated to one another in order to trade various market conditions and smooth the volatility of your overall portfolio.

My main portfolio and the majority of my trading profits have always come from riding prolonged trends using strategies that are similar to those outlined in "*The Honest Guide to Stock Trading*".

I am therefore not as interested in optimizing the candlestick patterns for maximum gains, but rather I want maximum win rates (because my trend following strategies have low win rates) and maximum returns in comparison to maximum drawdown (because my trend following strategies have relatively large drawdowns).

The term given to the variable that you are trying to improve upon when running your tests is the *objective function.*

Acknowledging what I have already said about wanting to develop short-term strategies that will compliment a trend-following portfolio, the candlestick patterns tested will be optimized to produce the best returns in relation to the lowest drawdowns.

Notice that these characteristics are in exact contrast to those of a trend following portfolio which has low win rates, spends a lot of time in the market and has large drawdowns.

The objective function that I will use will therefore be the CAR/MDD.

The CAR/MDD is simply the compounded annual return %, divided by the maximum drawdown %.

In essence, the CAR/MDD rewards returns and penalizes drawdown. This is exactly what we want to achieve when designing our candlestick pattern trading strategies.

Following are the test results for each of our candlestick patterns. Each test will begin by identifying whether the pattern precedes a market reversal (as gauged by the average 5 day return that follows the pattern) and proceed with testing whether adding further filters or rules can improve the patterns performance.

Although I share the formula for all rules as they are written in Amibroker, you will have little problem in modifying the formulas to suit the charting package of your choice.

Bullish Engulfing Pattern

The bullish engulfing pattern is a reversal pattern that is comprised of two candlesticks. The first day is a down day which indicates that sellers were controlling the market.

The second day opens lower than the first day close and closes higher than the first day open. The second day thus *engulfs* the first day. This is supposed to signify that bulls have overpowered the bears and thus rising prices should ensue.

The bullish engulfing pattern rules re-cap

- Price must be in a down-trend.
- The first day must be a down day.
- The second day must open lower than the first days close.
- The second day must close higher than the first days open.

Except for the definition of a 'downtrend', the above rules leave no room for interpretation. We must therefore define a down-trend before proceeding to carry out our tests.

As opposed to changing the definition of a down-trend by using different methods for different patterns, I will standardise the method used.

Wherever a candlestick pattern requires a prior uptrend or downtrend, I will define the uptrend or downtrend by stating that the pattern must be making an x day high or an x day low respectively.

In the case of the bullish engulfing pattern, tests find that if the first day of the pattern makes a 20 day low, the performance of the pattern is improved.

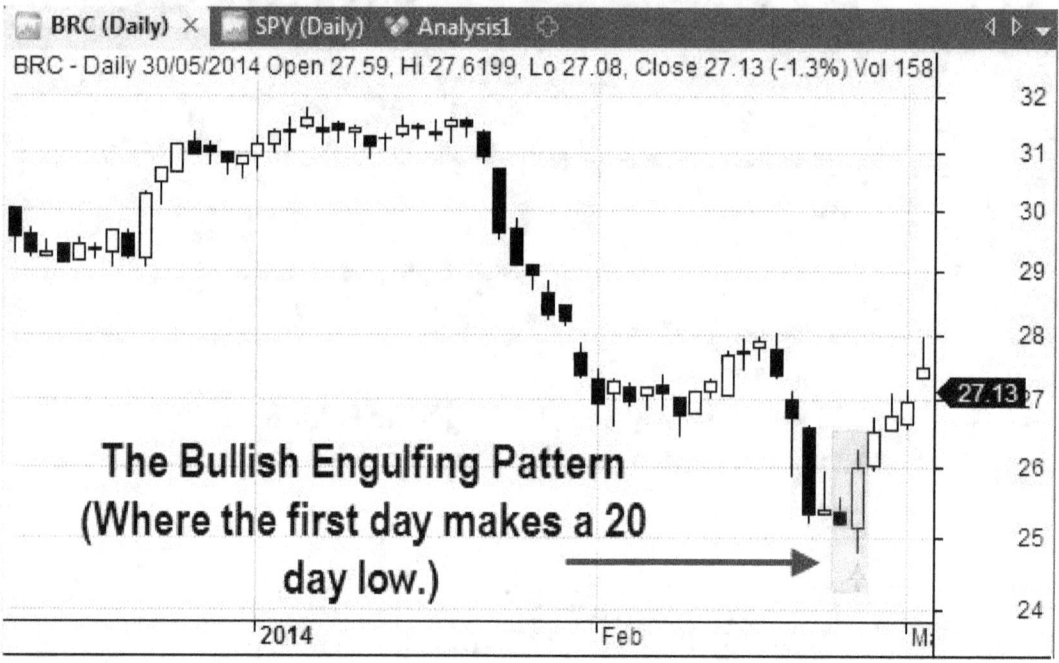

The Amibroker formula for defining a bullish engulfing pattern that makes a 20 day low is as follows:

///

```
DownTrend = L < Ref(LLV(L,20),-1);
BlackBody = C < O;
```

WhiteBody = **C** > **O**;
Engulfing = Max(**O**,**C**) > Ref(Max(**O**,**C**),-1) **AND** Min(**O**,**C**) < Ref(Min(**O**,**C**),-1);

BullishEngulfing = Ref(blackbody,-1) **AND** whitebody **AND** engulfing **AND** Ref(downtrend,-1);

//

When buying stocks that met the above rules and holding open positions for 5 days, the following equity curve was produced during our sample period:

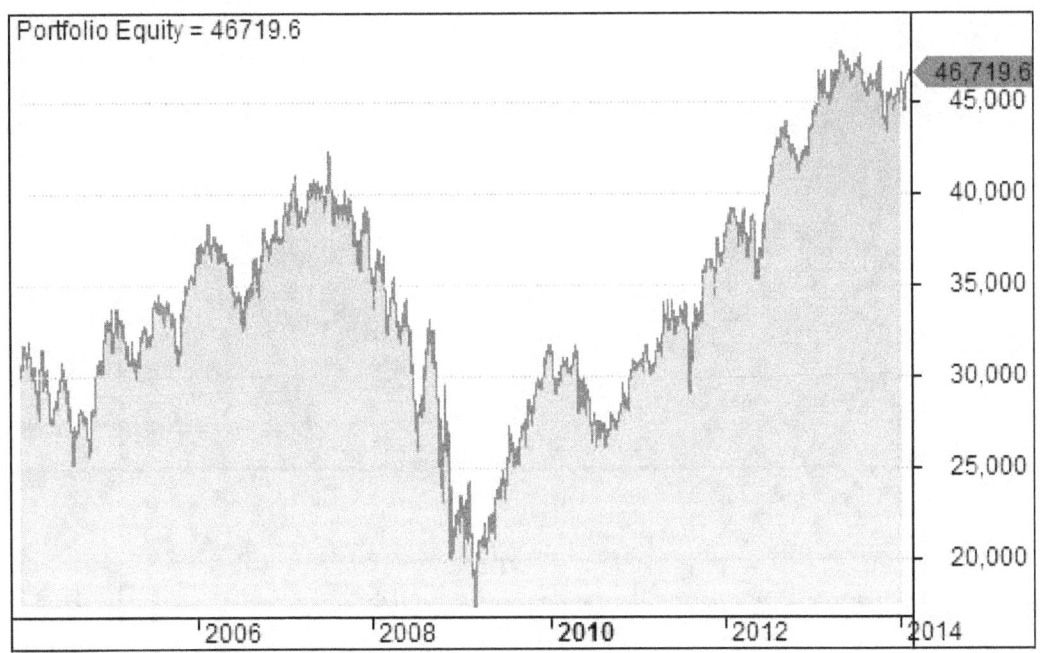

Notable performance metrics include a 49.84% win-rate and an average 5 day return of 0.12%.

Initial test results of the bullish engulfing pattern are poor. They in no way provide us with confidence that a reversal will follow the pattern.

When testing the bullish engulfing pattern during a variety of different market environments, we find that the performance of the pattern can be slightly improved if we only trade it when the SPY has a 40 day MA above a 120 day MA.

I also tested the pattern during either market corrections or during market strength (as gauged by the SPY RSI(8) reading), but these tests found no conclusive improvement to the results.

Once applying a market environment filter that only allows the bullish engulfing pattern to be traded if the SPY is in a long-term up-trend, we produced the following equity curve during the sample period:

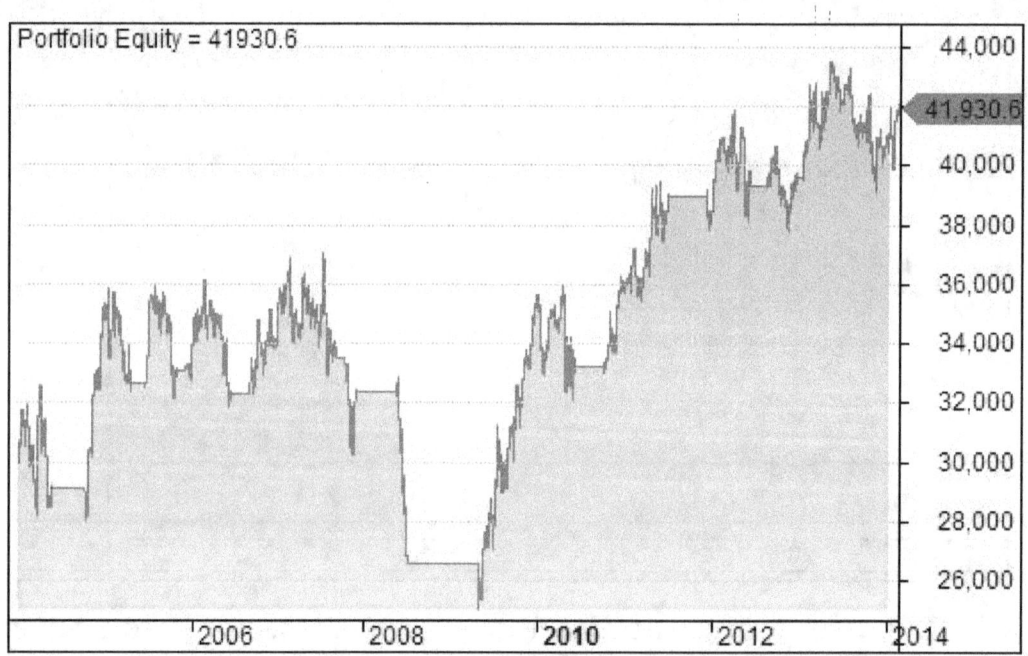

Remaining tests will include a rule which states that the bullish engulfing pattern can only be traded if the SPY is also in a long-term up-trend.

Tests of the bullish engulfing pattern with a variety of other filters find little evidence that the pattern can be improved by using traditional technical indicators.

Whether we only traded the pattern if it occurred at a key moving average, or whether we only traded the pattern when the stochastic oscillator or RSI were oversold, the pattern performance was rarely improved.

I also tested the pattern with a variety of rules based upon the relative size of the volume or the relative size of the price range; again there were no significant improvements to the pattern's performance.

A filter that *was* found to be effective was based upon a theory that the bullish engulfing pattern is more likely to perform well if it occurs in a stock that is trading higher than it was one year ago.

To test the theory I used a ROC filter with a 252 day look-back period. The rule stated that the bullish engulfing pattern was only a valid signal if the ROC (252) was above 0 on the first day of the pattern.

Once applying the ROC filter, the average 5 day return of open positions rises to 0.20%

The following charts are taken from the test results. For illustrative purposes I will show you a couple of the best trades. (This wouldn't be a trading book if I didn't cherry pick at least one or two examples!)

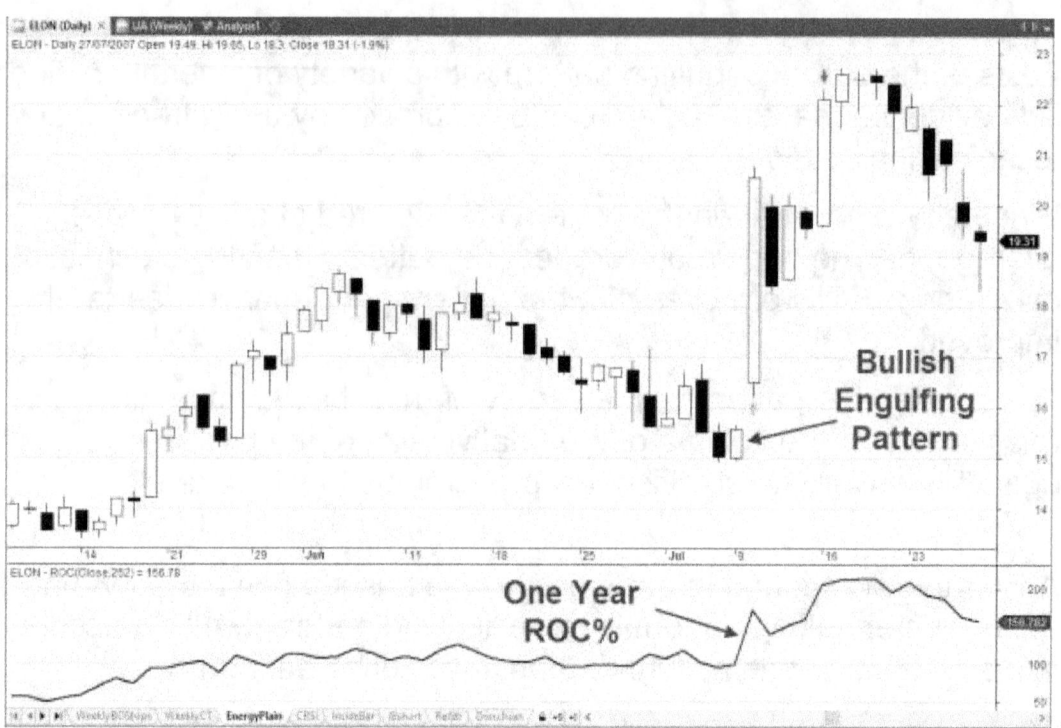

ELON (Daily1) × UA (Weekly) Analysis1
ELON - Daily 27/07/2007 Open 19.49, Hi 19.66, Lo 19.3, Close 19.31 (-1.9%)

Bullish
Engulfing
Pattern

One Year
ROC%

ELON - ROC(Close,252) = 156.78

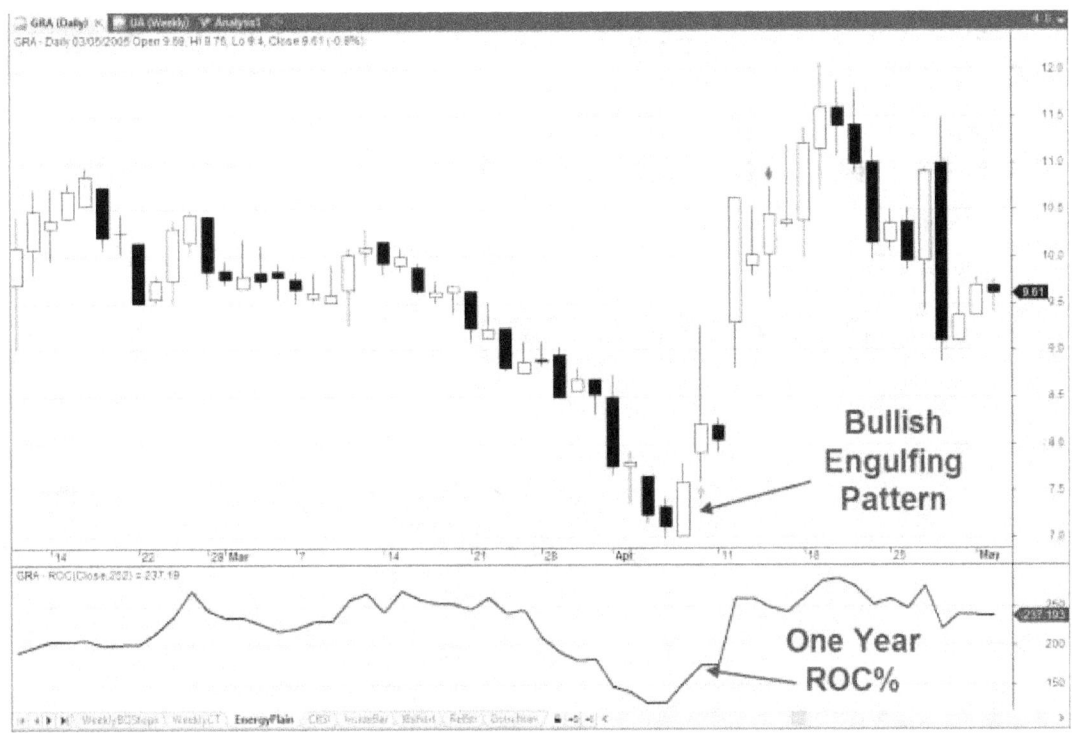

GRA (Daily) × | UA (Weekly) | Analysis1

GRA - Daily 03/05/2008 Open 9.59, HI 9.76, Lo 9.4, Close 9.61 (-0.8%)

Bullish
Engulfing
Pattern

GRA - ROC(Close,252) = 237.19

One Year
ROC%

Weekly/BOStops | Weekly/CT | EnergyPlain | CBS | IncludeBar | WaitAt | Reflat | Dotschian

Remaining tests will include a rule which states that the bullish engulfing pattern can only be traded if the one year (252 days) Rate of Change % is higher than 0.

Applying stop-losses and profit targets to the bullish engulfing pattern
The previous tests have found that the bullish engulfing pattern produces a better 5 day performance if it is only traded when the SPY is in a long-term uptrend and the individual stock is higher than it was one year ago.

The next tests that I carried out were to determine whether the strategy can be improved by the inclusion of stop-losses and profit targets.

But before getting to the stop-losses and profit targets, I first wanted to determine whether the bullish engulfing pattern performs better when we have following day confirmation that the bulls are in control of the market.

To define that the bulls are in control on the day following the bullish engulfing pattern, I applied the following rule to the strategy:

Only buy a bullish engulfing pattern if the following day high is at least 5 cents higher than the high made by the second day of the pattern.

For example:

The above rule is taught as standard in many trading seminars. Why? I don't know. Waiting for following day confirmation simply doesn't work for this particular setup.

It might feel safer to wait for confirmation, but as I explained in "*The Honest Guide to Stock Trading*"...you make money by taking the trades which feel scary, not safe.

Indeed, tests show us that waiting for next day strength before buying a bullish engulfing pattern will result in the pattern producing **fewer** winning trades, and **smaller** profits.

In fact, when applying the 5 cent above high buy-stop order to our current strategy, the CAR/MDD becomes a paltry 0.06.

I wouldn't trust the majority of trading education sites if they were run by mother, but when the material being taught includes rules that *hurt* the performance of a strategy, it isn't just the integrity of these so called experts that I wonder about....it's their sanity too!

Next time somebody offers you advice regarding topics such as the best place to put a stop-loss or the best filter to add to a system, ask them exactly how much better said stop-losses or filters have performed in the past.

If you can't get an exact answer, be adamant that the person giving you the advice is not qualified to be doing so.

In fact, knowing that so much of the trading education available is sub-standard, it is often a trading strategy in itself to take the exact opposite trade to what the conventional wisdom would suggest.

Take the above rule as an example. If instead of only buying the bullish engulfing pattern when the price goes up after the pattern, what if we only buy the bullish engulfing pattern when price went down after the pattern?

The following test included a rule which only bought the bullish engulfing pattern if the price traded 5 cents *lower* than the low of the pattern. For example:

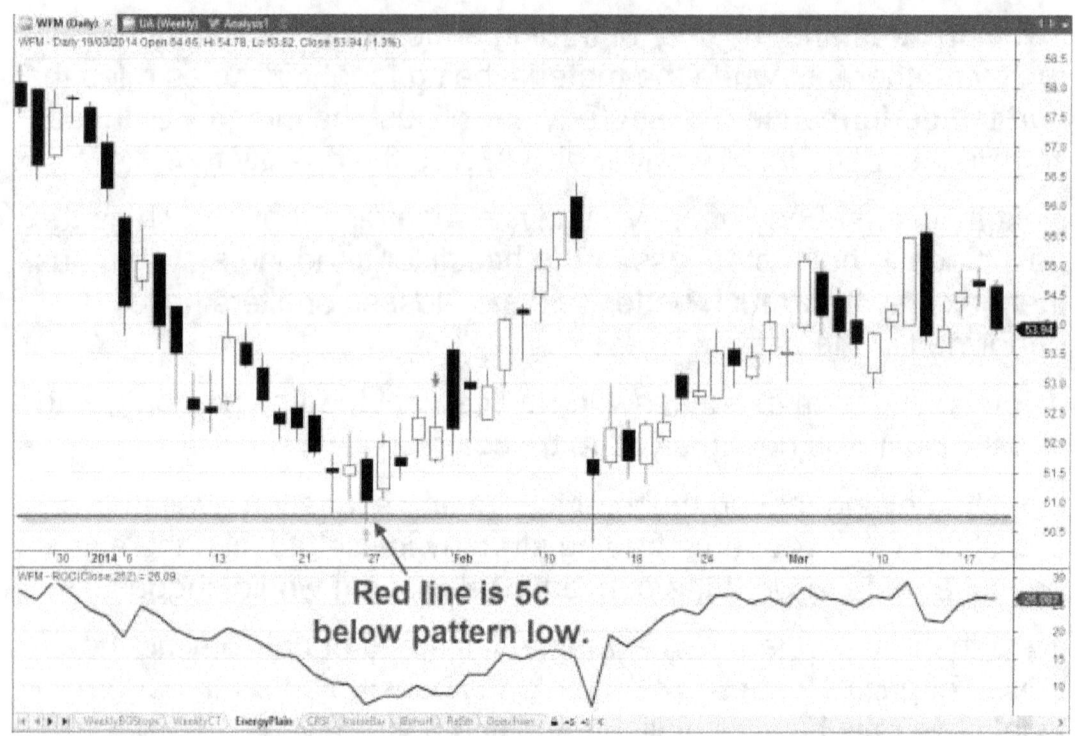

Red line is 5c
below pattern low.

It should come as no surprise that the above rule is far better than the rules you will most frequently read about on trading forums.

During the sample period, **if you only buy the engulfing pattern _low_ on the day that follows the pattern; our current strategy has a 54.43% win-rate and an average 5 day return of 0.43%.**

These results are significantly better than the results achieved if only buying the pattern _high_.

That brings us to the topic of stop-losses and profit targets. As it currently stands, each of the tests that I have so far run have simply opened all positions on the day that follows the bullish engulfing pattern and closed all open positions 5 days later.

However, it is unlikely that holding positions for 5 days is the optimum method for managing each trade.

To improve the final strategy, I got rid of the 5 day position hold rule and instead carried out a series of tests which applied a variety of stop-losses and profit targets to the strategy.

For this strategy and each of the remaining strategies in the book, I will test stop-losses and profit-targets that are between 1% and 10% above or below the entry price. The stop-loss and profit-target parameter tests will be carried out in increments of 1.

Finally, I will always include a rule which automatically closes a position after 20 days if neither a stop-loss nor profit-target is executed.

The reason for doing this is that if we hold a position for too long after the completion of a pattern, we can have less confidence that any edge found is related to the pattern in the first place.

Rather than publish the results of each test, (there are 16 patterns to get through and I don't want you to fall asleep!) I will focus on the test results which showed a significant improvement to the strategy.

Tests find that the highest CAR/MDD when trading the bullish engulfing pattern strategy can be found if applying a 2% profit target and a 5% stop-loss to each position.

The final rules of the bullish engulfing pattern trading strategy

- **Price must be above $5.00**
- **20 day Volume average must be above 100,000.**
- **On the first day of the bullish engulfing pattern, the SPY must have a 40 day MA above a 120 day MA.**
- **The ROC(252) of the stock must be above 0 on the first day of the pattern.**
- **The low of the first day of the pattern must be the lowest low in the past 20 days.**
- **If all rules are met, place a limit order that is 5c below the low of the pattern (good for one day).**

- **Apply a profit target that is 3% higher than the entry price.**
- **Apply a stop-loss that is 10% below the entry price.**
- **If neither the stop-loss nor profit-target is executed, exit positions on the close after 20 days.**
- **Once a position is closed, 3 days must pass before we are allowed to trade a signal in the same stock.**

To code the strategy in Amibroker we can enter the following formula:

//

```
SetTradeDelays(0,0,0,0);
SetOption("initialequity",30000);
SetOption ("MaxOpenPositions" , 5);
SetOption ("allowsamebarexit",false);
SetPositionSize(6000,spsValue);
SetBacktestMode(backtestregular);

DownTrend = L < Ref(LLV(L,20),-1);
BlackBody = C < O;
WhiteBody = C > O;
engulfing = Max(O,C) > Ref(Max(O,C),-1) AND Min(O,C) <
Ref(Min(O,C),-1);

BullishEngulfing = Ref(blackbody,-1) AND whitebody
AND engulfing AND Ref(downtrend,-1);

NonAdjVol = (V * C)/OI ;

Index = Foreign ("SPY","C",True);
Indexfastma = MA (Index, 40);
Indexslowma = MA (Index, 120);

UT = indexfastma > indexslowma;
```

```
Buysetup = BullishEngulfing
AND oi > 5
AND ut
AND MA(nonadjvol,20) > 100000
AND Ref(ROC(C,252),-1) > 0;

buystop = Ref(ValueWhen(buysetup,(LLV(L,2) - 0.05)),-1);

Buy = Ref(buysetup,-1) AND Cross(buystop,L);

SellPrice = Close;

BuyPrice = Min(Open,buystop);

Sell = 0;

PT = Optimize("pt%",3,1,10,1);
SL = Optimize("SL%",10,1,10,1);

ApplyStop  (stopTypeProfit,stopModePercent,pt,1,False,3);
ApplyStop  (stopTypeloss,stopModepercent,SL,1,False,3);
ApplyStop (stopTypeNBar,stopModeBars,19,0,False,3);

PositionScore = 100 + ref(nonadjvol,-1);
/////////////////////////////////////////////////////////////////////
```

Test results for the bullish engulfing pattern trading strategy

The following tables and charts show us the performance metrics of the bullish engulfing pattern when applying the above rules.

Notable metrics include a 76.74% win-rate, 1.10% average gain per trade and a CAR/MDD of 0.78.

Statistics			
	All trades	**Long trades**	**Short trades**
Initial capital	30000.00	30000.00	30000.00
Ending capital	46981.76	46981.76	30000.00
Net Profit	16981.76	16981.76	0.00
Net Profit %	56.61 %	56.61 %	0.00 %
Exposure %	13.53 %	13.53 %	0.00 %
Net Risk Adjusted Return %	418.26 %	418.26 %	N/A
Annual Return %	4.51 %	4.51 %	0.00 %
Risk Adjusted Return %	33.34 %	33.34 %	N/A
Total transaction costs	1339.46	1339.46	0.00
All trades	258	258 (100.00 %)	0 (0.00 %)
Avg. Profit/Loss	65.82	65.82	N/A
Avg. Profit/Loss %	1.10 %	1.10 %	N/A
Avg. Bars Held	9.63	9.63	N/A
Winners	198 (76.74 %)	198 (76.74 %)	0 (0.00 %)
Total Profit	37934.98	37934.98	0.00
Avg. Profit	191.59	191.59	N/A
Avg. Profit %	3.20 %	3.20 %	N/A
Avg. Bars Held	7.83	7.83	N/A
Max. Consecutive	14	14	0
Largest win	1196.60	1196.60	0.00
# bars in largest win	14	14	0
Losers	60 (23.26 %)	60 (23.26 %)	0 (0.00 %)
Total Loss	-20953.21	-20953.21	0.00
Avg. Loss	-349.22	-349.22	N/A
Avg. Loss %	-5.85 %	-5.85 %	N/A
Avg. Bars Held	15.55	15.55	N/A
Max. Consecutive	3	3	0
Largest loss	-796.00	-796.00	0.00
# bars in largest loss	8	8	0
Max. trade drawdown	-815.40	-815.40	0.00
Max. trade % drawdown	-13.60 %	-13.60 %	0.00 %
Max. system drawdown	-2276.82	-2276.82	0.00
Max. system % drawdown	-5.80 %	-5.80 %	0.00 %
Recovery Factor	7.46	7.46	N/A
CAR/MaxDD	0.78	0.78	N/A
RAR/MaxDD	5.75	5.75	N/A
Profit Factor	1.81	1.81	N/A
Payoff Ratio	0.55	0.55	N/A

Charts

1. Portfolio Equity

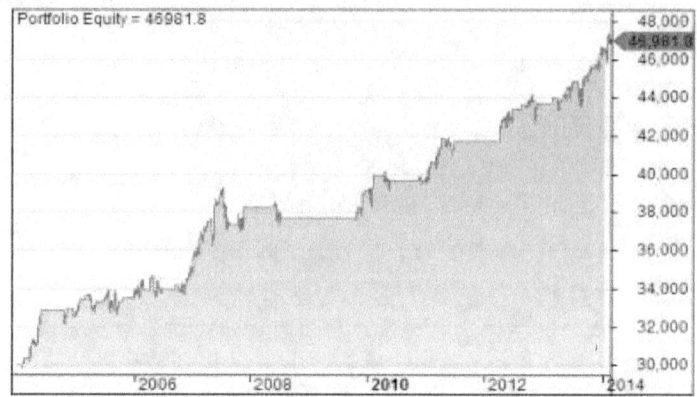

2. Underwater Equity

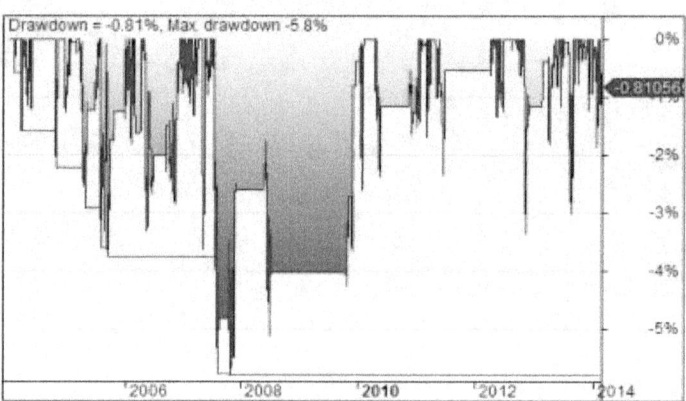

3. Profit Table

Year	Jan	Feb	Mar	Apr	May	Jun	Jul	Aug	Sep	Oct	Nov	Dec	Yr%
2004	0.0%	1.2%	2.6%	-0.5%	5.9%	0.0%	0.0%	0.0%	0.0%	-1.0%	1.3%	-1.0%	8.7%
2005	2.7%	0.0%	0.2%	-2.2%	1.6%	0.5%	1.4%	-2.1%	0.2%	0.7%	0.0%	-0.1%	2.7%
2006	1.5%	1.3%	-1.4%	2.1%	-1.5%	-0.3%	0.0%	0.0%	0.5%	0.1%	1.0%	0.8%	4.0%
2007	2.4%	2.8%	1.3%	0.9%	3.0%	0.6%	-1.4%	-2.4%	0.0%	0.5%	2.0%	-0.1%	9.9%
2008	0.0%	0.0%	0.0%	0.0%	0.5%	-2.0%	0.0%	0.0%	0.0%	0.0%	0.0%	0.0%	-1.5%
2009	0.0%	0.0%	0.0%	0.0%	0.0%	0.0%	0.0%	0.0%	0.0%	-0.1%	1.5%	2.4%	3.8%
2010	-1.7%	3.8%	0.0%	-0.0%	-0.8%	0.1%	0.0%	0.0%	0.0%	0.0%	0.2%	-0.3%	1.2%
2011	1.3%	1.2%	1.9%	1.2%	0.3%	-1.1%	0.6%	0.0%	0.0%	0.0%	0.0%	0.0%	5.4%
2012	0.0%	0.0%	0.0%	2.9%	-0.2%	1.3%	0.0%	0.4%	0.0%	1.3%	-1.0%	-0.2%	4.6%
2013	0.0%	0.2%	0.6%	-0.1%	-0.1%	0.9%	1.2%	-2.5%	3.1%	0.9%	0.3%	2.2%	6.8%
2014	-0.5%	1.3%	N/A	N/A	N/A	N/A	N/A	N/A	N/A	N/A	N/A	N/A	0.8%
Avg	0.5%	1.1%	0.5%	0.4%	0.9%	0.0%	0.2%	-0.7%	0.4%	0.2%	0.5%	0.4%	

65

The Morning Star Pattern

The morning star pattern is a 3 day reversal pattern that is supposed to signify the bottom of a downtrend.

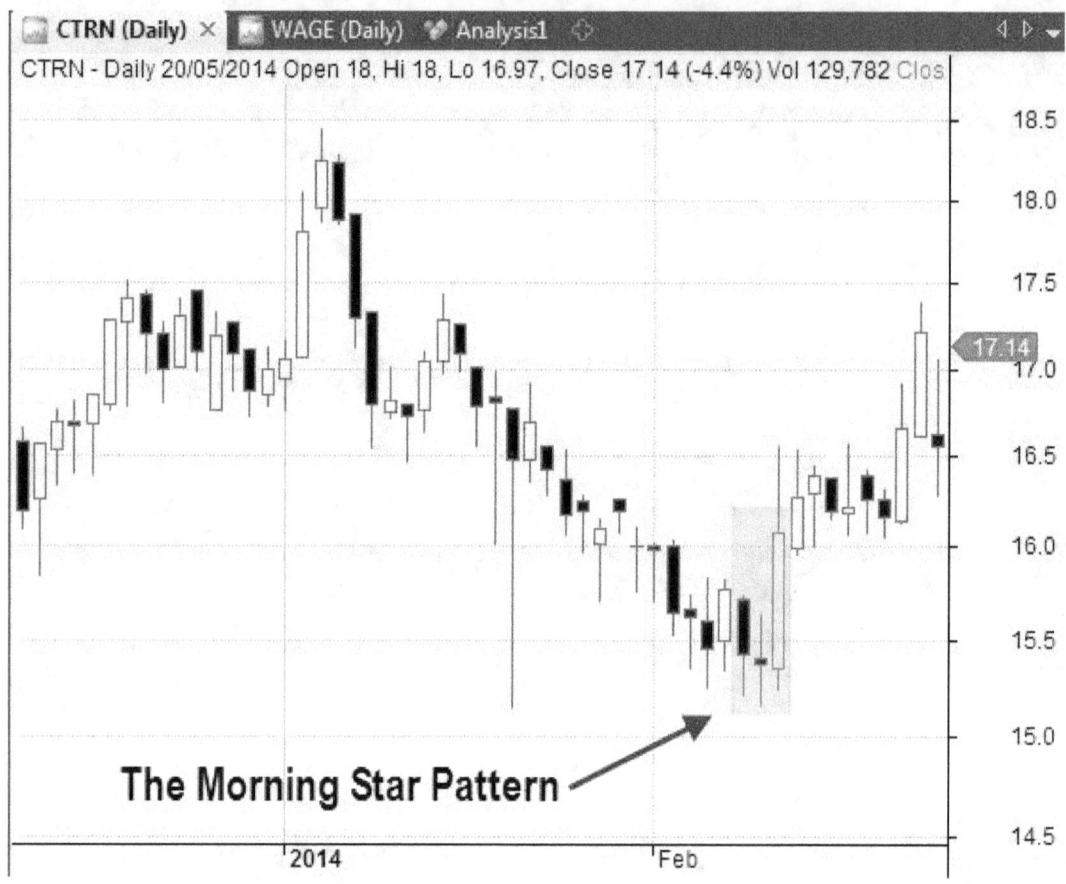

CTRN (Daily) ✕   WAGE (Daily) ✤ Analysis1 ✛

CTRN - Daily 20/05/2014 Open 18, Hi 18, Lo 16.97, Close 17.14 (-4.4%) Vol 129,782 Clos

The Morning Star Pattern

The morning star pattern rules re-cap

- Price has been in a downtrend.
- The first day of the pattern is a large down day (a black or red candle).
- The second day of the pattern gaps down from the first day and creates a candle that doesn't close higher than the first day close.

- The second day is also an indecision day signified by a small real body in relation to its entire day range.
- The third day of the pattern is a large up day (a white or green candle) that closes higher than the half-way point of the first day.

The morning star pattern code

Before we can code the morning star pattern we must be more specific regarding any rules which are currently open to interpretation.

Firstly, I tested a variety of x day lows that would define a 'downtrend'. Tests found that the morning star pattern performs well if the first day of the pattern makes a 2 day low.

Remaining tests will include a rule which states that the first day of the morning star pattern must make a 2 day low.

The definition of a 'small real body' and a 'large up or down day' also needs to be more specific. The following rules will be used:

A 'large' day is defined as a day that has at least 1.5% difference between the open and close.

A 'small real body' is defined as a day that has less than a 0.3% difference between the open and close.

The Amibroker formula for defining each of the aforementioned rules is as follows:

//

WhiteBody = **C > O**;

downTrend = **L** < Ref(LLV(**L**,2),-1);
BlackBody = **C** < **O**;
Big = abs((**Close** - **Open**)/**Open**) > 0.015;
rng = abs((**C-O**)/**O**);
SmallRealBody = rng < 0.003 **AND** rng >0;
RealBodyGapDown = Max(**O,C**) < Min(Ref(**O**,-1),Ref(**C**,-1));
isPrevLargeBlack = Ref(big,-1) **AND** Ref(blackbody,-1);
isPrevDownTrend = Ref(downtrend,-1);
GapDownFromBlack = realBodyGapDown **AND** isPrevLargeBlack
AND isPrevDowntrend;
StarDown = smallRealBody **AND** gapDownFromBlack;

MorningStar = Ref(starDown,-1) **AND** whitebody **AND** big **AND** C >
Ref((**O** + **C**)/2,-2);

//

The morning star pattern test results (5 day holding period)
When buying stocks that met the above rules and holding open
positions for 5 days, the following equity curve was produced during
our sample period:

70

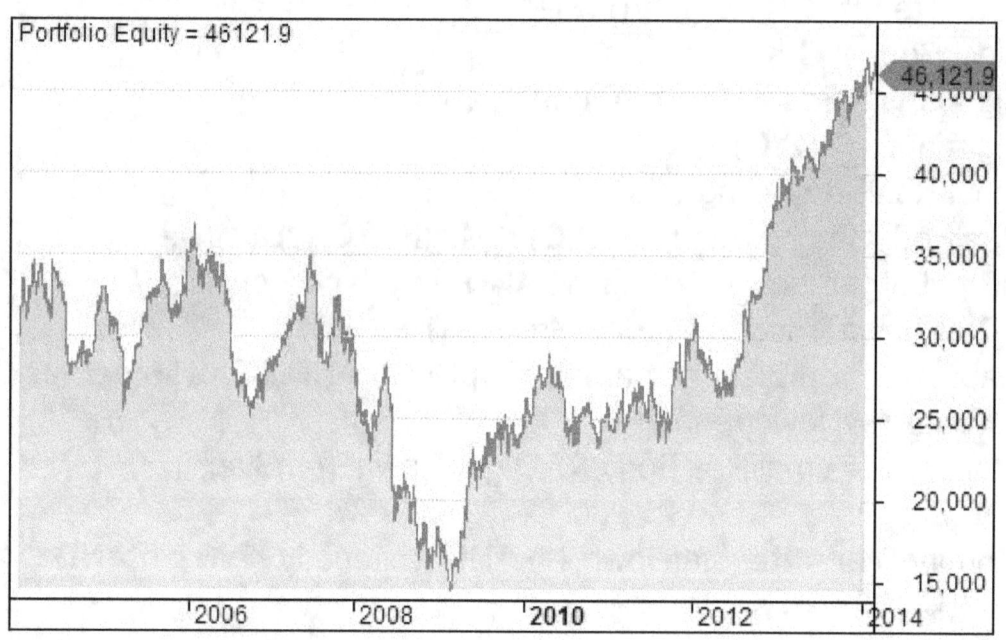

Portfolio Equity = 46121.9

Notable performance metrics include a 51.57% win-rate and an average 5 day return of 0.15%.

What is the best market environment for trading the morning star pattern?

Tests of the morning star pattern when filtering by each of the market environments defined in chapter 4 found no evidence that the pattern can be improved when filtering by market type.

Remaining tests will not include a market environment filter.

Applying indicator filters to the morning star pattern

I extensively tested the morning star pattern with a variety of filters that included only trading the pattern at certain moving averages or only trading the pattern if the stock was oversold (as gauged by the RSI, Stochastics or Bollinger bands etc).

None of the above filters improved the performance of the pattern during the sample period. However, a particular rule which did improve the performance of the pattern was found.

A cursory analysis of the 600 or so trades made during the sample seemed to indicate that the morning star pattern would often precede a reversal, but not before first falling to retest the low of the pattern during the next few days.

In which case, buying the open of the day which followed the pattern was not a very effective way of entering new trades. Instead, I applied the following rule:

After a morning star pattern, place a buy order at the same price as the lowest price made by the pattern. This buy order is valid for 5 days, after which it would be cancelled.

For example:

The buy order explained above will be applied to the strategy during the next tests.

Tests of the current strategy with a variety of stop-losses and profit-targets find that the best CAR/MDD can be achieved if applying a 3% stop-loss and a 9% profit target.

Tests have shown that a morning star pattern trading strategy can be improved by adding the following rules:

- **The price must be above $5.00**
- **The 20 day Volume average must be above 100,000.**
- **The first day of the morning star pattern must make a 2 day low.**
- **When the above rules are met, place a buy order at the same price as the low of the pattern. If the buy order is not executed within 5 days of the pattern, cancel it.**
- **If the buy order is executed, place a profit target 9% above your entry price. Place a stop-loss 3% beneath your entry price.**
- **If neither the stop-loss or profit target is executed, close positions on the open of the 20th day.**
- **Once a position is closed, 3 days must pass before we are allowed to trade a signal in the same stock.**

To code the strategy in Amibroker we can use the following formula:

//

```
SetTradeDelays(0,0,0,0);
SetOption("initialequity",30000);
SetOption ("MaxOpenPositions" , 5);
SetOption ("allowsamebarexit",false);
SetPositionSize(6000,spsValue);
```

```
SetBacktestMode(backtestregular);

WhiteBody = C > O;
downTrend = L < Ref(LLV(L,2),-1);
BlackBody = C < O;
Big = abs((Close - Open)/Open) > 0.015;
rng = abs((C-O)/O);
SmallRealBody = rng < 0.003 AND rng >0;
RealBodyGapDown = Max(O,C) < Min(Ref(O,-1),Ref(C,-1));
isPrevLargeBlack = Ref(big,-1) AND Ref(blackbody,-1);
isPrevDownTrend = Ref(downtrend,-1);
GapDownFromBlack = realBodyGapDown AND isPrevLargeBlack
AND isPrevDowntrend;
StarDown = smallRealBody AND gapDownFromBlack;

MorningStar = Ref(starDown,-1) AND whitebody AND big AND C >
Ref((O + C)/2,-2);

NonAdjVol = (V * C)/OI ;

Index = Foreign ("SPY","C",True);
Indexfastma = MA (Index, 40);
Indexslowma = MA (Index, 120);

Buysetup = morningstar
AND oi > 5
AND MA(nonadjvol,20) > 100000;

Sell =0;

Buystop = ValueWhen(Buysetup,LLV(L,3));

recentsig = BarsSince(buysetup) <= 5;

Buy = recentsig AND Cross(Buystop,L);
```

```
BuyPrice = Min(Open,buystop);
SellPrice = Close;

PT = Optimize("pt%",9,1,10,1);
SL = Optimize("SL%",3,1,10,1);

ApplyStop (stopTypeProfit,stopModePercent,pt,1,False,3);
ApplyStop (stopTypeloss,stopModepercent,sl,1,False,3);
ApplyStop(stopTypeNBar,stopModeBars,19,0,False,3);

PositionScore = 100 + Ref(nonadjvol,-1);
////////////////////////////////////////////////////////////////
```

Test results of the morning star pattern trading strategy
The following tables and charts show us the performance metrics of the morning star pattern when applying the above rules. **Notable metrics include a 32.28% win-rate, an average gain of 0.40% per trade and a CAR/MDD of 0.26.**

Statistics

	All trades	Long trades	Short trades
Initial capital	30000.00	30000.00	30000.00
Ending capital	52731.06	52731.06	30000.00
Net Profit	22731.06	22731.06	0.00
Net Profit %	75.77 %	75.77 %	0.00 %
Exposure %	29.08 %	29.08 %	0.00 %
Net Risk Adjusted Return %	260.52 %	260.52 %	N/A
Annual Return %	5.71 %	5.71 %	0.00 %
Risk Adjusted Return %	19.62 %	19.62 %	N/A
Total transaction costs	7082.90	7082.90	0.00
All trades	945	945 (100.00 %)	0 (0.00 %)
Avg. Profit/Loss	24.05	24.05	N/A
Avg. Profit/Loss %	0.40 %	0.40 %	N/A
Avg. Bars Held	5.80	5.80	N/A
Winners	305 (32.28 %)	305 (32.28 %)	0 (0.00 %)
Total Profit	157877.93	157877.93	0.00
Avg. Profit	517.63	517.63	N/A
Avg. Profit %	8.66 %	8.66 %	N/A
Avg. Bars Held	8.53	8.53	N/A
Max. Consecutive	5	5	0
Largest win	2313.93	2313.93	0.00
# bars in largest win	5	5	0
Losers	640 (67.72 %)	640 (67.72 %)	0 (0.00 %)
Total Loss	-135146.88	-135146.88	0.00
Avg. Loss	-211.17	-211.17	N/A
Avg. Loss %	-3.54 %	-3.54 %	N/A
Avg. Bars Held	4.50	4.50	N/A
Max. Consecutive	22	22	0
Largest loss	-1667.32	-1667.32	0.00
# bars in largest loss	2	2	0
Max. trade drawdown	-1667.32	-1667.32	0.00
Max. trade % drawdown	-27.78 %	-27.78 %	0.00 %
Max. system drawdown	-7220.07	-7220.07	0.00
Max. system % drawdown	-22.29 %	-22.29 %	0.00 %
Recovery Factor	3.15	3.15	N/A
CAR/MaxDD	0.26	0.26	N/A
RAR/MaxDD	0.88	0.88	N/A
Profit Factor	1.17	1.17	N/A
Payoff Ratio	2.45	2.45	N/A

Charts

1. Portfolio Equity

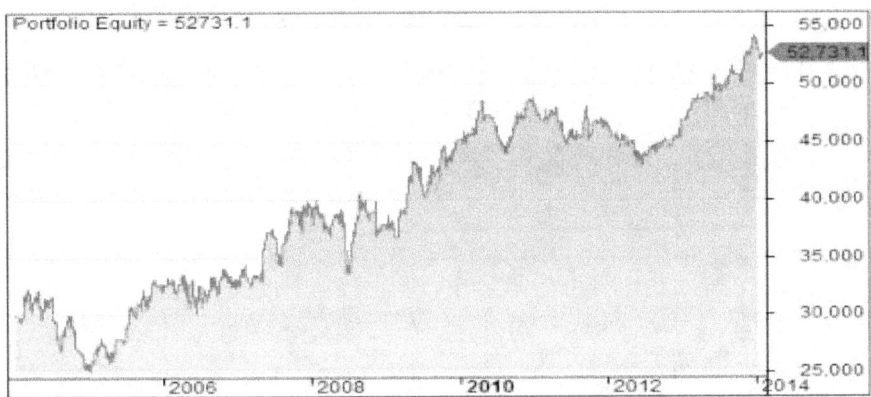

2. Underwater Equity

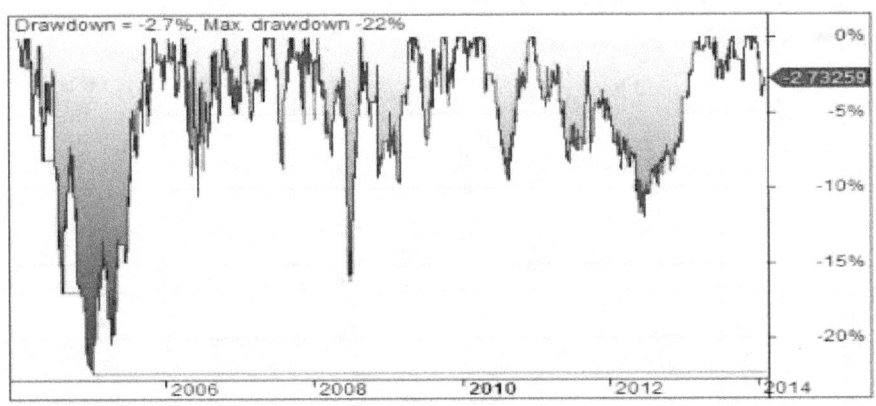

3. Profit Table

Year	Jan	Feb	Mar	Apr	May	Jun	Jul	Aug	Sep	Oct	Nov	Dec	Yr%
2004	-1.8%	7.6%	-0.9%	-2.1%	1.8%	1.3%	-11.3%	0.9%	3.4%	-8.0%	-2.0%	-3.7%	-15.0%
2005	4.1%	3.7%	-3.5%	-0.7%	6.0%	-1.3%	11.2%	0.7%	4.4%	-2.3%	3.4%	-0.9%	26.6%
2006	2.9%	-1.1%	-0.4%	-0.6%	-0.8%	0.4%	0.2%	1.4%	-1.1%	4.7%	-2.9%	-0.1%	2.4%
2007	1.4%	-1.2%	0.5%	0.2%	10.6%	0.1%	-4.6%	4.4%	4.1%	1.1%	2.3%	-0.0%	19.8%
2008	-0.5%	-2.5%	-2.4%	2.6%	0.5%	-10.3%	7.1%	8.8%	-1.3%	-2.7%	-3.8%	1.1%	-4.5%
2009	-0.0%	-2.7%	6.2%	6.1%	4.1%	-2.8%	-2.5%	4.0%	1.3%	-0.0%	0.3%	4.8%	19.7%
2010	1.2%	-0.5%	1.5%	3.8%	-1.3%	-2.6%	-3.0%	-1.6%	4.5%	2.2%	1.5%	1.4%	7.1%
2011	-2.1%	-1.1%	1.8%	0.6%	-2.5%	-2.8%	-0.0%	-0.2%	3.5%	-0.5%	0.1%	-0.7%	-4.0%
2012	-2.2%	-0.0%	-0.3%	-0.4%	-3.3%	0.6%	0.9%	-0.4%	1.4%	-0.2%	1.6%	1.5%	-1.0%
2013	2.4%	2.5%	1.4%	-0.2%	-0.2%	1.0%	1.0%	0.4%	1.5%	-1.4%	5.4%	2.1%	17.1%
2014	-1.8%	-0.4%	N/A	N/A	N/A	N/A	N/A	N/A	N/A	N/A	N/A	N/A	-2.2%
Avg	0.3%	0.4%	0.4%	0.9%	1.5%	-1.6%	-0.1%	1.9%	2.2%	-0.7%	0.6%	0.5%	

78

The Piercing Pattern

The piercing pattern is another candlestick formation that takes two days to complete. To remind you what a piercing pattern looks like when it forms on the chart, please study the following example:

JRS (Daily) × SPY (Daily) Analysis1
JRS - Daily 13/02/2014 Open 10.67, Hi 10.75, Lo 10.63, Close 10.75 (0.4%) Vol 57,600

JRS - Volume = 57,600.00

The piercing pattern rules recap

- Price has been in a downtrend.
- The first day of the pattern is a larger than average down-day.
- The second day of the pattern opens lower than the first day low.

- The second day closes at least halfway into the real body of the first day.

'A down-trend' is defined by the first day of the pattern making a 10 day low.

'A larger than average down-day' is defined as a day that closes at least 1.5% lower than it opened and has a real body that is at least 2 times greater than the size of the candle shadows.

The piercing pattern code

To code the above rules that are used to define the piercing pattern in Amibroker, we can use the following formula:

//

WhiteBody = **C** > **O**;
BlackBody = **C** < **O**;
BigBlack = (**Open** - **Close**)/**Open** > 0.015 **AND** (**Open** - **Close**) * 2 > **High** - **Low**;
DownTrend = **L** < Ref(LLV(**L**,10),-1);

PiercingPattern = Ref(bigblack,-1) **AND** whitebody **AND O** < Ref(**L**,-1)
AND C >= Ref((**O**+**C**)/2,-1) **AND C** < Ref(**O**,-1) **AND**
Ref(downtrend,-1);

///

Piercing pattern test results (5 day holding period)

The first test results will show you how well the piercing pattern performed over our sample period.

Remember that I determine how well the pattern signifies a reversal by holding each trade for 5 days and closing on the close of the 5th day that we have held the position:

For example:

ROSE - Daily 13/09/2013 Open 49.78, Hi 50.89, Lo 49.46, Close 49.88 (0.6%)

When trading all piercing patterns that met the above rules whilst holding open positions for 5 days, the following equity curve was produced during the sample period:

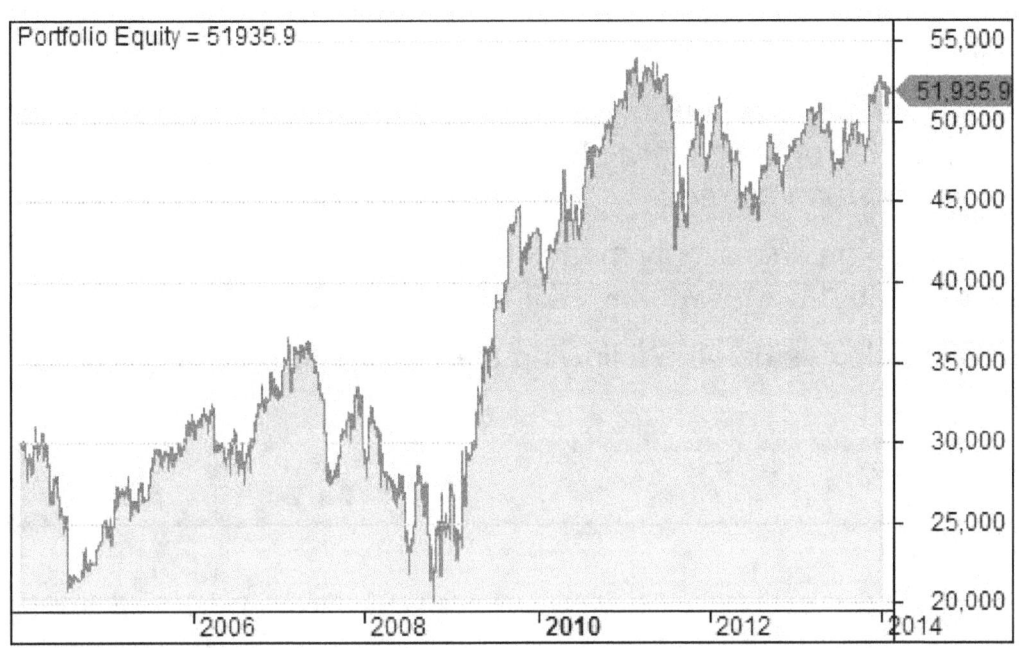

Portfolio Equity = 51935.9

Notable performance metrics include a 52.20% win-rate and an average 5 day return per trade of 0.23%.

We find that the piercing pattern produces a slight edge, but certainly nothing spectacular. Yet again, the actual probability of a reversal, at least during the next 5 days, is barely better than a coin toss.

Initial test results are testament to why you shouldn't read that piercing patterns are great reversal signals and blindly trade every one of them that you see.

What is the best market environment for trading the piercing pattern?
As the previous "portfolio equity" chart illustrates, the piercing pattern strategy with a 5 day holding period suffered a large drawdown in 2007/2008 and 2011.

After applying our market environment filters to the piercing pattern strategy with a 5 day holding period, it becomes clear that avoiding bear markets is a very useful way to improve the average gain per trade.

Tests show that the performance of the piercing pattern is improved if the first day of the pattern also occurred when the SPY was in a strong long-term uptrend.

To remind you, this simply means that the SPY has a 40 day MA above a 120 day MA with the RSI(8) reading above 70.

For example, we had the following piercing pattern setup in stock MWA.

MWA - Daily 15/01/2014 Open 9.11, Hi 9.21, Lo 9.03, Close 9.21 (1.9%)

Piercing Pattern

On the same day of the final candle in the pattern, the SPY chart looked like this:

When adding this market environment filter to our piercing pattern trading strategy we were able to **improve the win rate to a very respectable 57.25% and the average gain per trade to 0.70%.**

Although the net profit has been reduced (because we make far fewer trades), the equity curve now looks far smoother because we avoided the large drawdowns which previously occurred in 2008 and 2011.

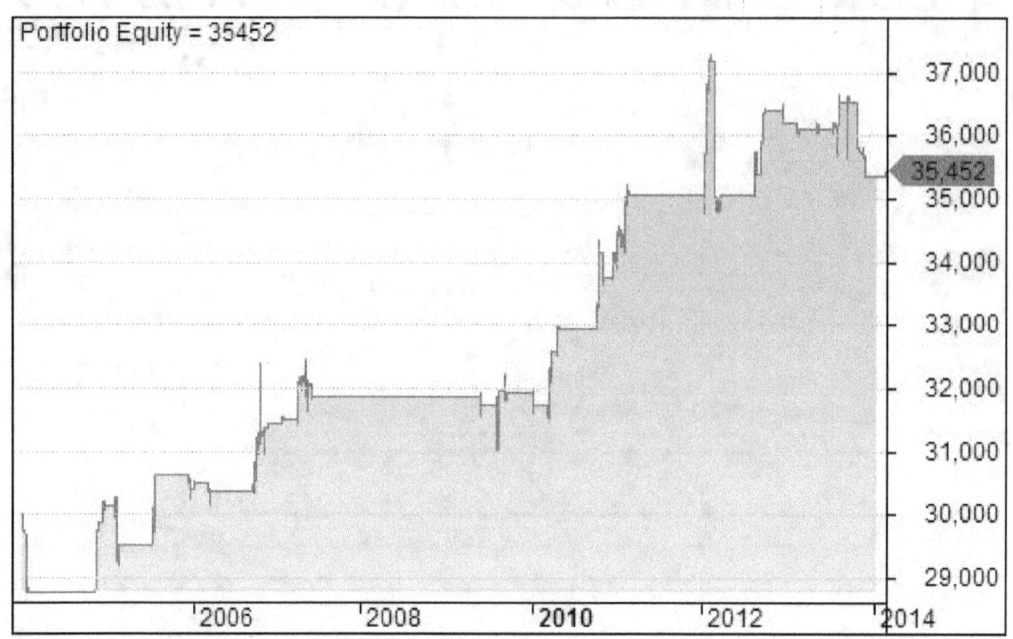

Portfolio Equity = 35452

Applying indicator filters to the piercing pattern.

Further tests that included running the piercing pattern (5 day holding period, SPY strong uptrend) found little evidence that the returns could be improved if applying further indicator based filters to the pattern.

Applying stop-losses and profit targets to the piercing pattern strategy.

Currently, the strategy that I have outlined has no profit targets or perhaps more importantly, no stop-losses.

Positions are entered, held for 5 days…and regardless of how far they may rise or fall in the meantime, we simply close the position after the 5 day holding period expires.

However, the next tests that I carried out included the more traditionally used price based stop-losses and profit targets.

If we look again at a piercing pattern, we can see that the low created by the second day would be a logical place to put a stop-loss, that's because if the price were to close below the low of the pattern, we can reasonably assume that the bulls are still not strong enough to reverse the market.

It makes perfect sense if we are testing the patterns while hypothesising that they are reversal patterns, that if the price closes below the low of the pattern soon after entering a trade, the pattern has been unsuccessful in reversing the market.

For example:

Adding this type of a stop-loss degrades performance.

The win rate of the strategy becomes only 53.38% and the average gain per trade is reduced to 0.44%.

To illustrate the negative effect that a stop-loss can sometimes have on a mean reverting trading strategy I also ran the strategy with a number of percent based stop-losses between 1% and 10%.

The results have been collated in the following graph. The percent used for the stop-loss is plotted on the *x* axis.

Notice that some tight stop-losses actually turn a winning system into a losing one.

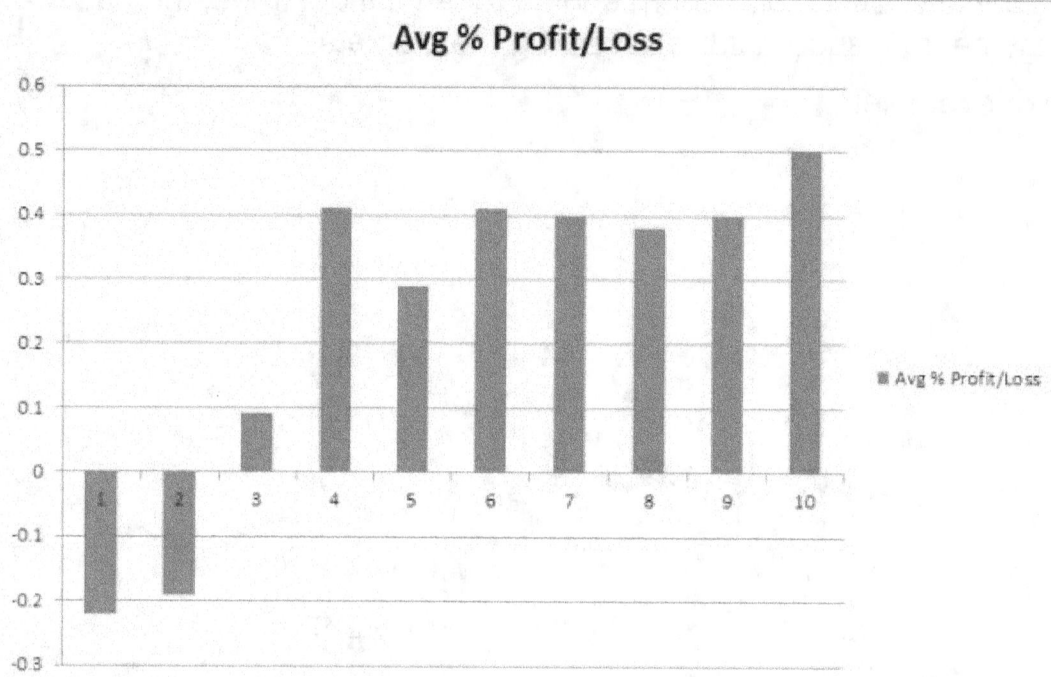

The next step was to try and also add some profit targets to the strategy. As before, if neither a stop-loss nor profit-target is hit within 20 days, we exit positions.

Unsurprisingly, if we have a very close profit target (2% or less) we find that average return per trade is negative, irrespective of the profit target used.

That is partly because we are limiting the opportunity a stock has to appreciate. It is also because contrary to the popular notion that placing a stop-loss below the low of a pattern is a good idea, our tests have illustrated that this isn't always the case.

Our tests showed that the best stop-loss and profit target to apply to piercing pattern trading strategy is 7% and 10% respectively.

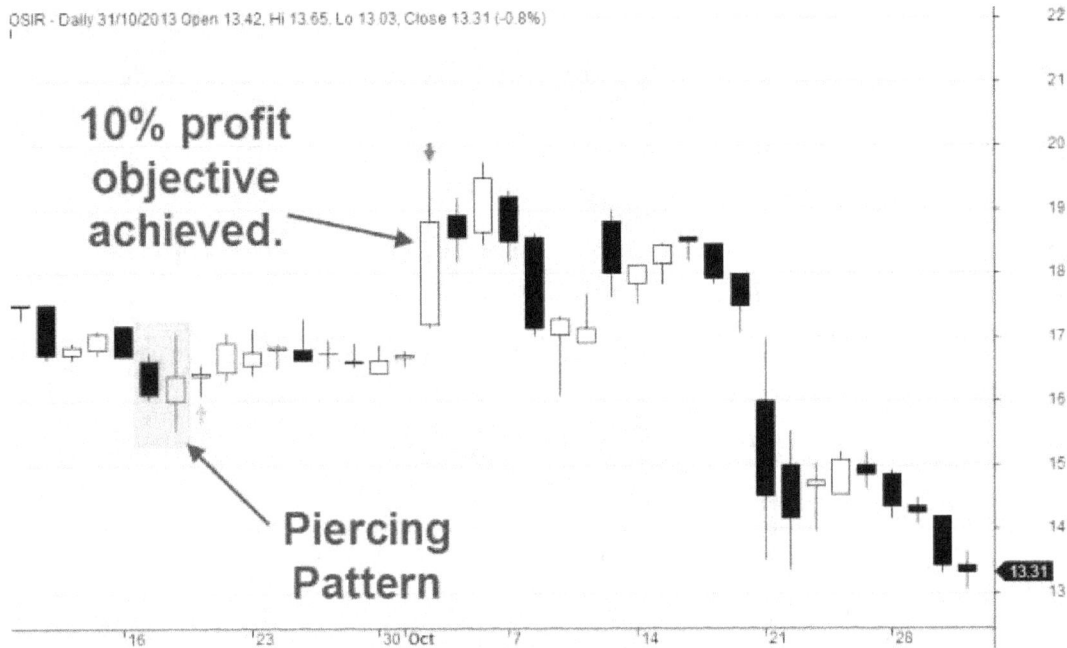

OSIR - Daily 31/10/2013 Open 13.42, Hi 13.65, Lo 13.03, Close 13.31 (-0.8%)

10% profit objective achieved.

Piercing Pattern

The final rules of the piercing pattern trading strategy.

Tests have shown that you can greatly improve the performance of trading the piercing pattern if you follow these rules:

- **Price must be above $5.00**
- **20 day Volume average must be above 100,000.**
- **On the first day of the piercing pattern, the SPY must have a 40 day MA above a 120 day MA and the 8 period RSI of the SPY must be above 70.**
- **The low of the first day of the pattern must be the lowest low in the past 10 days.**
- **If all rules are met, buy on the next day open.**
- **Apply a 10% profit target.**
- **Apply a 7% stop-loss.**

- **If neither the stop-loss nor profit target is executed, exit positions after 20 days.**
- **Once a position is closed, 3 days must pass before we are allowed to trade a signal in the same stock.**

Although there are only a handful of these patterns each year, the beauty of modern day computing power and charting packages is that rules can be easily coded and used to scan the entire universe of stocks that exist on the major exchanges.

A single scan will take seconds to provide you with a complete list of all stocks that meet each of the rules.

To code the strategy in Amibroker we can enter the following formula:

```
///////////////////////////////////////////////////////////////////////

SetTradeDelays(0,0,0,0);
SetOption("initialequity",30000);
SetOption ("MaxOpenPositions" , 5);
SetOption ("allowsamebarexit",false);
SetPositionSize(6000,spsValue);
SetBacktestMode(backtestregular);

WhiteBody = C > O;
BlackBody = C < O;
BigBlack = (Open - Close)/Open > 0.015 AND (Open - Close) * 2 >
High - Low;
DownTrend = L < Ref(LLV(L,10),-1);

PiercingPattern = Ref(bigblack,-1) AND whitebody AND O <
Ref(L,-1)
AND C >= Ref((O+C)/2,-1) AND C < Ref(O,-1) AND
Ref(downtrend,-1);
```

```
NonAdjVol = (V * C)/OI ;
Index = Foreign ("SPY","C",True);
Indexfastma = MA (Index, 40);
Indexslowma = MA (Index, 120);
STU = indexfastma > indexslowma AND RSIa(index,8) > 70;

Buysetup = PiercingPattern
AND oi> 5
AND stu
AND MA(nonadjvol,20) > 100000;

Sell = 0;
Buy = Ref(buysetup,-1);
BuyPrice = Open;
SellPrice = Close;
PT = Optimize("pt%",10,1,10,1);
SL = Optimize("SL%",7,1,10,1);
ApplyStop (stopTypeProfit,stopModePercent,pt,1,False,3);
ApplyStop (stopTypeloss,stopModepercent,sl,1,False,3);
ApplyStop(stopTypeNBar,stopModeBars,19,0,False,3);
PositionScore = 100 + Ref(nonadjVol,-1);
//////////////////////////////////////////////////////////////////
```

The test results of the improved piercing pattern

The most notable performance statistics of our strategy are a 49.11% win rate, an average gain per trade of 0.99% and a CAR/MDD of 0.25.

The following charts provide the complete performance metrics for our final strategy.

Statistics

	All trades	Long trades	Short trades
Initial capital	30000.00	30000.00	30000.00
Ending capital	36668.75	36668.75	30000.00
Net Profit	6668.75	6668.75	0.00
Net Profit %	22.23 %	22.23 %	0.00 %
Exposure %	10.33 %	10.33 %	0.00 %
Net Risk Adjusted Return %	215.16 %	215.16 %	N/A
Annual Return %	1.99 %	1.99 %	0.00 %
Risk Adjusted Return %	19.30 %	19.30 %	N/A
Total transaction costs	935.48	935.48	0.00
All trades	112	112 (100.00 %)	0 (0.00 %)
Avg. Profit/Loss	59.54	59.54	N/A
Avg. Profit/Loss %	0.99 %	0.99 %	N/A
Avg. Bars Held	12.59	12.59	N/A
Winners	55 (49.11 %)	55 (49.11 %)	0 (0.00 %)
Total Profit	27202.59	27202.59	0.00
Avg. Profit	494.59	494.59	N/A
Avg. Profit %	8.26 %	8.26 %	N/A
Avg. Bars Held	13.53	13.53	N/A
Max. Consecutive	5	5	0
Largest win	2512.18	2512.18	0.00
# bars in largest win	19	19	0
Losers	57 (50.89 %)	57 (50.89 %)	0 (0.00 %)
Total Loss	-20533.85	-20533.85	0.00
Avg. Loss	-360.24	-360.24	N/A
Avg. Loss %	-6.02 %	-6.02 %	N/A
Avg. Bars Held	11.68	11.68	N/A
Max. Consecutive	5	5	0
Largest loss	-991.04	-991.04	0.00
# bars in largest loss	8	8	0
Max. trade drawdown	-1288.96	-1288.96	0.00
Max. trade % drawdown	-20.49 %	-20.49 %	0.00 %
Max. system drawdown	-2447.24	-2447.24	0.00
Max. system % drawdown	-8.16 %	-8.16 %	0.00 %
Recovery Factor	2.73	2.73	N/A
CAR/MaxDD	0.24	0.24	N/A
RAR/MaxDD	2.37	2.37	N/A
Profit Factor	1.32	1.32	N/A
Payoff Ratio	1.37	1.37	N/A

1. Portfolio Equity

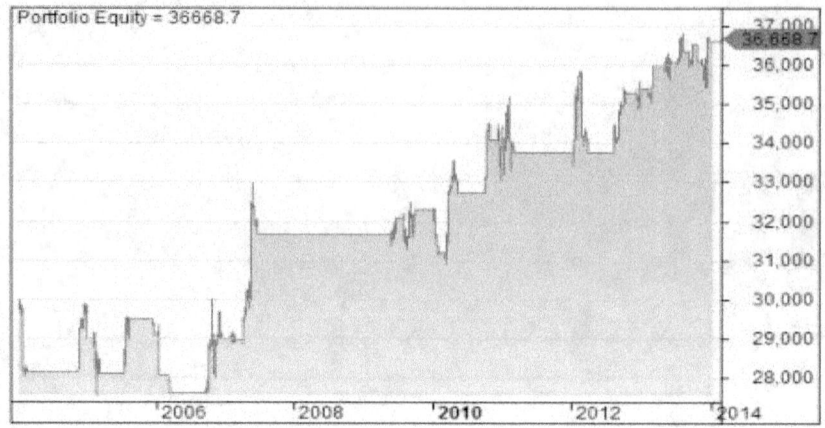

2. Underwater Equity

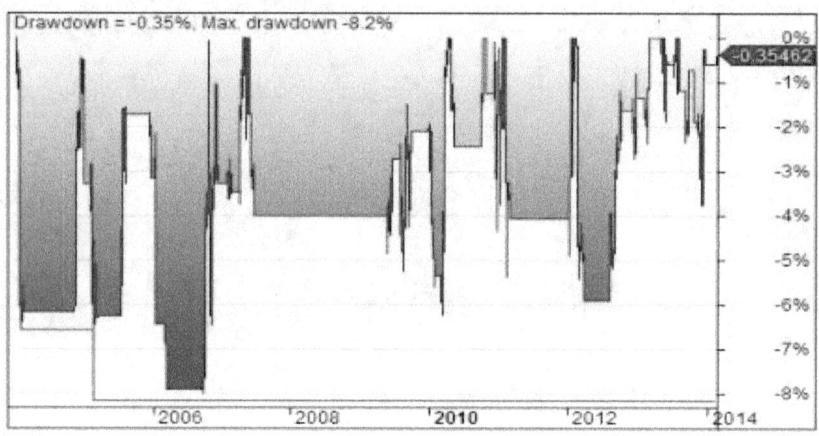

3. Profit Table

Year	Jan	Feb	Mar	Apr	May	Jun	Jul	Aug	Sep	Oct	Nov	Dec	Yr%
2004	-6.0%	-0.2%	0.0%	0.0%	0.0%	0.0%	0.0%	0.0%	0.0%	0.0%	4.5%	0.7%	-1.3%
2005	-2.0%	-2.4%	-0.7%	0.0%	0.0%	0.0%	3.7%	1.1%	0.0%	0.0%	0.0%	-1.5%	-1.9%
2006	-3.4%	0.0%	-1.6%	0.0%	0.0%	0.0%	0.0%	0.0%	0.1%	5.2%	0.2%	-0.5%	-0.1%
2007	0.0%	0.2%	-0.4%	3.0%	9.5%	-3.1%	0.0%	0.0%	0.0%	0.0%	0.0%	0.0%	9.2%
2008	0.0%	0.0%	0.0%	0.0%	0.0%	0.0%	0.0%	0.0%	0.0%	0.0%	0.0%	0.0%	0.0%
2009	0.0%	0.0%	0.0%	0.0%	0.0%	1.3%	0.0%	-1.6%	1.0%	1.3%	0.0%	0.0%	2.0%
2010	-2.8%	-0.6%	1.5%	5.7%	-2.3%	0.0%	0.0%	0.0%	0.0%	5.4%	-1.2%	-1.9%	3.4%
2011	1.2%	0.0%	-0.2%	0.0%	0.0%	0.0%	0.0%	0.0%	0.0%	0.0%	0.0%	0.0%	1.0%
2012	1.1%	4.0%	-3.9%	-1.0%	0.0%	0.0%	0.0%	0.8%	2.5%	1.2%	0.0%	0.4%	5.0%
2013	-0.1%	-0.5%	2.2%	0.0%	-0.7%	1.0%	1.6%	-0.8%	-0.9%	0.2%	-0.9%	2.2%	3.3%
2014	0.0%	0.2%	N/A	N/A	N/A	N/A	N/A	N/A	N/A	N/A	N/A	N/A	0.2%
Avg	-1.1%	0.1%	-0.3%	0.8%	0.7%	-0.1%	0.5%	-0.1%	0.3%	1.3%	0.3%	-0.1%	

The Hammer Pattern

The hammer is a 1 day pattern that occurs during a downtrend. It is similar to another candlestick pattern that is called the dragonfly doji pattern because the real body of the candlestick is small in relation to the lower shadow.

The difference between a dragonfly doji and the hammer is that the hammer pattern does not need to close at the high of the day, nor at the same price as the open. The rules are as follows:

The Hammer pattern rules re-cap

- Price must be in a downtrend.

95

- The hammer day must have a lower shadow at least 2 times longer than the real body.
- The upper shadow must be 10% less than the entire day range.
- The real body must close in the upper half of the entire day range.

The hammer pattern code

Once again we must eliminate any ambiguity that exists in our definition of the pattern. Tests found that in the case of a hammer pattern, the best results are again found if defining a down-trend by stating that the day preceding the hammer pattern must make a 10 day low.

For example:

Further preliminary tests also found that the performance of the hammer candlestick pattern is improved when it occurs

following a large down-day.

'A large down day' is defined as a day that closes at least 1.5% lower than it opened and has a real body that makes up at least 50% of the entire days range.

The Amibroker formula for the hammer pattern when using the above rules is as follows:

//

```
lowerShadow = Min(O,C) - L;
uppershadow = H - Max(O,C);
body = abs(O-C);
rngx = abs(H - L);
DownTrend = L < Ref(LLV(L,10),-1);
bigrealbody = abs(O-C) > 0.50*rngx;
largeBlackBody = C < O AND bigrealbody;
Big = abs((Close - Open)/Open) > 0.015;
isPrevLargeBlack = Ref(big,-1) AND Ref(largeblackbody,-1);
UmbrellaLine = uppershadow < rngx*0.1 AND lowershadow > body*2;

Hammer = umbrellaline AND Ref(downtrend,-1) and isprevlargeblack;
```

//

The hammer pattern psychology

Price is in a downtrend. The bears are in total control. The long lower shadow is evidence that the bears were still in control during the day, but by the end of the day the bulls had come back to the market causing demand to outstrip the intra-day supply.

The Hammer

Bears in control

Bears were still in control for part of the hammer day, but the long lower shadow is evidence that the bulls started overpowering the bears by the end of the day.

The hammer pattern test results (5 day holding period).
It's all very well for me to explain the supposed psychology of the individual patterns to you. But in all honesty, the pattern psychology that I describe is simply that which is also described in the established candlestick literature.

I agree that it is nice to have a valid reason as to why a pattern works, because it helps maintain confidence in trading the pattern and sticking to your trading strategy rules.

But always be conscious of the fact that as many patterns fail as they do succeed, irrespective of how sound the logic of the pattern may be.

Testing will provide a far greater understanding of how well a pattern might perform than a reasonable explanation for the patterns existence ever could.

The following chart shows the equity curve that was produced during our sample period when trading all hammer candlestick patterns that met our re-defined rules. All open positions were held for 5 days:

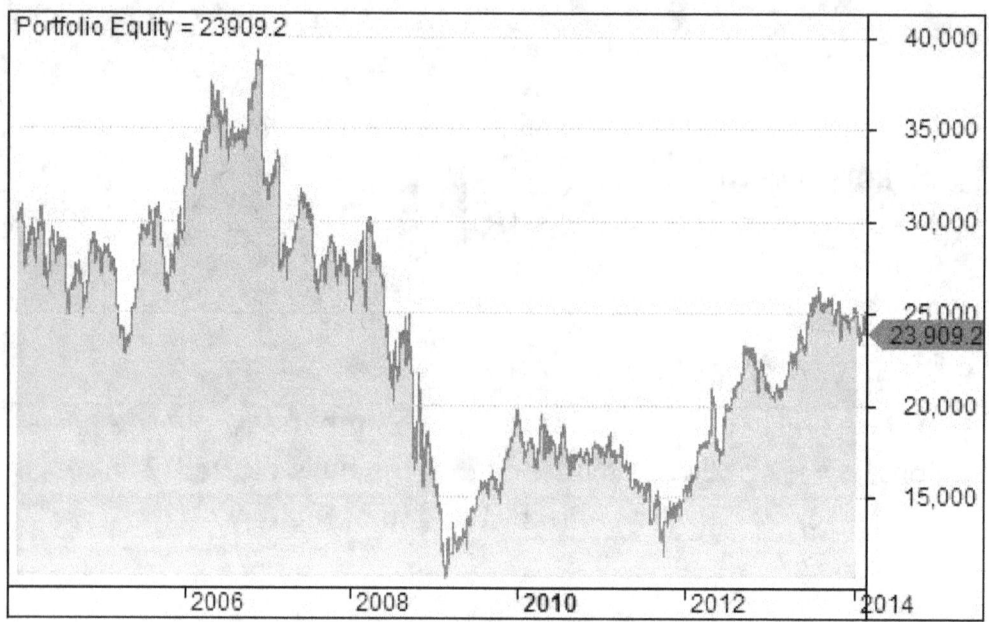

Notable performance metrics include a win-rate of 50.55% and an average gain per trade of -0.08%. Most obvious to note is that the hammer pattern seems to be a losing setup.

What is the best market environment for trading the hammer candlestick pattern?

My next tests were to determine whether the hammer candlestick pattern can be improved if we filter the market environment in which it is allowed.

Tests found that the hammer pattern performs marginally better if it occurs when the SPY is in a long term uptrend.

This means that we can trade the hammer candlestick pattern if the SPY has its 40 day MA above its 120 Day MA.

Applying indicator filters to the hammer candlestick pattern.

It is often stated that candlestick patterns provide stronger signals when they appear in the overbought or oversold condition; this is usually expressed using an indicator such as the stochastics or RSI being above or below a certain threshold.

Tests found that indeed the pattern can be improved if it is preceded by a day with a very low RSI(2) threshold. The exact filter is as follows:

Only trade a hammer candlestick pattern if the preceding day has a RSI(2) reading below 5.

I also tested the pattern while applying historical volatility filters, ConnorsRSI filters and moving average filters. None of these filters improved the returns of our basic strategy.

Another common suggestion is that the hammer pattern is improved if it occurs in conjunction with a large increase in volume. The argument being that the large volume is further evidence that a 'blow-off' day has finally seen the end of the bear's control.

I applied a rule which stated that either the hammer pattern or the day preceding the hammer pattern must be accompanied by volume greater than X% of a 20 day volume average. Our strategy was not improved in any of these tests.

Having said the above, all is not lost! A simple rule which did greatly improve the performance of the hammer candlestick pattern was found.

The rule was as follows:

Only buy the hammer candlestick pattern if the following day trades at the lowest low of the past 2 days:

For example:

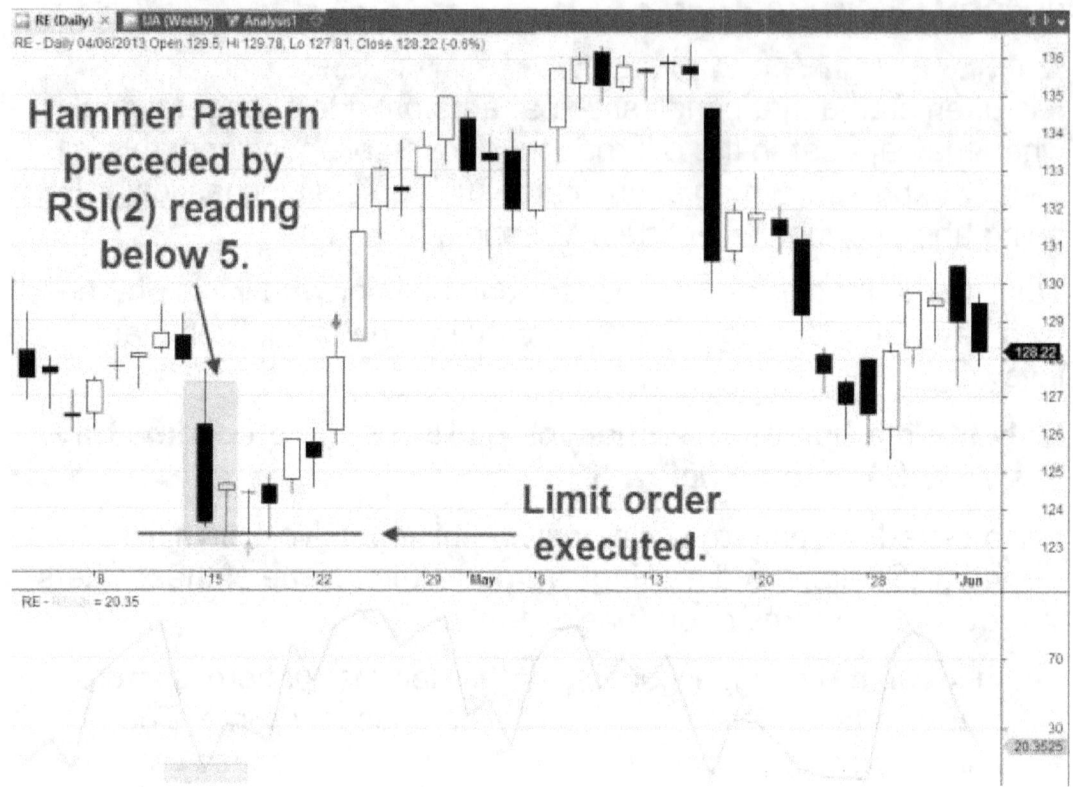

Remaining tests will include a rule which states that we only enter a position following the hammer pattern if the next day trades at, or opens lower than, the low of the past 2 days.

Applying stop-losses and profit targets to the hammer candlestick strategy

My next tests included applying a variety of percentage based stop-losses and profit-targets. Again, I have also added a rule which closes all positions after 20 days if the stop-loss or profit-target isn't executed.

These tests find the optimum stop-loss and profit target to apply to the hammer candlestick pattern strategy is 9% and 2% respectively.

The final rules of the hammer candlestick pattern trading strategy.
Tests have shown that the hammer pattern can be improved upon if we use the following rules:

- **The price must be above $5.00**
- **The 20 day volume average must be above 100,000.**
- **The day before the hammer pattern must have had the lowest low of the past 10 days.**
- **The day before the hammer must close at least 1.5% lower than it opened and have a real body that is at least 50% the size of the entire day's range.**
- **If the above rules are met, place a buy order at the lowest low of the past 2 days. This buy order is valid for 1 day, after which it is cancelled.**
- **Apply a 9% stop-loss.**
- **Apply a 2% profit-target.**
- **Exit all open positions after 20 days.**
- **Once a position is closed, 3 days must pass before we are allowed to trade a signal in the same stock.**

To code the strategy in Amibroker we can use the following formula:

//

```
SetTradeDelays(0,0,0,0);
SetOption("initialequity",30000);
SetOption ("MaxOpenPositions" , 5);
SetOption ("allowsamebarexit",false);
SetPositionSize(6000,spsValue);
SetBacktestMode(backtestregular);

lowerShadow = Min(O,C) - L;
uppershadow = H - Max(O,C);
```

```
body = abs(O-C);
rngx = abs(H - L);
DownTrend = L < Ref(LLV(L,10),-1);
bigrealbody = abs(O-C) > 0.50*rngx;
largeBlackBody = C < O AND bigrealbody;
Big = abs((Close - Open)/Open) > 0.015;
isPrevLargeBlack = Ref(big,-1) AND Ref(largeblackbody,-1);
UmbrellaLine = uppershadow < rngx*0.1 AND lowershadow >
body*2;
NonAdjVol = (V * C)/OI ;
Hammer = umbrellaline AND Ref(downtrend,-1) and
isprevlargeblack;


Index = Foreign ("SPY","C",True);
Indexfastma = MA (Index, 40);
Indexslowma = MA (Index, 120);

UT = indexfastma > indexslowma;

Buysetup = Hammer
AND oi > 5
AND ut
AND Ref(RSI(2),-1) < 5
AND MA(nonadjvol,20) > 100000
AND NOT OnLastTwoBarsOfDelistedSecurity;

Buystop = Ref(ValueWhen(Buysetup,LLV(L,2)),-1);

Buy = Ref(buysetup,-1) AND Cross(Buystop,L);

BuyPrice = Min(Open,buystop);

Sell = OnSecondLastBarOfDelistedSecurity;
```

```
SellPrice = Close;

PT = Optimize("pt%",2,1,10,1);
SL = Optimize("SL%",9,1,10,1);

ApplyStop (stopTypeProfit,stopModePercent,pt,1,False,3);
ApplyStop (stopTypeloss,stopModepercent,sl,1,False,3);
ApplyStop(stopTypeNBar,stopModeBars,19,0,False,3);

PositionScore = 100 + Ref(nonadjvol,-1);
```

//

Test results of the hammer pattern trading strategy.
The following tables and charts show us the performance metrics of
the hammer pattern when applying the above rules. **Notable
metrics include an 85.04% win-rate, an average return per trade
of 0.76% and a CAR/MDD of 0.38.**

Statistics

	All trades	Long trades	Short trades
Initial capital	30000.00	30000.00	30000.00
Ending capital	35742.56	35742.56	30000.00
Net Profit	5742.56	5742.56	0.00
Net Profit %	19.14 %	19.14 %	0.00 %
Exposure %	3.51 %	3.51 %	0.00 %
Net Risk Adjusted Return %	544.78 %	544.78 %	N/A
Annual Return %	1.74 %	1.74 %	0.00 %
Risk Adjusted Return %	49.47 %	49.47 %	N/A
Total transaction costs	774.56	774.56	0.00
All trades	127	127 (100.00 %)	0 (0.00 %)
Avg. Profit/Loss	45.22	45.22	N/A
Avg. Profit/Loss %	0.76 %	0.76 %	N/A
Avg. Bars Held	4.80	4.80	N/A
Winners	108 (85.04 %)	108 (85.04 %)	0 (0.00 %)
Total Profit	14544.34	14544.34	0.00
Avg. Profit	134.67	134.67	N/A
Avg. Profit %	2.25 %	2.25 %	N/A
Avg. Bars Held	3.89	3.89	N/A
Max. Consecutive	22	22	0
Largest win	436.54	436.54	0.00
# bars in largest win	2	2	0
Losers	19 (14.96 %)	19 (14.96 %)	0 (0.00 %)
Total Loss	-8801.78	-8801.78	0.00
Avg. Loss	-463.25	-463.25	N/A
Avg. Loss %	-7.74 %	-7.74 %	N/A
Avg. Bars Held	10.00	10.00	N/A
Max. Consecutive	3	3	0
Largest loss	-554.34	-554.34	0.00
# bars in largest loss	5	5	0
Max. trade drawdown	-578.42	-578.42	0.00
Max. trade % drawdown	-9.62 %	-9.62 %	0.00 %
Max. system drawdown	-1712.18	-1712.18	0.00
Max. system % drawdown	-4.62 %	-4.62 %	0.00 %
Recovery Factor	3.35	3.35	N/A
CAR/MaxDD	0.38	0.38	N/A
RAR/MaxDD	10.70	10.70	N/A
Profit Factor	1.65	1.65	N/A

105

1. Portfolio Equity

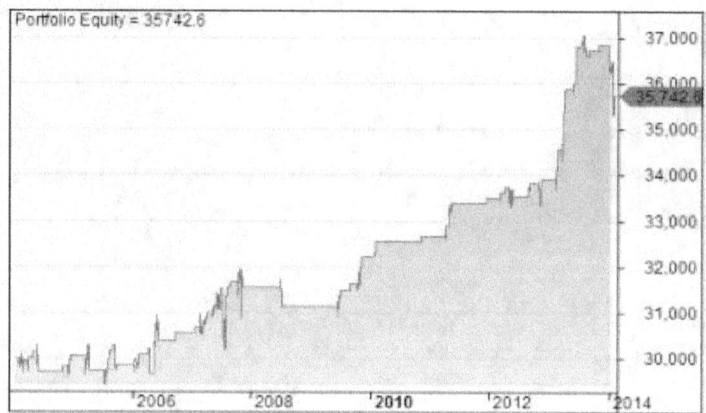

2. Underwater Equity

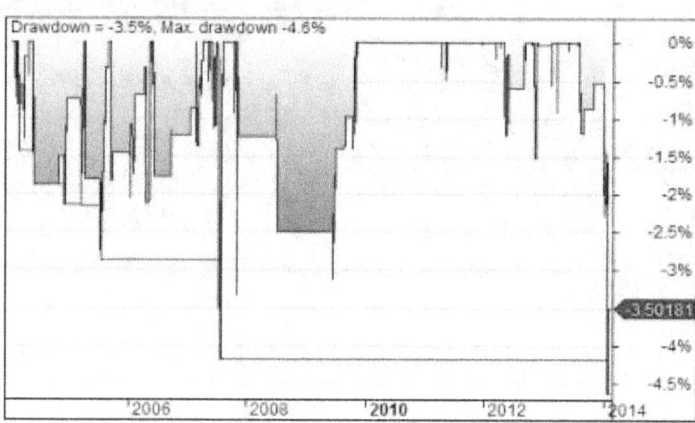

3. Profit Table

Year	Jan	Feb	Mar	Apr	May	Jun	Jul	Aug	Sep	Oct	Nov	Dec	Yr%
2004	0.1%	-0.3%	0.4%	0.4%	-1.4%	0.0%	0.0%	0.0%	0.0%	0.4%	-0.6%	1.4%	0.2%
2005	0.0%	0.0%	-0.1%	-1.0%	0.0%	0.0%	-0.4%	1.9%	-1.2%	0.2%	0.0%	0.0%	-0.7%
2006	0.4%	0.4%	0.0%	-1.4%	3.3%	-0.8%	0.0%	0.0%	0.6%	0.0%	0.0%	0.0%	2.3%
2007	0.4%	-0.1%	0.5%	0.8%	0.5%	-0.2%	-1.1%	3.0%	0.0%	0.8%	-1.2%	0.0%	3.2%
2008	0.0%	0.0%	0.0%	0.0%	0.0%	0.0%	-1.3%	0.0%	0.0%	0.0%	0.0%	0.0%	-1.3%
2009	0.0%	0.0%	0.0%	0.0%	0.0%	0.8%	0.4%	0.0%	0.4%	-0.1%	1.9%	0.0%	3.4%
2010	0.3%	0.7%	0.0%	0.0%	0.0%	0.0%	0.0%	0.0%	0.0%	0.0%	0.4%	0.0%	1.4%
2011	0.0%	0.0%	0.0%	0.7%	1.6%	0.0%	0.0%	0.0%	0.0%	0.0%	0.0%	0.3%	2.6%
2012	0.0%	0.0%	0.3%	0.3%	-0.9%	0.3%	0.0%	0.0%	0.8%	-0.1%	0.4%	0.0%	1.2%
2013	0.0%	0.6%	1.4%	3.7%	0.0%	2.6%	0.3%	-0.9%	0.3%	0.0%	0.3%	0.0%	8.6%
2014	-2.8%	-0.2%	N/A	N/A	N/A	N/A	N/A	N/A	N/A	N/A	N/A	N/A	-3.0%
Avg	-0.1%	0.1%	0.3%	0.3%	0.3%	0.3%	-0.2%	0.4%	0.1%	0.1%	0.1%	0.2%	

The Bullish Kicker Pattern

The bullish kicker is a 2 day pattern that is supposed to signify impending market strength.

The bullish kicker pattern rules re-cap.

- Price has been in a downtrend.
- The first day is a down day.
- The second day opens equal to or higher than the first day's high.
- The second day low is higher than the first day high.

The bullish kicker pattern code

We again begin with defining the subjective rule that price has been in a down-trend. In the case of the bullish kicker pattern:

The best results were found when the first day of the pattern made the lowest low in the past 5 days.

The Amibroker formula for the bullish kicker pattern is as follows:

///

DownTrend = **L** < Ref(LLV(**L**,5),-1);

BullKicker = Ref(**O**,-1) > Ref(**C**,-1) **AND O** >= Ref(**H**,-1) **AND C > O AND L** > Ref(**H**,-1) **AND** Ref(downtrend,-1);

///

The bullish kicker pattern psychology

The bullish kicker pattern provides us with a very visual demonstration of a change in investor sentiment. If we study the next chart it is clear that the bears were in control of the market.

However, when the market gaps considerably higher and the bears power isn't even enough to test the previous days price range, we can reasonably assume that the bulls have come back to the market with some conviction.

ALL (Daily) × SPY (Daily) Analysis1

ALL - Daily 04/04/2014 Open 56.89, Hi 57.28, Lo 56.4, Close 56.41 (-0.3%) Vol 2,615,8(

Lowest low in
past 5 days. ⟶

Bullish kicker pattern.
(Notice the sudden
gap higher.)

21   27   Feb   10   18   24

The bullish kicker test results (5 day holding period)

I won't bore you with the detail, but even after optimizing the definition of our downtrend, the bullish kicker is barely a profitable signal when positions are only held for 5 days.

Notable metrics include a 52.68% win rate and an average gain per trade of just 0.09%. These results are not what you might have expected from such a visually strong pattern.

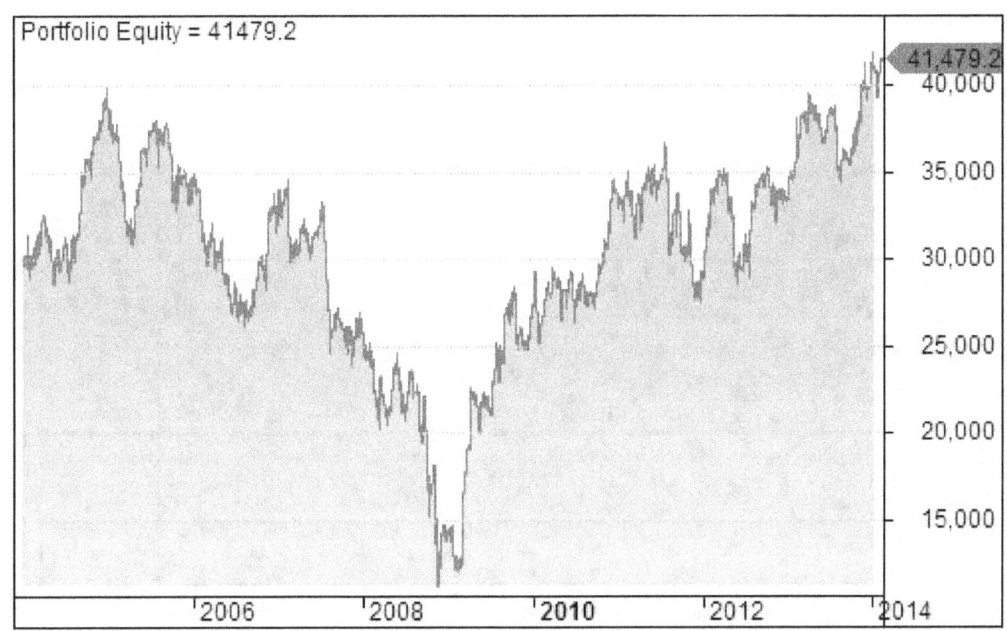

Portfolio Equity = 41479.2

The best market environment for trading the bullish kicker pattern happens to be when the SPY is in a long-term down-trend.

Having said that, the performance is the pattern is choppy at best. Even still, applying the above market environment filter slightly improves the win-rate to 53.41% and the average return per trade to 0.37%.

This is the strategy equity curve if only trading the pattern when the SPY has its 40 day MA **below** its 120 day MA:

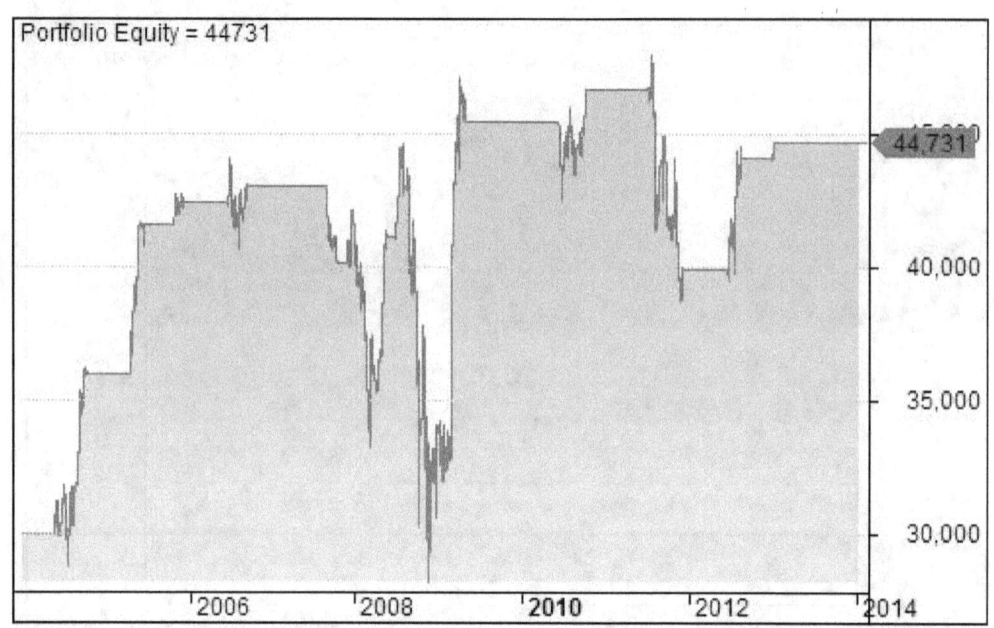

Portfolio Equity = 44731

44,731

40,000

35,000

30,000

'2006   '2008   **2010**   '2012   '2014

Applying indicator filters to the bullish kicker candlestick pattern.

As things currently stand, I have some serious doubts that the kicker pattern is the 'strongest candlestick signal' that there is.

Perhaps adding some further filters will improve the performance.

Firstly, I tested the bullish kicker pattern when it occurred in the oversold stochastic condition. Contrary to popular beliefs, the pattern is in no way improved if only traded when a stock is also oversold (as gauged by the Stochastics indicator).

In fact, tests show that the one time when you *don't* want to trade the pattern is when the stochastics are oversold!

The following chart lists the stochastic values on the horizontal axis. Notice that when the current strategy includes a rule which states that the stochastic oscillator must be oversold (anywhere under 25), the returns are either breakeven or actually negative.

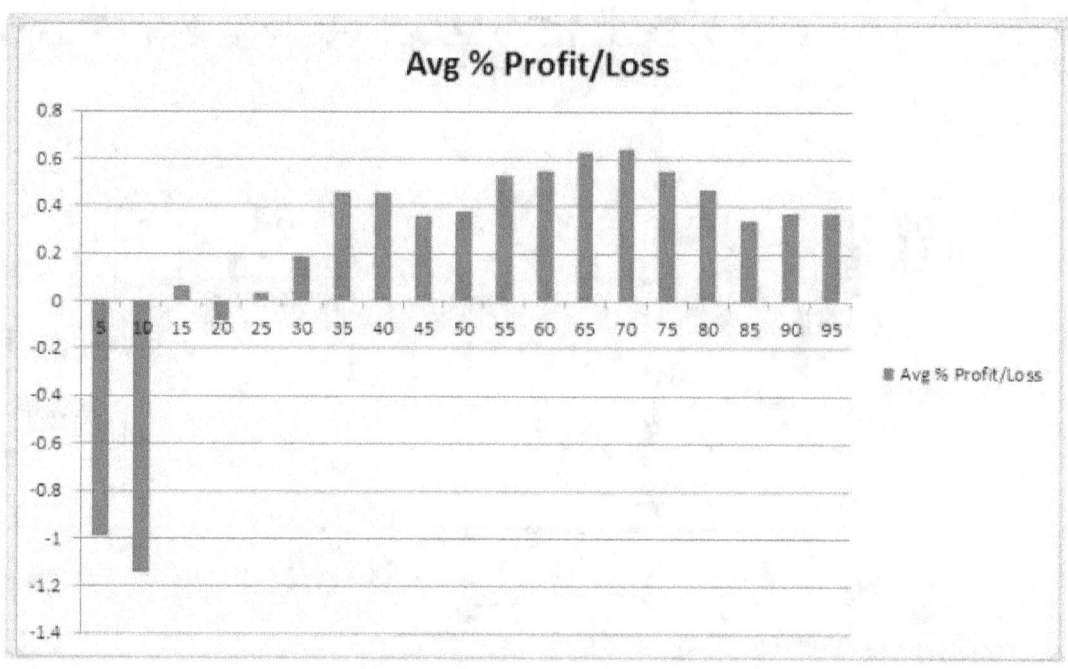

Avg % Profit/Loss

While trading the strategy in the oversold stochastic condition is not advisable, there are further filters which do improve the strategy performance.

One of the filters that I tested was based upon the 1 day ROC%. The exact rule is that we are only allowed to trade the bullish kicker pattern if the first day of the pattern has a ROC(C,1) reading which is less than -2%.

After applying our ROC filter to the 5 day holding period strategy (only trade during a long-term down-trend) we have the following results:

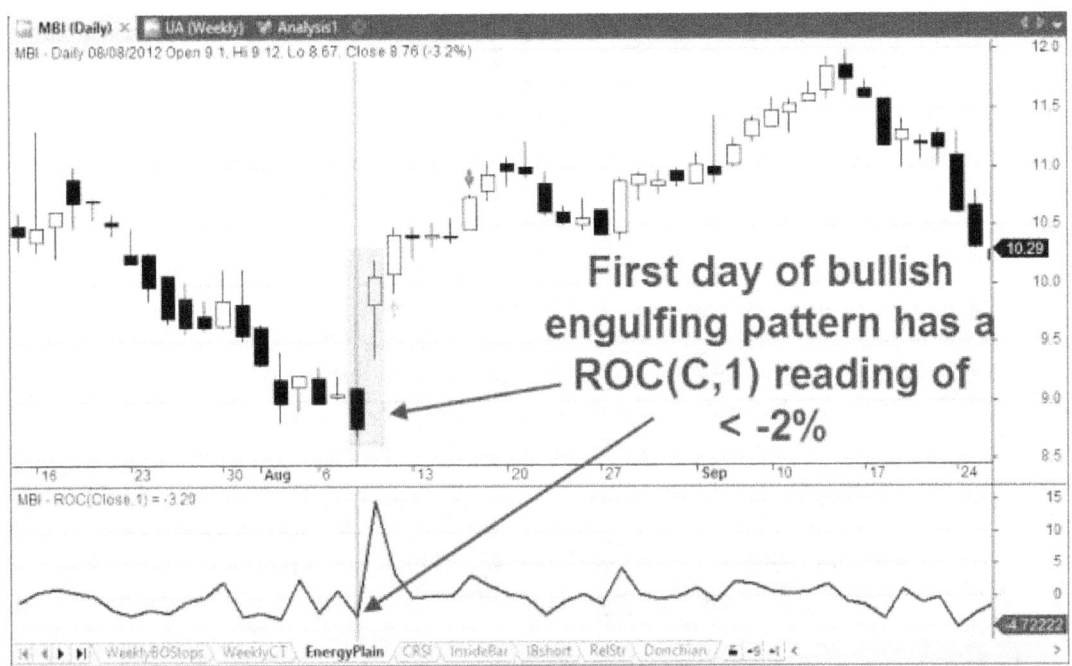

Notable performance metrics include a 53.95% win rate and an average return per trade of 0.96%.

With a CAR/MDD of 0.24, the risk adjusted performance is also better than you would have achieved if simply buying and holding the market.

Applying stop-losses and profit targets to the bullish kicker trading strategy

Perhaps applying stop-losses and profit targets to the strategy will help to improve the performance. As with each pattern tested in this book, the first logical place to put our stop-loss would be below the low of the pattern itself.

For example, a stop-loss below the bullish kicker candlestick pattern can be seen in the next chart.

Bullish Kicker

A stop-loss would be a close below this low.

When simply holding all positions for our default 5 day period - but including a stop-loss below the pattern, the performance is little changed.

When using percent based profit-targets and stop-losses, the optimum values to use are 8% for both the stop-loss and profit-target.

When applying the above exit rules, the equity curve produced during the test is as follows:

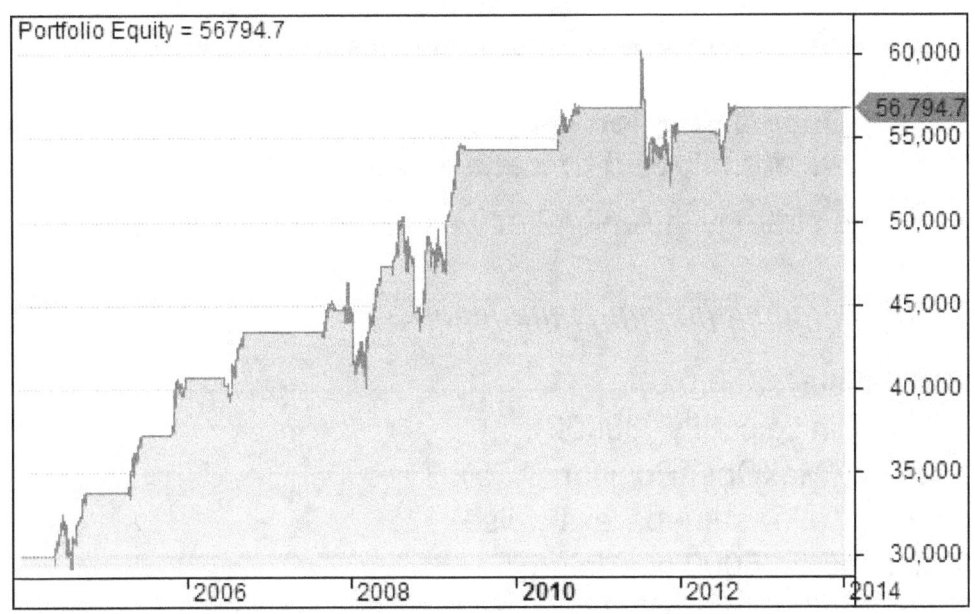

Notable performance metrics include a 58.09% win-rate, an average gain per trade of 1.49% and a CAR/MDD of 0.48.

The final rules of the bullish kicker pattern trading strategy.

Tests have shown that a standard bullish kicker trading strategy can be improved if we apply the following rules:

- **The price must be above $5.00**
- **The 20 day Volume average must be above 100,000.**
- **The low of the bullish kicker must be the lowest low in the past 5 days.**
- **The pattern must occur when the SPY has its 40 day MA below its 120 Day MA.**
- **On the first day of the pattern, the ROC(C,1) must be below -2%.**
- **Profit targets are 8% above the entry price.**
- **Stop-loss are 8% below the entry price.**

- **If the price has not closed below the stop-loss or above the profit target within 20 days, close positions.**
- **Once a position is closed, 3 days must pass before we are allowed to trade a signal in the same stock.**

To code the strategy in Amibroker we can enter the following formula:

//

```
SetTradeDelays(0,0,0,0);
SetOption("initialequity",30000);
SetOption ("MaxOpenPositions" , 5);
SetOption ("allowsamebarexit",false);
SetPositionSize(6000,spsValue);
SetBacktestMode(backtestregular);


DownTrend = L < Ref(LLV(L,5),-1);

BullKicker = Ref(O,-1) > Ref(C,-1) AND O >= Ref(H,-1)
AND C > O AND L > Ref(H,-1) AND Ref(downtrend,-1);

NonAdjVol = (V * C)/OI ;

Index = Foreign ("SPY","C",True);
Indexfastma = MA (Index, 40);
Indexslowma = MA (Index, 120);

DT = indexfastma < indexslowma;

Buysetup = bullkicker
AND oi > 5
AND dt
AND Ref(ROC(C,1),-1) < -2
AND MA(nonadjvol,20) > 100000;
```

```
Sell =  0;

BuyPrice = Open;

Buy = Ref(buysetup,-1);

SellPrice = Close;

PT = Optimize("pt%",8,1,10,1);
SL = Optimize("SL%",8,1,10,1);

ApplyStop (stopTypeProfit,stopModePercent,pt,1,False,3);
ApplyStop (stopTypeloss,stopModepercent,sl,1,False,3);
ApplyStop(stopTypeNBar,stopModeBars,19,0,False,3);


PositionScore = 100 + ref(nonadjvol,-1);
```

//

Test results of the bullish kicker candlestick trading strategy.
The following tables and charts show us the complete performance
metrics of the bullish kicker pattern when applying the above rules.

Statistics

	All trades	Long trades	Short trades
Initial capital	30000.00	30000.00	30000.00
Ending capital	56794.67	56794.67	30000.00
Net Profit	26794.67	26794.67	0.00
Net Profit %	89.32 %	89.32 %	0.00 %
Exposure %	11.71 %	11.71 %	0.00 %
Net Risk Adjusted Return %	762.88 %	762.88 %	N/A
Annual Return %	6.48 %	6.48 %	0.00 %
Risk Adjusted Return %	55.35 %	55.35 %	N/A
Total transaction costs	2403.88	2403.88	0.00
All trades	303	303 (100.00 %)	0 (0.00 %)
Avg. Profit/Loss	88.43	88.43	N/A
Avg. Profit/Loss %	1.49 %	1.49 %	N/A
Avg. Bars Held	8.35	8.35	N/A
Winners	176 (58.09 %)	176 (58.09 %)	0 (0.00 %)
Total Profit	84078.51	84078.51	0.00
Avg. Profit	477.72	477.72	N/A
Avg. Profit %	8.00 %	8.00 %	N/A
Avg. Bars Held	8.36	8.36	N/A
Max. Consecutive	15	15	0
Largest win	2375.32	2375.32	0.00
# bars in largest win	2	2	0
Losers	127 (41.91 %)	127 (41.91 %)	0 (0.00 %)
Total Loss	-57283.84	-57283.84	0.00
Avg. Loss	-451.05	-451.05	N/A
Avg. Loss %	-7.53 %	-7.53 %	N/A
Avg. Bars Held	8.35	8.35	N/A
Max. Consecutive	13	13	0
Largest loss	-1168.54	-1168.54	0.00
# bars in largest loss	2	2	0
Max. trade drawdown	-1168.54	-1168.54	0.00
Max. trade % drawdown	-19.45 %	-19.45 %	0.00 %
Max. system drawdown	-7968.58	-7968.58	0.00
Max. system % drawdown	-13.50 %	-13.50 %	0.00 %
Recovery Factor	3.36	3.36	N/A
CAR/MaxDD	0.48	0.48	N/A
RAR/MaxDD	4.10	4.10	N/A
Profit Factor	1.47	1.47	N/A

121

Charts

1. Portfolio Equity

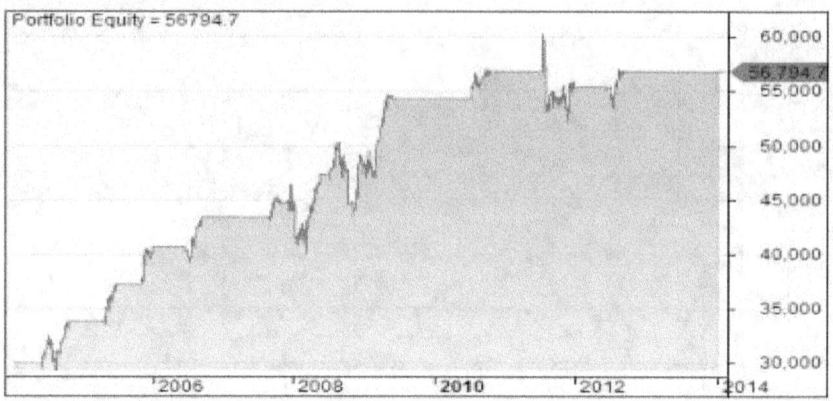

2. Underwater Equity

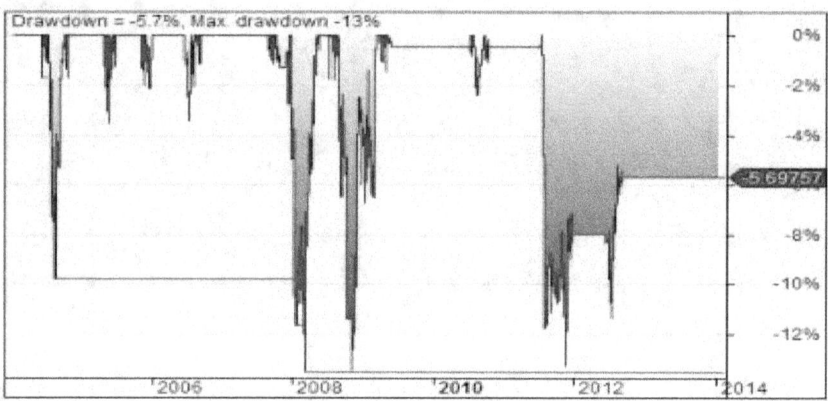

3. Profit Table

Year	Jan	Feb	Mar	Apr	May	Jun	Jul	Aug	Sep	Oct	Nov	Dec	Yr%
2004	0.0%	0.0%	0.0%	0.0%	-0.2%	6.3%	-2.7%	-0.6%	5.5%	4.1%	0.0%	0.0%	**12.8%**
2005	0.0%	0.0%	0.0%	-0.1%	5.6%	4.5%	0.0%	0.0%	0.0%	1.3%	7.0%	-0.3%	**19.1%**
2006	0.9%	0.0%	0.0%	0.0%	0.0%	-1.1%	2.9%	2.7%	2.1%	0.0%	0.0%	0.0%	**7.7%**
2007	0.0%	0.0%	0.0%	0.0%	0.0%	0.0%	0.0%	0.0%	1.9%	1.4%	-0.4%	2.5%	**5.5%**
2008	-10.2%	1.7%	1.3%	5.4%	5.8%	0.0%	2.3%	3.9%	-3.8%	-7.3%	2.3%	4.5%	**4.6%**
2009	-0.2%	-1.3%	6.8%	6.9%	1.1%	-0.2%	0.0%	0.0%	0.0%	0.0%	0.0%	0.0%	**13.5%**
2010	0.0%	0.0%	0.0%	0.0%	0.0%	0.0%	2.0%	-0.1%	2.5%	-0.1%	0.0%	0.0%	**4.4%**
2011	0.0%	0.0%	0.0%	0.0%	0.0%	0.0%	3.4%	-6.4%	-1.7%	1.8%	-1.0%	1.8%	**-2.4%**
2012	0.0%	0.0%	0.0%	0.0%	0.0%	-0.2%	-0.1%	2.6%	0.2%	0.0%	0.0%	0.0%	**2.5%**
2013	0.0%	0.0%	0.0%	0.0%	0.0%	0.0%	0.0%	0.0%	0.0%	0.0%	0.0%	0.0%	**0.0%**
2014	0.0%	0.0%	N/A	N/A	N/A	N/A	N/A	N/A	N/A	N/A	N/A	N/A	**0.0%**
Avg	-0.9%	0.0%	0.8%	1.2%	1.2%	0.9%	0.8%	0.2%	0.7%	0.1%	0.8%	0.9%	

123

The Bullish Harami Pattern

The bullish harami pattern is commonly known in the west as a bullish inside day. It is a 2 day pattern where the first day is a continuation of a downtrend and creates a large down day.

The second day creates a smaller body and the open and closing price are contained within the open and closing price of the first day.

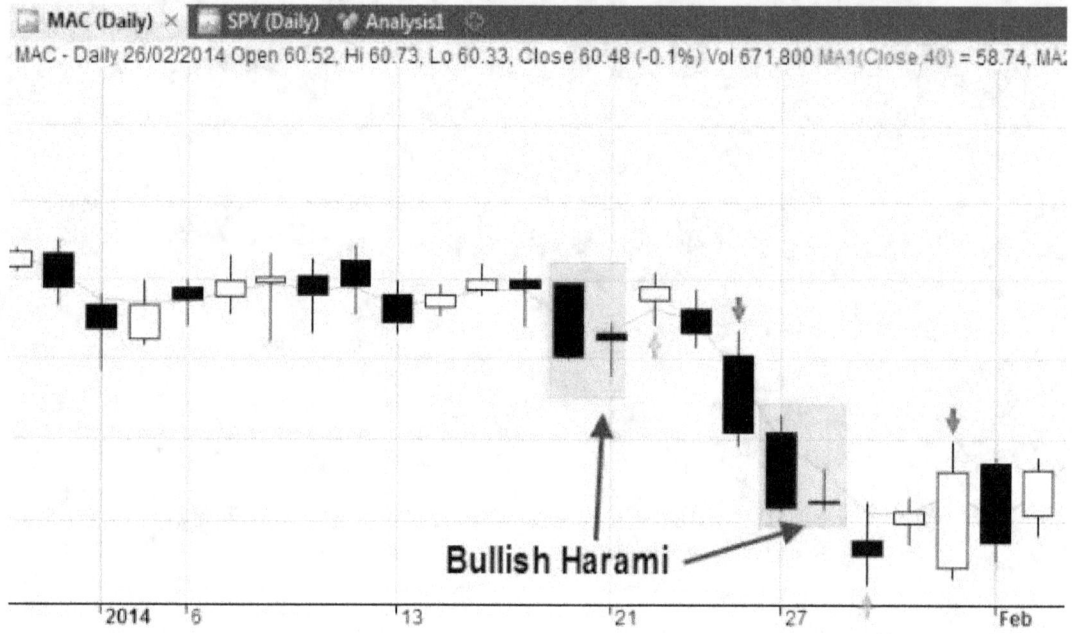

MAC (Daily) × SPY (Daily) Analysis1

MAC - Daily 26/02/2014 Open 60.52, Hi 60.73, Lo 60.33, Close 60.48 (-0.1%) Vol 671,800 MA1(Close,40) = 58.74, MA:

Bullish Harami

The bullish harami rules re-cap

- The price must be in a downtrend.
- The first day is a large down day.
- The second day is a small range day.
- The second day opens lower than the first days open and closes higher than the first days close.
- The second day can either be an up day or a down day. (I shall test both rules to determine whether one is better than the other.)

- Some people require that the high and low of the second day are within the first day range as well. (I will also test that rule too.)

There are a few areas of ambiguity regarding our current pattern definition. We need to clearly define a 'down-trend', a 'large down day' and a 'small range day' before we can begin testing.

We also need to establish from the outset whether the pattern is improved if the second day is an up day or a down day, or whether it is improved if we stipulate that the high and low of the second day are within the high and low of the first day.

Firstly, adding a rule that states that the low and high of the second day are within the low and high of the first day has no significant effect on the results. However, stipulating that the second day is an up day does make a significant difference to the results.

We will add a rule that states that **we can only trade the bullish harami pattern if the second day closes positive.**

The area of most stability for our definition of a down-trend is between 6 and 12 days. We will take the middle value, meaning that **a down-trend is defined as the first day of the pattern making the lowest low of the past 9 days.**

A 'large down day' is defined as a day that has closed at least 1.5% lower than it opened.

A 'small range day' is defined as a day that has less than a 0.3% difference between the open and close.

I should point out that these definitions can be altered without breaking the rules of the bullish harami as outlined in much of the established candlestick literature.

The following code is what I shall use, but you can tweak certain parameters where you see fit.

The Amibroker code for the bullish harami pattern when containing the rules outlined above is as follows:

///

```
BlackBody = C < O;
Big = abs((Close - Open)/Open) > 0.015;
rng = abs((C-O)/O);
SmallRealBody = rng < 0.003 AND rng > 0;
DownTrend = L < Ref(LLV(L,9),-1);

BullishHarami = Ref(big AND blackbody,-1) AND smallRealBody
AND Min(O,C) > Ref(C,-1) AND Max(O,C) < Ref(O,-1) AND
Ref(downtrend,-1) AND O < C;
```

///

The bullish harami pattern psychology

A strong down-trend has been in effect and seems to be gathering even more force as evidenced by the large down day.

However, whereas we expect the trend to continue lower because of the large down day, instead we see the bulls open the market higher than the close of the previously bearish candle. This is the evidence we need to presume that the shorts are covering their positions.

When the market finally closes while making a small range day, we can see that the prior market expansion has now contracted. That contraction is further reason for bears to believe that the strong down-trend which they have been riding has come to end.

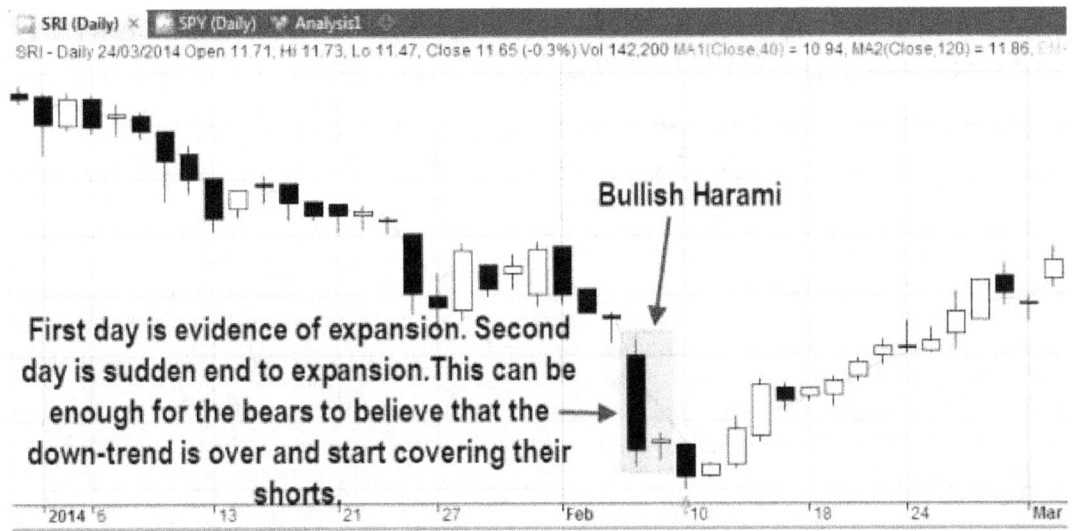

SRI (Daily) × SPY (Daily) Analysis1

SRI - Daily 24/03/2014 Open 11.71, Hi 11.73, Lo 11.47, Close 11.65 (-0.3%) Vol 142,200 MA1(Close,40) = 10.94, MA2(Close,120) = 11.86,

Bullish Harami

First day is evidence of expansion. Second day is sudden end to expansion. This can be enough for the bears to believe that the down-trend is over and start covering their shorts.

2014 6   13   21   27   Feb   10   18   24   Mar

The bullish Harami test results (5 day holding period)

When trading the bullish Harami pattern using the rules outlined so far and holding all positions for 5 days, we get the following equity curve:

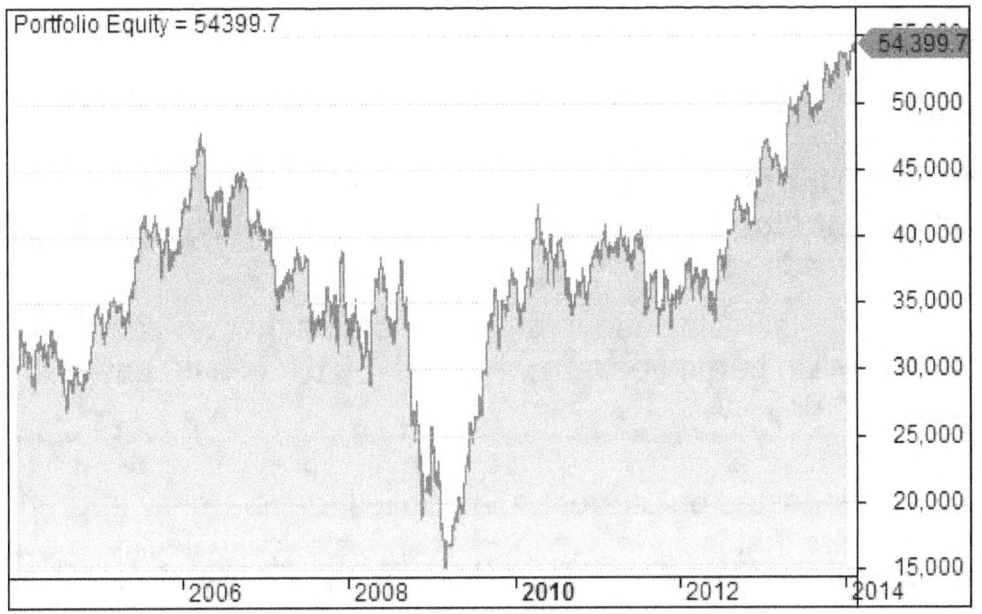

Portfolio Equity = 54399.7

128

Notable performance metrics include a 51.67% win-rate and an average 5 day return per trade of 0.17%.

What is the best market condition for trading the bullish harami pattern? The best market environment to trade the bullish harami pattern is when the SPY is in a long-term up-trend.

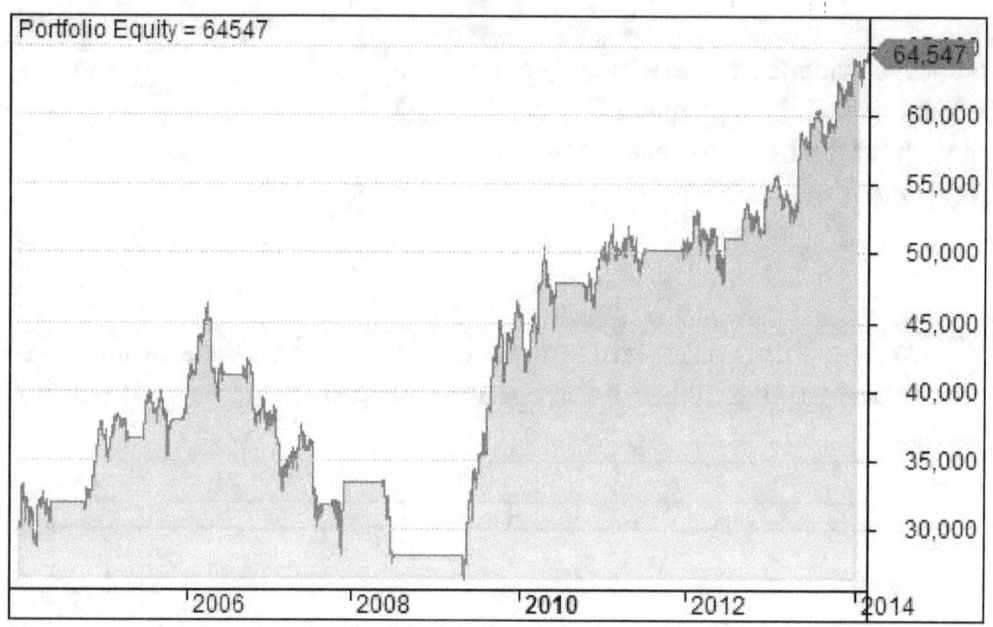

Notable performance metrics when applying the market environment filter are a 51.65% win-rate and an average 5 day return per trade of 0.35.

Remaining tests will include a rule which states that we can only trade the bullish harami pattern when the SPY has a 40 day MA above a 120 day MA.

Applying indicator filters to the bullish harami candlestick pattern Again, I have tested our current rules while independently applying a range of filters that include, Connors RSI, historical volatility, moving averages, volume, stochastics, Bollinger bands, keltner bands, ATR and Rate of Change.

Without excessive curve-fitting, only a few of the aforementioned indicators improved the CAR/MDD of our current strategy.

However, applying a simple moving average filter to the strategy showed a marked improvement across multiple parameters that were set between 10 and 200.

I wanted to know if the performance of the pattern was improved by stipulating that the closing price of the bullish harami day was above the (x) day MA.

The following chart lists the (x) day MA on the x axis and the corresponding 5 day average return per trade is shown on the y axis.

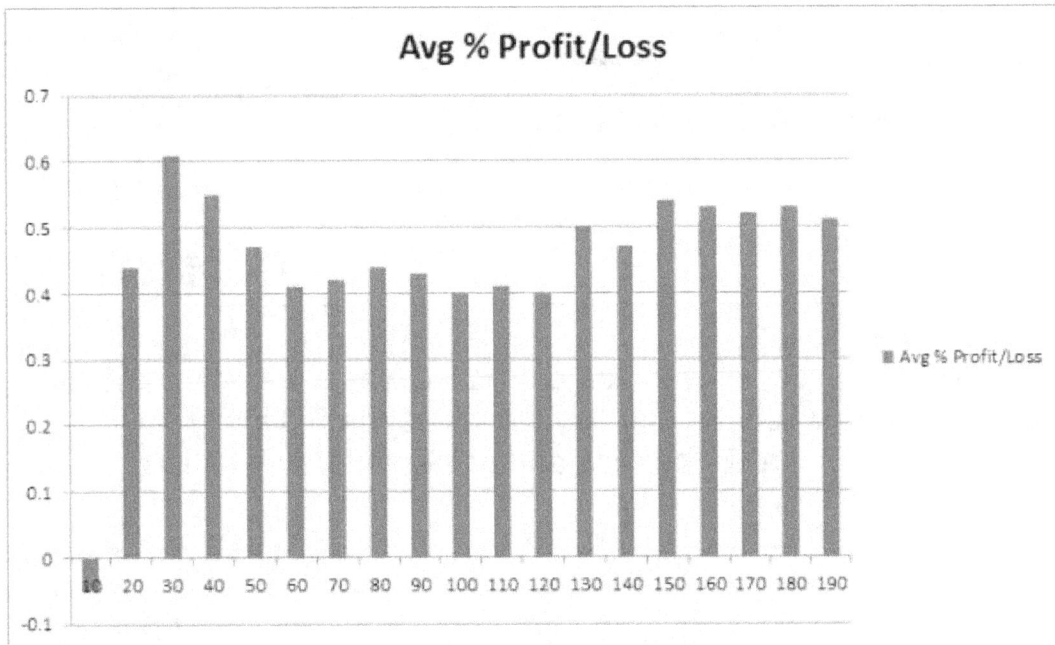

As the chart illustrates, except for the 10 day MA, we can improve the average gain per trade of our existing strategy if stipulating that the pattern must occur when a stock is trading above a certain MA.

The area of most stability is between 140 and 200, we shall take the middle range and apply the following rule:

We can only trade the bullish harami pattern if it is trading above the 170 day MA.

For example:

Another rule which showed some promise was if we only trade the harami pattern when the first day closes beneath a lower BollingerBand set at 20 periods and one standard deviation.

For example:

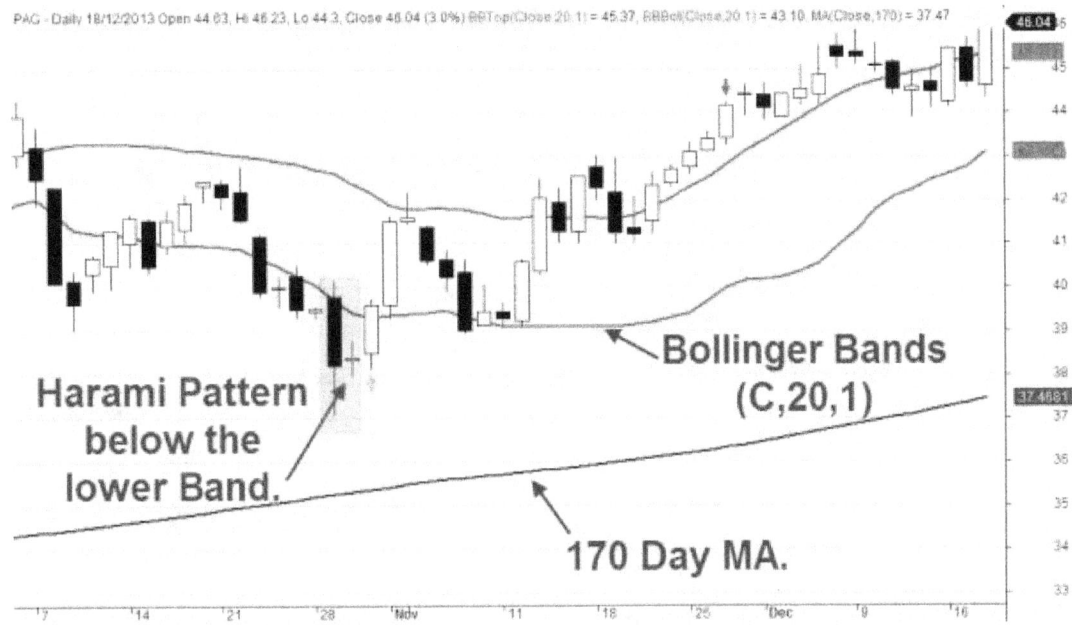

Harami Pattern below the lower Band.

Bollinger Bands (C,20,1)

170 Day MA.

Applying stop-losses and profit targets to the bullish harami candlestick pattern trading strategy

Before testing the various stop-losses and profit targets, I wanted to first decide whether the bullish harami performs better if we wait for confirmation that the market is moving higher.

One of the most popular ideas is to buy the bullish harami if the high of the second day in the pattern is broken the next day.

For example, the following losing trade would not have been permitted if we stated that we would only buy if the price breached the high of the harami candle:

NYT (Daily) ✕   SPY (Daily)   Analysis1

NYT - Daily 17/03/2014 Open 16.62, Hi 16.79, Lo 16.11, Close 16.21 (-1.9%) Vol 774,9

Instead of simply buying the open following a signal, we place an order to buy if the price breaks the high of the second day.

2014   '13   '21   '27   Feb   '10   '18

Tests show that applying a rule which only permits buying the bullish harami pattern if the following day trades higher than the harami high will improve the average gain made per trade.

As with each of the previous patterns we have so far tested, stop-losses below the low of the pattern hurt performance.

Tests of the strategy that included a stop-loss below the low of the pattern and a range of profit targets that offered between a 0.5/1 and 10/1 risk reward ratio all drastically hurt the performance of the strategy too.

When testing profit targets and stop-losses that are between 1% and 10% above or below the entry price we find that the optimum parameters to use are 7% and 2% respectively.

The final rules of the bullish harami pattern trading strategy

Tests have shown that a standard bullish harami trading strategy can be improved if we apply the following rules:

- **The price must be above $5.00**
- **The 20 day Volume average must be above 100,000.**
- **The low of the first day in the bullish harami pattern must be the lowest low in the past 9 days.**
- **On the first day of the pattern, the SPY must have a 40 day MA above a 120 day.**
- **The closing price on the day of the signal must be above the 170 day MA.**
- **The closing price on the day of the signal must be below a lower BollingerBand set to 20 periods and one standard deviation.**
- **If the rules are met, place a buy stop order at the high of the harami candle.**
- **Apply a 7% profit target above the entry price.**
- **Apply a 2% stop-loss below the entry price.**
- **If no targets or Stop-losses are executed, exit positions after 20 days.**
- **Once a position is closed, 3 days must pass before we are allowed to trade a signal in the same stock.**

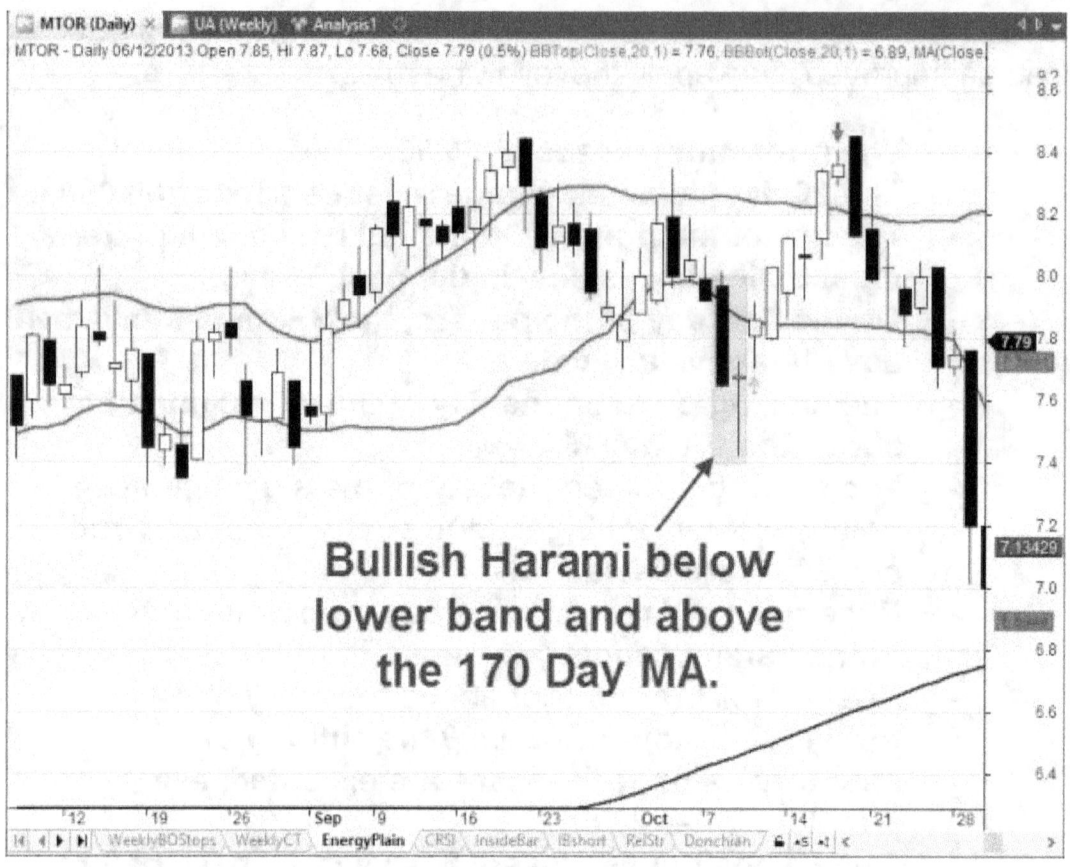

MTOR - Daily 06/12/2013 Open 7.85, Hi 7.87, Lo 7.68, Close 7.79 (0.5%) BBTop(Close,20,1) = 7.76, BBBot(Close,20,1) = 6.89, MA(Close

Bullish Harami below lower band and above the 170 Day MA.

To code the strategy in Amibroker we can use the following formula:

//

```
SetTradeDelays(0,0,0,0);
SetOption("initialequity",30000);
SetOption ("MaxOpenPositions" , 5);
SetOption ("allowsamebarexit",false);
SetPositionSize(6000,spsValue);
SetBacktestMode(backtestregular);

BlackBody = C < O;
Big = abs((Close - Open)/Open) > 0.015;
rng = abs((C-O)/O);
```

```
SmallRealBody = rng < 0.003 AND rng > 0;
DownTrend = L < Ref(LLV(L,9),-1);

BullishHarami = Ref(big AND blackbody,-1) AND smallRealBody
AND Min(O,C) > Ref(C,-1)
AND Max(O,C) < Ref(O,-1) AND Ref(downtrend,-1) AND O < C;

NonAdjVol = (V * C)/OI ;

Index = Foreign ("SPY","C",True);
Indexfastma = MA (Index, 40);
Indexslowma = MA (Index, 120);

UT = indexfastma > indexslowma;

Buysetup = bullishharami
AND oi > 5
AND ut
AND C > MA(C,170)
AND C < BBandBot(C,20,1)
AND MA(nonadjvol,20) > 100000;

buystop = Ref(ValueWhen(buysetup,H),-1);

Buy = Ref(buysetup,-1) AND Cross(H,buystop);

Sell = 0;

BuyPrice = Max(Open,buystop);

SellPrice = Close;

PT = Optimize("pt%",7,1,10,1);
SL = Optimize("SL%",2,1,10,1);
```

```
ApplyStop (stopTypeProfit,stopModePercent,pt,1,False,3);
ApplyStop (stopTypeloss,stopModepercent,sl,1,False,3);
ApplyStop(stopTypeNBar,stopModeBars,19,0,False,3);

PositionScore = 100 + Ref(nonadjvol,-1);
//////////////////////////////////////////////////////////
```

Test results for the bullish harami trading strategy

The following tables and charts show us the performance metrics of the bullish harami pattern when applying the above rules. **Notable metrics include a 38.71% win rate, an average gain per trade of 1.29% and a CAR/MDD of 0.52.**

	All trades	Long trades	Short trades
Initial capital	30000.00	30000.00	30000.00
Ending capital	44384.79	44384.79	30000.00
Net Profit	14384.79	14384.79	0.00
Net Profit %	47.95 %	47.95 %	0.00 %
Exposure %	6.38 %	6.38 %	0.00 %
Net Risk Adjusted Return %	751.39 %	751.39 %	N/A
Annual Return %	3.93 %	3.93 %	0.00 %
Risk Adjusted Return %	61.57 %	61.57 %	N/A
Total transaction costs	1241.41	1241.41	0.00
All trades	186	186 (100.00 %)	0 (0.00 %)
Avg. Profit/Loss	77.34	77.34	N/A
Avg. Profit/Loss %	1.29 %	1.29 %	N/A
Avg. Bars Held	6.02	6.02	N/A
Winners	72 (38.71 %)	72 (38.71 %)	0 (0.00 %)
Total Profit	30904.03	30904.03	0.00
Avg. Profit	429.22	429.22	N/A
Avg. Profit %	7.17 %	7.17 %	N/A
Avg. Bars Held	8.01	8.01	N/A
Max. Consecutive	5	5	0
Largest win	1622.08	1622.08	0.00
# bars in largest win	2	2	0
Losers	114 (61.29 %)	114 (61.29 %)	0 (0.00 %)
Total Loss	-16519.23	-16519.23	0.00
Avg. Loss	-144.91	-144.91	N/A
Avg. Loss %	-2.42 %	-2.42 %	N/A
Avg. Bars Held	4.76	4.76	N/A
Max. Consecutive	16	16	0
Largest loss	-698.52	-698.52	0.00
# bars in largest loss	4	4	0
Max. trade drawdown	-868.15	-868.15	0.00
Max. trade % drawdown	-14.07 %	-14.07 %	0.00 %
Max. system drawdown	-2389.25	-2389.25	0.00
Max. system % drawdown	-7.55 %	-7.55 %	0.00 %
Recovery Factor	6.02	6.02	N/A
CAR/MaxDD	0.52	0.52	N/A
RAR/MaxDD	8.15	8.15	N/A
Profit Factor	1.87	1.87	N/A
Payoff Ratio	2.96	2.96	N/A

1. Portfolio Equity

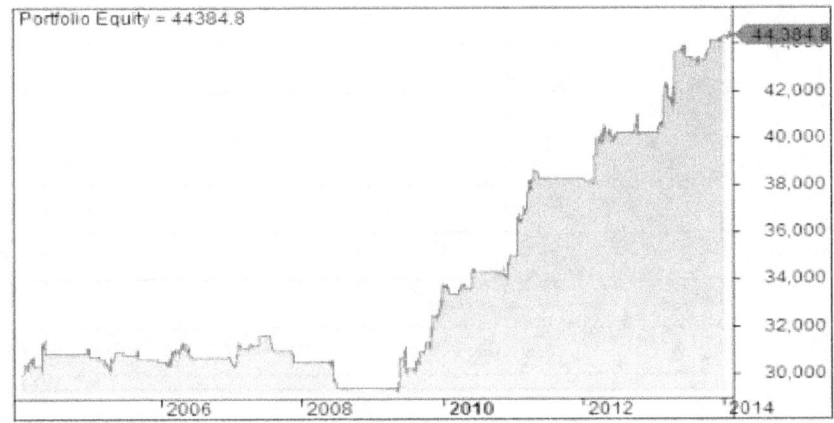

2. Underwater Equity

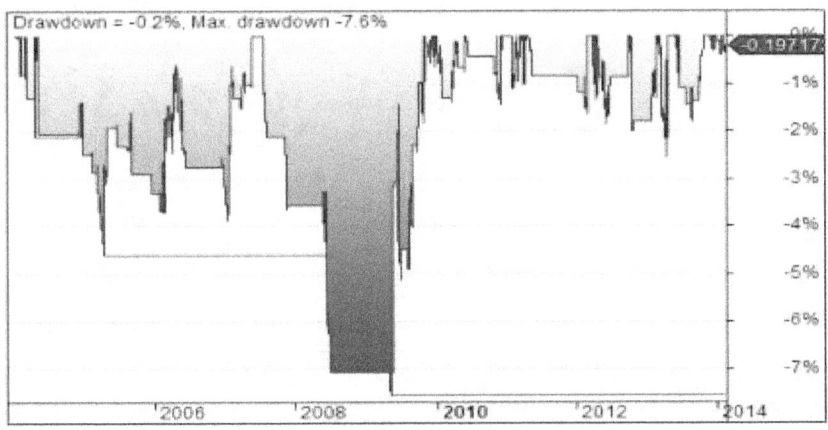

3. Profit Table

Year	Jan	Feb	Mar	Apr	May	Jun	Jul	Aug	Sep	Oct	Nov	Dec	Yr%
2004	1.4%	-0.0%	-0.2%	2.7%	-0.8%	0.0%	0.0%	0.0%	0.0%	0.0%	0.0%	0.6%	3.5%
2005	-1.0%	-0.4%	-0.8%	0.8%	1.0%	-0.4%	0.0%	-0.1%	-0.5%	0.0%	0.0%	-0.4%	-1.8%
2006	0.0%	0.5%	1.1%	0.9%	-1.2%	-0.8%	0.0%	0.0%	0.0%	0.0%	0.0%	0.0%	0.6%
2007	-0.9%	2.4%	0.0%	0.1%	1.1%	0.4%	-0.7%	-1.4%	0.0%	0.0%	-1.5%	0.0%	-0.5%
2008	0.0%	0.0%	0.0%	0.0%	0.0%	-2.8%	-0.9%	0.0%	0.0%	0.0%	0.0%	0.0%	-3.7%
2009	0.0%	0.0%	0.0%	0.0%	-0.0%	5.2%	-2.3%	0.7%	1.6%	0.7%	4.3%	1.4%	12.0%
2010	2.2%	-0.7%	0.0%	0.6%	0.0%	2.2%	0.0%	0.0%	0.0%	0.0%	-0.8%	2.8%	6.4%
2011	0.0%	4.9%	3.9%	1.1%	-0.7%	0.0%	0.0%	0.0%	0.0%	0.0%	0.0%	0.0%	9.4%
2012	-0.4%	-0.3%	5.1%	1.3%	-0.6%	-0.2%	0.2%	0.0%	0.0%	-0.1%	0.1%	0.0%	5.0%
2013	0.0%	0.9%	3.6%	-1.0%	5.0%	-0.2%	-0.3%	-0.6%	0.4%	1.2%	0.7%	0.2%	9.9%
2014	-0.1%	0.4%	N/A	N/A	N/A	N/A	N/A	N/A	N/A	N/A	N/A	N/A	0.3%
Avg	0.1%	0.7%	1.3%	0.7%	0.4%	0.3%	-0.4%	-0.2%	0.1%	0.2%	0.3%	0.5%	

The Inverted Hammer

The inverted hammer is yet another candlestick pattern that is supposed to signify the possible reversal of a down-trend.

The inverted hammer pattern rules re-cap

- Price has been in a downtrend.
- The upper shadow must be at least 2 times larger than the real body.
- The lower shadow must be less than 10% of the entire day range.
- The real body must be in the lower half of the entire day range.
- The real body has an open and close that are lower than the previous days open and close. (A real body gap down)
- The inverted hammer can be an up day or a down day. It is often written that if the inverted hammer closes higher

than the open it has more bullish implications. (Our tests will tell us of that is true.)

We again find that some of the rules regarding the identification of the inverted hammer pattern leave room for ambiguity.

For the price to be considered in a down-trend, tests have shown that the best results are found when a down-trend is defined by the low of the inverted hammer being the lowest low of the past 1-6 days.

We will stipulate that the inverted hammer must be making a 3 day low.

Initial tests have also shown that the inverted hammer is a better signal when it closes higher than the open. **All subsequent tests will stipulate that the inverted hammer must close higher than the open.**

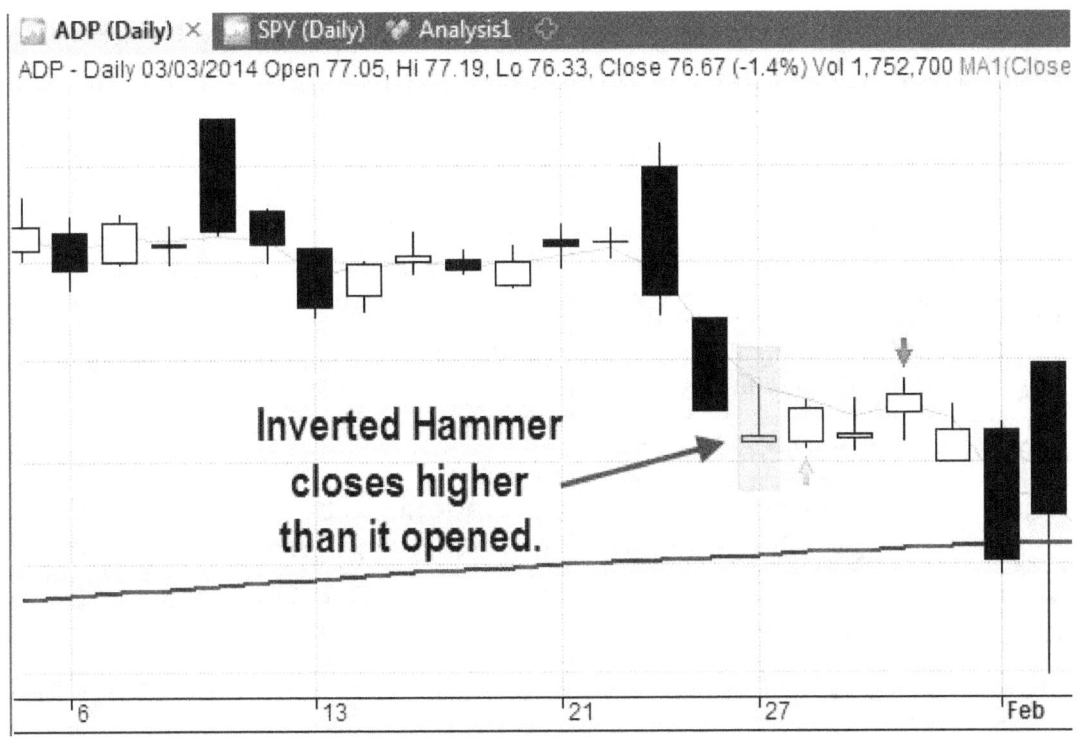

ADP - Daily 03/03/2014 Open 77.05, Hi 77.19, Lo 76.33, Close 76.67 (-1.4%) Vol 1,752,700 MA1(Close

Inverted Hammer closes higher than it opened.

The Amibroker formula that contains each of the inverted hammer pattern recognition rules just described is as follows:

///

LongUpperShadow = **H** - Max(**O**,**C**) > (**H** - **L**)*0.67;
rng = abs((**C**-**O**)/**O**);
SmallRealBody = rng < 0.003 **AND** rng > 0;
DownTrend = **L** < Ref(LLV(**L**,3),-1);
rngy = **H**-**L**;
lowerShadow = Min(**O**,**C**) - **L**;
shaven = lowerShadow < rngy*0.1;
RealBodyGapDown = Max(**O**,**C**) < Min(Ref(**O**,-1),Ref(**C**,-1));

InvertedHammer = smallRealBody **AND** shaven **AND** realBodyGapDown

144

AND longuppershadow **AND** downtrend **AND O < C**;

//

The inverted hammer pattern psychology

On the face of it, the inverted hammer doesn't immediately look like a bullish pattern. When studying the characteristics of the pattern we see that the long upper shadow is evidence that buyers were able to gain control of the market for part of the day, but by the end of the day the sellers have had enough force to close the market near the low of the day's trading range.

If anything, this seems bearish!

The established candlestick literature suggests that we must see *confirmation* that the bulls are strong on the day *following* a signal. Before we go any further, it is worth testing whether it pays to wait for confirmation or not.

To define confirmation I will simply use the most commonly used rule that's written about on trading forums and educational sites. I.E. if price can breach the high of the inverted hammer on the day following the pattern, we have confirmation that the bulls are in control.

Tests results show that waiting for confirmation that the market is strong on the day following the inverted hammer pattern **does** improve performance.

If we simply buy the open of the day following the inverted hammer, our win-rate is 54.40% and the average 5 day return per trade is 0.47%.

If we **wait** for the price to breach the high of the inverted hammer pattern on the following day, or if the following day opens higher than the high of the inverted hammer, **we get a 66.25% win-rate and an average 5 day return per trade of 0.70%.**

For example:

LBY - Daily 10/12/2013 Open 22.35, Hi 22.36, Lo 21.79, Close 21.93 (-1.4%)

BuyStop Order 1c
above the high of
the pattern

Or

HSBC (Daily) × | SPY (Daily) | Analysis1

HSBC - Daily 24/02/2014 Open 52.49, Hi 53.17, Lo 52.37, Close 53.04 (-2.4%) Vol 2,308,823 MA1(Close,40) =

Inverted
Hammer

Next day opens higher
than the inverted hammer
high, so we buy the open.

Remaining tests will include a rule which states that we can only buy an inverted hammer pattern if the following day trades higher than the inverted hammer high.

The inverted hammer pattern test results (5 day holding period)
When applying the rules defined thus far to the inverted hammer pattern and hold all positions for a 5 day period, we get the following equity curve:

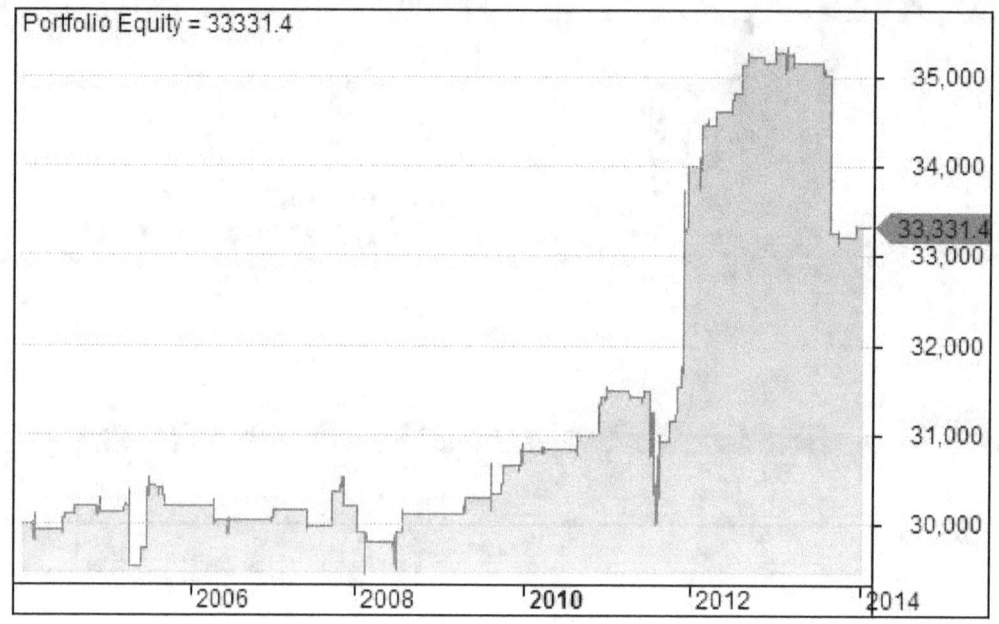

What is the best market condition for trading the inverted hammer candlestick?
It is worth pointing out that the inverted hammer pattern is not the most commonly found of all candlestick patterns. After applying the buy stop order to the system rules, we are only left with 80 trades in the sample. It might therefore be wise to not include any market environment filter.

Remaining tests will not include a SPY filter.

Applying indicator filters to the inverted hammer candlestick pattern

Again, because the sample size is already quite small I have not included any further filters.

The final tests were to determine what the optimum stop-losses and profit target values have been during the sample period.

These tests found that applying a 7% stop-loss and a 6% profit-target provided the greatest CAR/MDD.

For example:

Tests have shown that an inverted hammer candlestick pattern trading strategy can be improved by adding the following rules;

- **The price must be above $5.00**
- **The 20 day Volume average must be above 100,000.**

- **The low of the inverted hammer pattern must be the lowest low in the past 3 days.**
- **Upon getting a valid signal, orders are placed to buy the high of the inverted hammer candlestick plus 1 cent.**
- **If the price opens higher than the high of the inverted hammer on the next day, we enter on the open.**
- **If no buy order is filled on the day following a signal, we move on to the next trade.**
- **Apply a 7% stop-loss.**
- **Apply a 6% profit-target.**
- **Close all open positions after 20 days.**
- **Once a position is closed, 3 days must pass before we are allowed to trade a signal in the same stock.**

Another winning trade example:

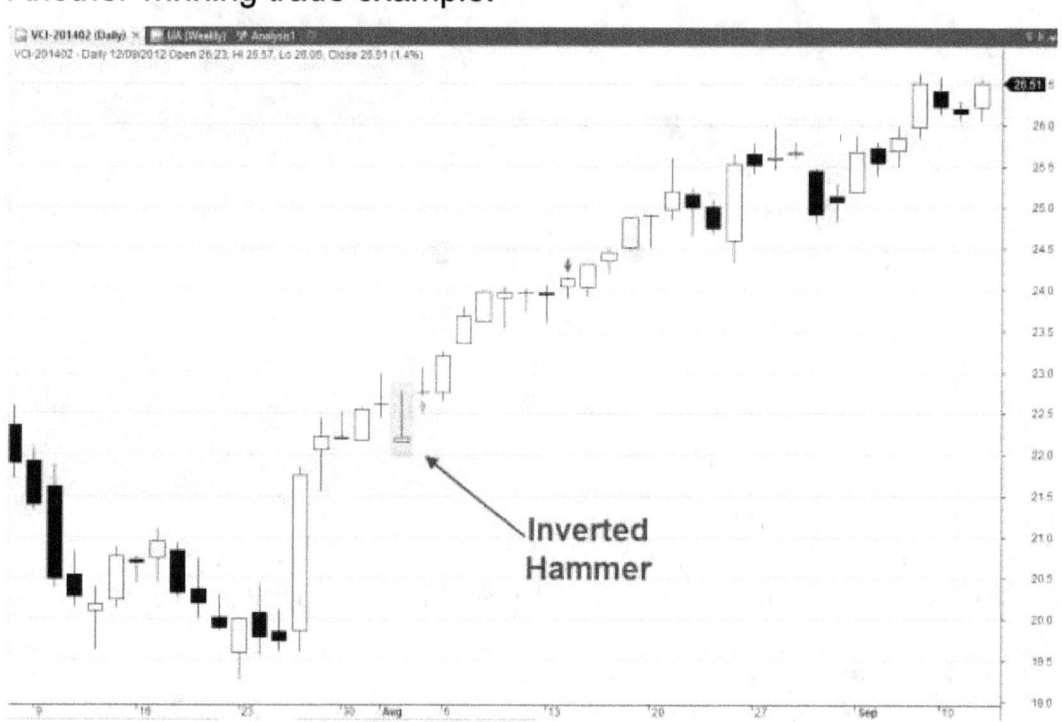

A losing trade:

To code the strategy in Amibroker we can use the following formula:

//

```
SetTradeDelays(0,0,0,0);
SetOption("initialequity",30000);
SetOption ("MaxOpenPositions" , 5);
SetOption ("allowsamebarexit",false);
SetPositionSize(6000,spsValue);
SetBacktestMode(backtestregular);

LongUpperShadow = H - Max(O,C) > (H - L)*0.67;
rng = abs((C-O)/O);
SmallRealBody = rng < 0.003 AND rng > 0;
DownTrend = L < Ref(LLV(L,3),-1);
rngy = H-L;
```

```
lowerShadow = Min(O,C) - L;
shaven = lowerShadow < rngy*0.1;
RealBodyGapDown = Max(O,C) < Min(Ref(O,-1),Ref(C,-1));

InvertedHammer = smallRealBody AND shaven AND
realBodyGapDown
AND longuppershadow AND downtrend AND O < C;

NonAdjVol = (V * C)/OI ;

Buysetup = invertedhammer
AND oi > 5
AND MA(nonadjvol,20) > 100000;

Sell = 0;

Buystop = Ref(ValueWhen(buysetup,H + 0.01),-1);

Buy = Ref(Buysetup,-1) AND Cross(H,Buystop);

BuyPrice = Max(Buystop,Open);

SellPrice = Close;

PT = Optimize("pt%",6,1,10,1);
SL = Optimize("SL%",7,1,10,1);

ApplyStop (stopTypeProfit,stopModePercent,pt,1,False,3);
ApplyStop (stopTypeloss,stopModepercent,sl,1,False,3);
ApplyStop(stopTypeNBar,stopModeBars,19,0,False,3);

PositionScore = 100 + Ref(nonadjvol,-1);
//////////////////////////////////////////////////////////
```

Test results for the inverted hammer trading strategy

The following tables and charts show us the performance metrics of
the inverted hammer pattern when applying the above rules.

Notable metrics include a 67.50% win rate, an average return per trade of 2.12% and a CAR/MDD of 0.65.

Statistics

	All trades	Long trades	Short trades
Initial capital	30000.00	30000.00	30000.00
Ending capital	40155.57	40155.57	30000.00
Net Profit	10155.57	10155.57	0.00
Net Profit %	33.85 %	33.85 %	0.00 %
Exposure %	6.17 %	6.17 %	0.00 %
Net Risk Adjusted Return %	548.31 %	548.31 %	N/A
Annual Return %	2.91 %	2.91 %	0.00 %
Risk Adjusted Return %	47.13 %	47.13 %	N/A
Total transaction costs	518.52	518.52	0.00
All trades	80	80 (100.00 %)	0 (0.00 %)
Avg. Profit/Loss	126.94	126.94	N/A
Avg. Profit/Loss %	2.12 %	2.12 %	N/A
Avg. Bars Held	12.60	12.60	N/A
Winners	54 (67.50 %)	54 (67.50 %)	0 (0.00 %)
Total Profit	18060.52	18060.52	0.00
Avg. Profit	334.45	334.45	N/A
Avg. Profit %	5.59 %	5.59 %	N/A
Avg. Bars Held	11.83	11.83	N/A
Max. Consecutive	9	9	0
Largest win	744.29	744.29	0.00
# bars in largest win	15	15	0
Losers	26 (32.50 %)	26 (32.50 %)	0 (0.00 %)
Total Loss	-7904.95	-7904.95	0.00
Avg. Loss	-304.04	-304.04	N/A
Avg. Loss %	-5.08 %	-5.08 %	N/A
Avg. Bars Held	14.19	14.19	N/A
Max. Consecutive	5	5	0
Largest loss	-1383.84	-1383.84	0.00
# bars in largest loss	5	5	0
Max. trade drawdown	-1450.80	-1450.80	0.00
Max. trade % drawdown	-23.99 %	-23.99 %	0.00 %
Max. system drawdown	-1696.21	-1696.21	0.00
Max. system % drawdown	-4.45 %	-4.45 %	0.00 %
Recovery Factor	5.99	5.99	N/A
CAR/MaxDD	0.65	0.65	N/A
RAR/MaxDD	10.60	10.60	N/A
Profit Factor	2.28	2.28	N/A
Payoff Ratio	1.10	1.10	N/A

1. Portfolio Equity

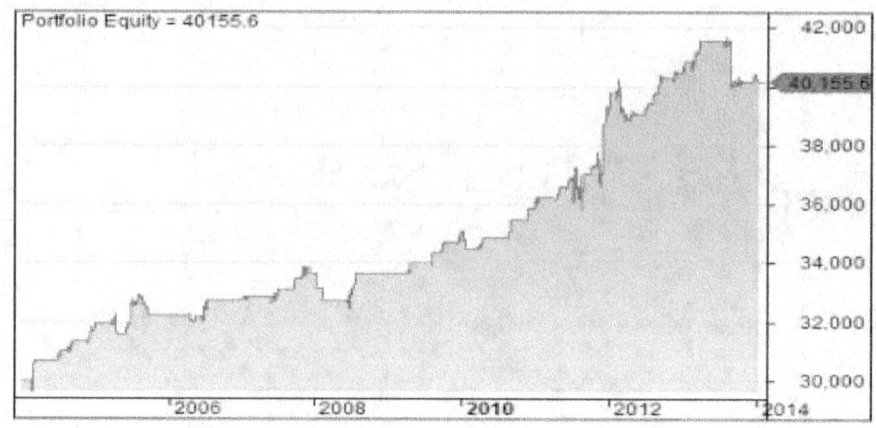

2. Underwater Equity

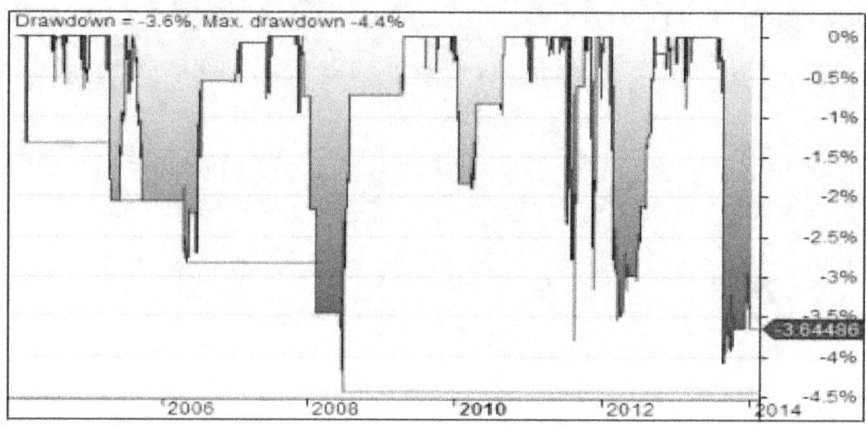

3. Profit Table

Year	Jan	Feb	Mar	Apr	May	Jun	Jul	Aug	Sep	Oct	Nov	Dec	Yr%
2004	0.0%	-0.5%	2.9%	0.0%	0.0%	0.1%	0.9%	-0.2%	1.3%	0.0%	-0.2%	2.0%	**6.4%**
2005	0.0%	0.0%	-0.0%	-1.1%	0.0%	2.1%	1.1%	0.1%	-1.1%	0.0%	0.0%	0.0%	**0.9%**
2006	0.0%	0.0%	0.0%	-0.7%	0.5%	0.8%	0.9%	0.0%	0.0%	0.0%	0.0%	0.0%	**1.5%**
2007	0.1%	0.3%	0.0%	0.0%	0.0%	0.3%	0.5%	0.0%	0.5%	0.6%	1.2%	-0.8%	**2.8%**
2008	-1.4%	-1.3%	0.0%	0.0%	0.0%	-0.2%	3.0%	0.0%	0.0%	0.0%	0.0%	0.0%	**0.0%**
2009	0.0%	0.0%	0.0%	0.4%	0.7%	0.0%	0.0%	1.0%	0.0%	1.0%	0.0%	0.2%	**3.3%**
2010	-0.8%	0.0%	0.0%	1.0%	0.0%	0.0%	0.0%	0.0%	1.9%	0.0%	0.0%	0.9%	**3.1%**
2011	1.1%	0.0%	0.0%	0.3%	0.6%	0.7%	-0.1%	0.6%	0.0%	1.0%	3.4%	1.1%	**9.0%**
2012	1.9%	-0.7%	-1.2%	0.3%	-0.2%	0.4%	0.5%	1.2%	1.0%	0.0%	0.6%	-0.1%	**3.7%**
2013	0.9%	-0.2%	1.9%	0.0%	0.0%	0.0%	-0.2%	0.1%	-3.3%	-0.0%	0.0%	0.7%	**-0.2%**
2014	-0.7%	0.0%	N/A	N/A	N/A	N/A	N/A	N/A	N/A	N/A	N/A	N/A	**-0.7%**
Avg	**0.1%**	**-0.2%**	**0.3%**	**0.0%**	**0.2%**	**0.4%**	**0.6%**	**0.3%**	**0.0%**	**0.3%**	**0.5%**	**0.4%**	

Section 2. Bearish Candlestick Patterns

The remaining chapters of the book will include the most commonly referenced candlestick patterns that are supposed to be a sign of impending market **falls**.

For this reason, each of the patterns that we test in the remaining chapters will be incorporated into strategies that short the market.

Before we begin, I should probably first stress that shorting the market has some inherent dangers that are not associated with buying the market.

The most obvious of which being that you can lose more than 100% of your initial risk when short. This is because when you buy something, the worst that can happen is that it will go to zero dollars.

But imagine that you shorted a stock for $10… that same stock could go to $100 or more and you'd have lost 1000% of your initial risk or more.

Furthermore, shares are not always available to be shorted. This is problematic when doing back-tests because we have no way of determining whether we would have been able to actually make the trades made in the test during a live market.

Finally, a study of historical data emphatically suggests that equity markets have a long-term bias to the upside. When short, you are ultimately fighting a trend that has endured for decades. This immediately puts a short-only strategy at a great disadvantage.

Bear markets happen of course, but they are often characterised as being more pronounced but shorter in duration than bull markets. This is why I recommend only seeing the following strategies as a way to supplement a predominantly long portfolio and to smooth your overall returns.

Implement a short-only strategy at your own peril!

With each of the above points made, it makes sense to change some of the basic rules that have so far governed our strategies.

The changes are as follows;

- We are only allowed to short stocks that are at least $20.00
- We are only allowed to short stocks that have a 20 daily volume average of at least 250,000.

Finally, we are looking to supplement our long-only portfolio by taking advantage of short-term market falls. For this reason, we will redefine the parameters used in our market environment filter. The exact changes are as follows:

Trend strength definition for down-trends when going short

- **Strong down-trend** when **5 day MA < 15 day MA** and **RSI(3)** is **below** 30.
- **Down-trend/short-term rally** when **5 day MA < 15 day MA** and **RSI(3)** is **above** 70.

Making the above changes will allow us to short some stocks while simultaneously buying others. This is useful because rather than our short positions acting as our only means of profiting, they can also be part of a hedged portfolio.

The Bearish Engulfing Pattern

The bearish engulfing pattern is simply the reverse of a bullish engulfing pattern. It is a 2 day pattern that occurs in the context of an up-trend. The pattern is supposed to signify that sellers (bears) are taking control of the market away from the buyers (bulls).

The bearish engulfing pattern rules re-cap

- Price must be in an up-trend.
- The first day must be an up day.
- The second day must open higher than the first days close.
- The second day must close lower than the first days open.

The bearish engulfing has basic and specific rules. As ever, the only area of ambiguity is when defining the prior trend. We will keep to our previous tests and define an uptrend by stating that price must be making an (X) day high during the pattern.

Tests show that the bearish engulfing can be improved if the first day of the pattern has made a 5 day high.

First day of the bearish
engulfing pattern also
makes a 5 day high.

The bearish engulfing pattern code

The Amibroker formula for defining the bearish engulfing pattern that makes a 5 day high is as follows:

///

Uptrend = **H** > Ref(HHV(**H**,5),-1);
WhiteBody = **C** > **O**;
BlackBody = **C** < **O**;
Engulfing = Max(**O**,**C**) > Ref(Max(**O**,**C**),-1) **AND** Min(**O**,**C**) < Ref(Min(**O**,**C**),-1);

BearishEngulfing = Ref(whitebody,-1) **AND** blackbody **AND** engulfing
AND Ref(uptrend,-1);

///

Close your eyes! The following results are indicative of the difficulties in shorting the market. They also illustrate quite forcefully that equity markets have a long term bias to the upside.

When shorting the market after a 5 day high bearish engulfing pattern, the following equity curve was produced during our sample period:

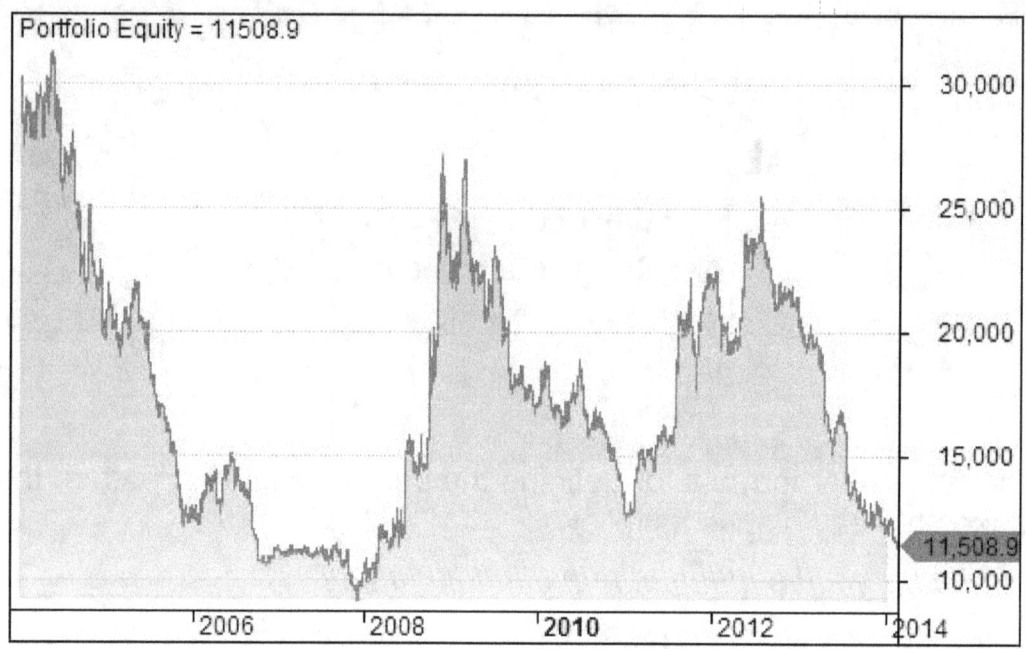

Blindly trading the bearish engulfing pattern is nothing more than a way of killing your account by a thousand cuts. Or should I say 1460 cuts.

Part of the problem is indeed that the bearish engulfing pattern is so common that during the tests, we lose nearly a quarter of our account on transaction fees.

Of the 1460 bearish engulfing patterns that were shorted during the test period, only 46.87% were profitable trades, the average

5 day return per trade is -0.22%.

There is little need to publish any further metrics; we lose a heap of money, that's all we need to know!

A typical trade looks like this:

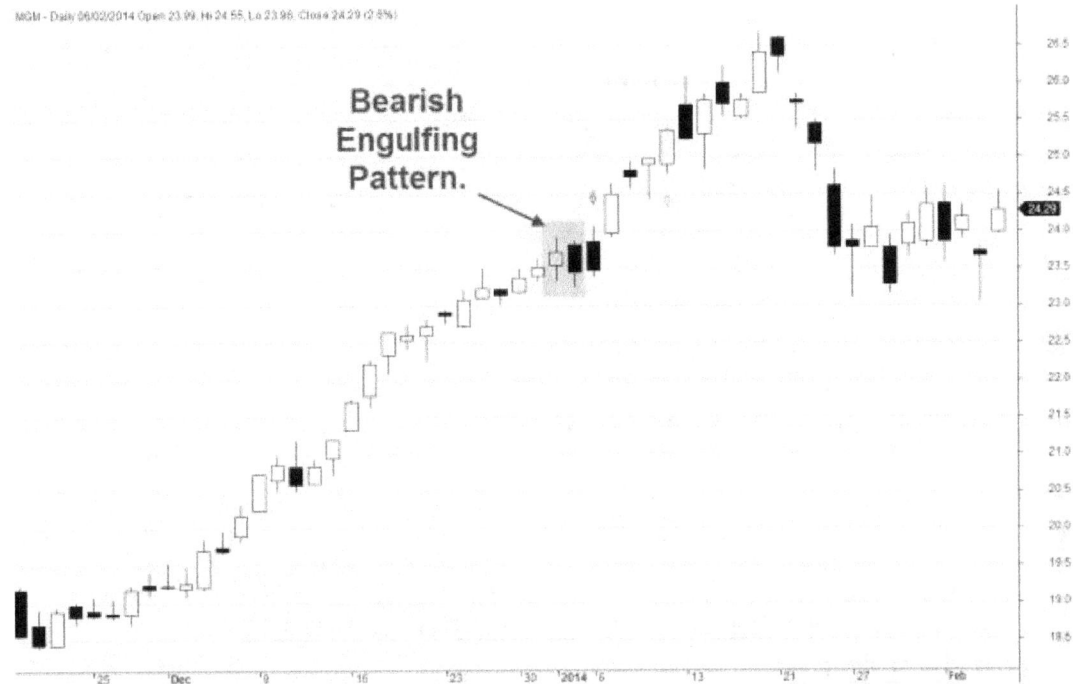

To illustrate the inherent danger with shorting the market (especially low priced stocks), the next chart illustrates that unlike when buying a company; we can lose more than 100% of our initial risk:

3,040,900 MA1(Close,40) = 27.40, MA2(Close,10) = 32.47, EMA(Close,20) = 31.59, EMA1(Close,30) = 29.98

Bearish Engulfing

160% Gap UP!!

What is the best market condition for trading the bearish engulfing pattern?

Remembering that a good few of our bullish patterns performed significantly better when the SPY was in an up-trend, it should come as no surprise that the first bearish pattern that we test happens to perform far better when the SPY is in a **downtrend that is currently rallying**.

Remember that this is now defined by the SPY having a **5 day MA beneath a 15 day MA** and the **RSI (3)** being **above 70**.

When applying the above filter to our current strategy we get the following returns:

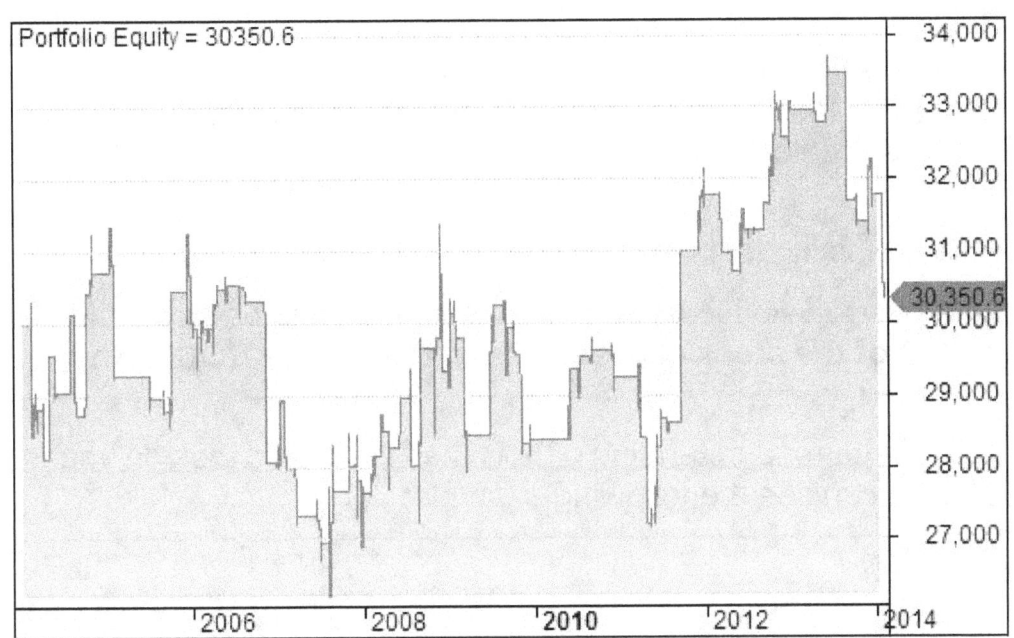

Applying the above market environment filter to our strategy and holding positions for 5 days has managed to turn a pattern that would have wiped out roughly 66% of our account, to a pattern that makes a miniscule gain. Not exactly earth shattering stuff, but it's a start.

Of particular interest is that we avoided catastrophic losses during the bull markets, while making significant gains during the bear markets of 2008 and 2011. This is precisely what we would want a short strategy to do.

Holding positions for 5 days and applying the market environment filter has also **increased the win-rate of the bearish engulfing pattern from 41.17% to 52.06% and the average gain per trade from -0.22% to 0.02%.**

Applying indicator filters to the bearish engulfing pattern
One of the best technical indicator filters that I tested with the bearish engulfing pattern was a 20 day and 60 day Rate of Change

filter.

The test results imply that a stock which has had a **one month** performance that is greater than the **quarterly performance** of the SPY has a greater likelihood of falling when the bearish pattern occurs.

For the remaining tests, we shall include the following rule:

We are only allowed to trade the bearish engulfing pattern if the **20 day ROC of the stock is greater than the 60 day ROC of the SPY.**

To get a better understanding of how the filter would look on your charts, we can see the following example:

UNXL - Daily 09/05/2013 Open 34.6, Hi 35.09, Lo 33.14, Close 34.48 (-1.2%) Vol 452,500 MA1(Close

Bearish Engulfing Pattern

UNXL - ROC(Close,60) = 107.09

On second day of the pattern, the 60 day ROC was 164...
On the same day, the SPY 60 day ROC was only 9.31

Applying stop-losses and profit targets to the bearish engulfing pattern

Firstly, I wanted to determine whether the pattern performed better if it was confirmed by weakness the following day. To test this out, I applied the following rule:

Only short the bearish engulfing pattern if the following day trades lower than the low of the second day in the pattern.

For example, the following chart highlights a bearish engulfing pattern that we would not have traded because the day following the pattern didn't trade below the pattern low:

166

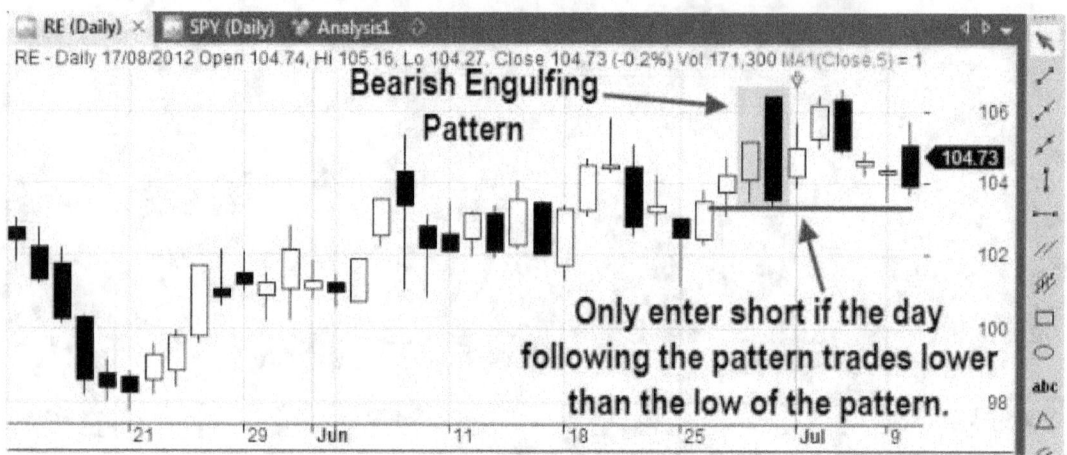

Tests showed that waiting for confirmation that the market is heading lower will degrade the performance of the strategy.

I also tested the current strategy with a number of percentage based stop-losses and profit targets ranging from 1% - 10%. The following image is of a 3D optimization graph which plots the stop-loss and profit target parameters used and the corresponding CAR/MDD.

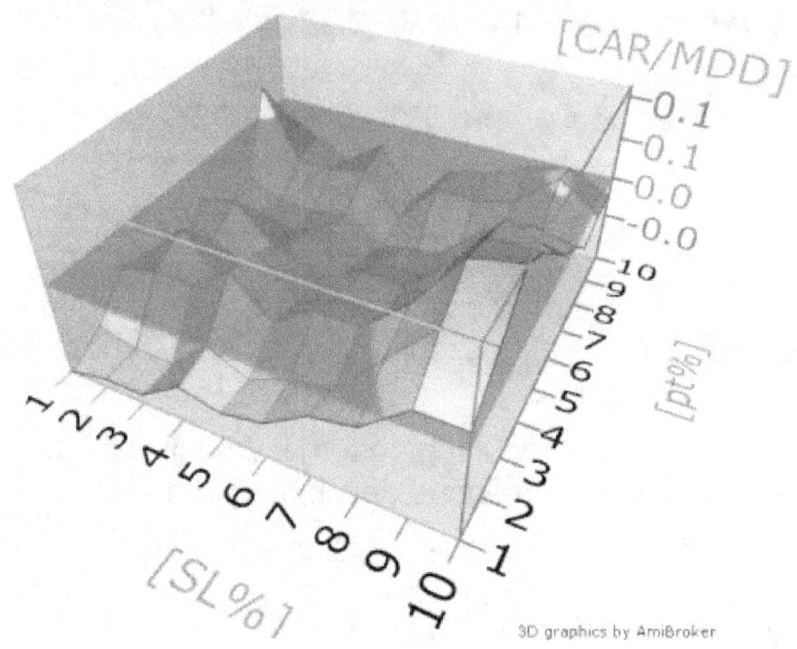

167

The above graph tells us a couple of things. Firstly, we don't want to place our stop-losses too close to our entry. Secondly, the best results are found if applying a stop-loss which is farther away from the entry price than the profit-target. In other words, the risk/reward ratio on the trade is negative.

Our final test that I carried out was to reduce the default number of days which we use to close positions which hadn't executed a stop-loss or profit-target. Instead of closing all open positions after 20 days, I tested what would happen if we closed all open positions after 10 days.

Here are the results:

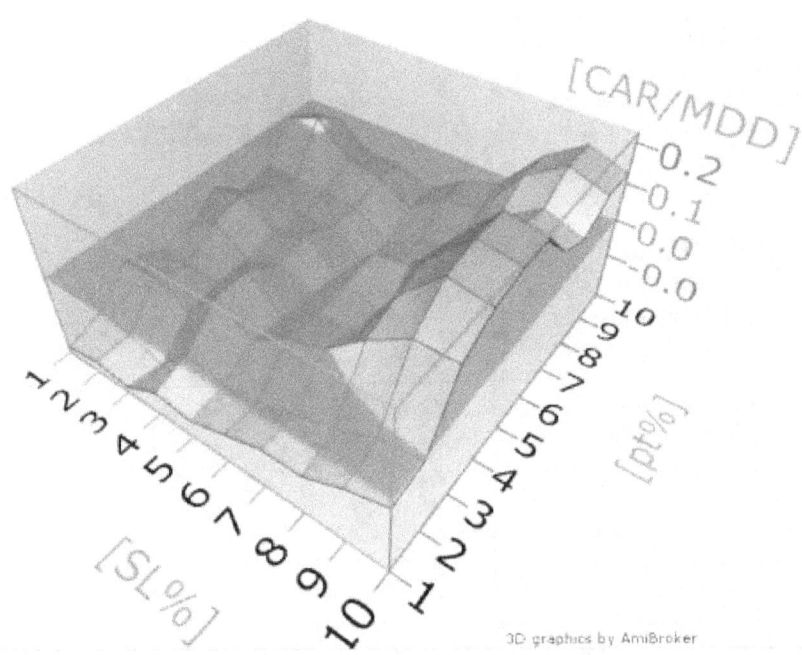

The above graph suggests that we should close any open positions after 10 days instead of 20. This is not particularly suprising when we consider that the equity markets have a long-term bias to the upside. In essence, we taking that knowledge and using it to optimize out test results.

Even still, there is no reason to believe that the equity markets will suddenly revesre a century long bias so for the remainder of the bearish camdlestick pattern tests, the final strategy rules will always apply a 10 day exit to any open positions.

Remaining tests of all bearish patterns will include a rule which states that open positions be closed after 10 days.

For this particular strategy, the optimum profit target and stop-loss parameters are 5% and 9% respectively.

The final rules of the bearish engulfing trading strategy

- **The price must be above $20.00.**
- **The 20 day volume average must be above 250,000.**
- **The high of the first day in the pattern must be the highest high in the past 5 days.**
- **The SPY must have a 5 day MA beneath a 15 day MA and an RSI(3) above 70 on the day that the bearish**

- **engulfing pattern completes.**
- **The 20 day ROC of the stock must be greater than the 60 day ROC of the SPY.**
- **Upon getting a valid signal, orders are placed to short the stock on the open of the following day.**
- **Apply a profit target that is 5% below the entry price.**
- **Apply a stop-loss that is 9% above the entry price.**
- **Close all open positions after 10 days.**
- **Once a position is closed, 3 days must pass before we are allowed to trade a signal in the same stock.**

To code the strategy in Amibroker we can use the following formula:

//

```
SetTradeDelays(0,0,0,0);
SetOption("initialequity",30000);
SetOption ("MaxOpenPositions" , 5);
SetOption ("allowsamebarexit",false);
SetPositionSize(6000,spsValue);
SetBacktestMode(backtestregular);

NonAdjVol = (V * C)/OI ;

Index = Foreign ("SPY","C",True);
Indexfastma = MA (Index, 5);
Indexslowma = MA (Index, 15);

WTD = indexfastma < indexslowma AND RSIa(index,3) > 70;

Uptrend = H > Ref(HHV(H,5),-1);
WhiteBody = C > O;
BlackBody = C < O;
Engulfing = Max(O,C) > Ref(Max(O,C),-1) AND Min(O,C) <
Ref(Min(O,C),-1);
```

```
BearishEngulfing = Ref(whitebody,-1) AND blackbody AND
engulfing
AND Ref(uptrend,-1);

Shortsetup = BearishEngulfing
AND oi > 20
AND MA(nonadjvol,20) > 250000
AND wtd
AND ROC(C,20) > ROC(index,60);

Cover = 0;

Short = Ref(shortsetup,-1);

shortPrice = Open;
coverPrice = Close;

PT = Optimize("pt%",5,1,10,1);
SL = Optimize("SL%",9,1,10,1);

ApplyStop (stopTypeProfit,stopModePercent,pt,1,False,3);
ApplyStop (stopTypeloss,stopModepercent,sl,1,False,3);
ApplyStop(stopTypeNBar,stopModeBars,9,0,False,3);

PositionScore = 100 + Ref(nonadjvol,-1);
//////////////////////////////////////////////////////////////////
```

Test results for the bearish engulfing trading strategy
The following tables and charts show us the performance metrics of
the bearish engulfing pattern when applying the above rules.
**Notable metrics include a 57.98% win rate, an average gain per
trade of 0.60% and a CAR/MDD of 0.17.**

Statistics

	All trades	Long trades	Short trades
Initial capital	30000.00	30000.00	30000.00
Ending capital	39246.16	30000.00	39246.16
Net Profit	9246.16	0.00	9246.16
Net Profit %	30.82 %	0.00 %	30.82 %
Exposure %	12.90 %	0.00 %	12.90 %
Net Risk Adjusted Return %	238.92 %	N/A	238.92 %
Annual Return %	2.68 %	0.00 %	2.68 %
Risk Adjusted Return %	20.76 %	N/A	20.76 %
Total transaction costs	1209.47	0.00	1209.47
All trades	257	0 (0.00 %)	257 (100.00 %)
Avg. Profit/Loss	35.98	N/A	35.98
Avg. Profit/Loss %	0.60 %	N/A	0.60 %
Avg. Bars Held	8.78	N/A	8.78
Winners	149 (57.98 %)	0 (0.00 %)	149 (57.98 %)
Total Profit	39072.92	0.00	39072.92
Avg. Profit	262.23	N/A	262.23
Avg. Profit %	4.38 %	N/A	4.38 %
Avg. Bars Held	6.15	N/A	6.15
Max. Consecutive	14	0	14
Largest win	867.11	0.00	867.11
# bars in largest win	2	0	2
Losers	108 (42.02 %)	0 (0.00 %)	108 (42.02 %)
Total Loss	-29826.76	0.00	-29826.76
Avg. Loss	-276.17	N/A	-276.17
Avg. Loss %	-4.62 %	N/A	-4.62 %
Avg. Bars Held	12.41	N/A	12.41
Max. Consecutive	7	0	7
Largest loss	-1041.12	0.00	-1041.12
# bars in largest loss	8	0	8
Max. trade drawdown	-1084.50	0.00	-1084.50
Max. trade % drawdown	-18.00 %	0.00 %	-18.00 %
Max. system drawdown	-5486.96	0.00	-5486.96
Max. system % drawdown	-15.85 %	0.00 %	-15.85 %
Recovery Factor	1.69	N/A	1.69
CAR/MaxDD	0.17	N/A	0.17
RAR/MaxDD	1.31	N/A	1.31
Profit Factor	1.31	N/A	1.31
Payoff Ratio	0.95	N/A	0.95

1. Portfolio Equity

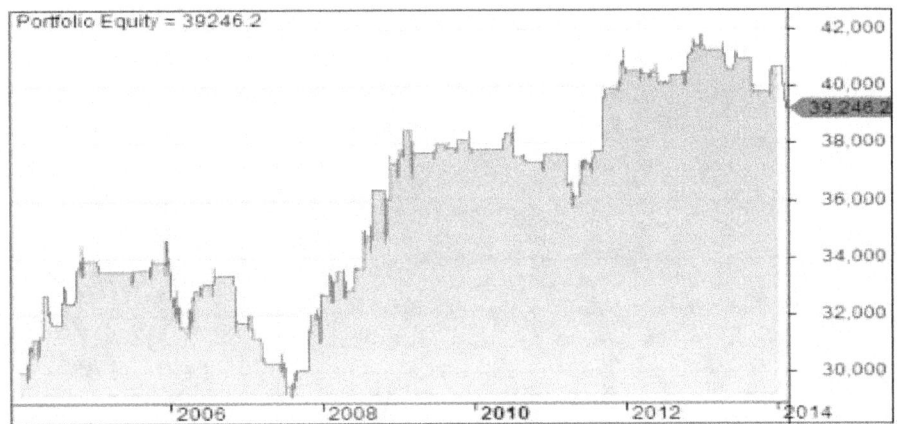

2. Underwater Equity

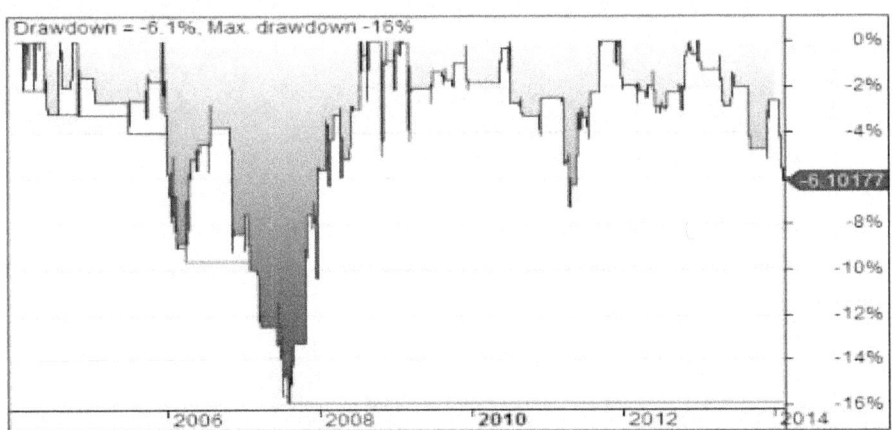

3. Profit Table

Year	Jan	Feb	Mar	Apr	May	Jun	Jul	Aug	Sep	Oct	Nov	Dec	Yr%
2004	0.0%	2.7%	-0.3%	6.4%	-2.0%	-1.2%	0.2%	2.1%	0.0%	4.6%	0.1%	0.0%	**13.0%**
2005	-1.0%	-0.1%	0.0%	0.0%	0.0%	0.0%	0.1%	0.0%	0.5%	0.4%	0.0%	0.6%	**0.4%**
2006	-6.0%	-1.4%	0.1%	3.1%	0.9%	0.8%	-0.1%	0.9%	0.0%	0.0%	-4.9%	0.0%	**-6.9%**
2007	0.9%	-2.6%	-2.1%	-0.7%	0.0%	0.2%	-2.6%	1.1%	0.6%	0.5%	6.1%	-1.9%	**-0.9%**
2008	4.0%	1.4%	1.1%	-2.6%	0.6%	2.3%	3.3%	-0.2%	5.0%	-4.1%	3.3%	3.6%	**18.7%**
2009	1.2%	1.8%	-2.0%	0.0%	0.0%	0.1%	0.7%	-0.5%	0.1%	0.8%	0.0%	-0.9%	**1.3%**
2010	0.0%	0.0%	0.0%	0.0%	0.5%	1.0%	-2.1%	0.0%	-0.6%	0.0%	0.0%	0.8%	**-0.4%**
2011	0.0%	0.0%	-0.4%	-4.5%	1.0%	3.5%	-0.5%	1.4%	5.8%	0.0%	0.0%	2.4%	**8.7%**
2012	-0.9%	0.0%	-0.3%	-0.1%	0.0%	-0.7%	-0.2%	0.8%	0.0%	0.4%	2.6%	-0.4%	**1.3%**
2013	-0.4%	0.0%	0.0%	-0.9%	-0.7%	1.3%	-0.4%	0.0%	-2.8%	0.0%	0.0%	2.2%	**-1.8%**
2014	0.0%	-3.6%	N/A	N/A	N/A	N/A	N/A	N/A	N/A	N/A	N/A	N/A	**-3.6%**
Avg	-0.2%	-0.2%	-0.4%	0.1%	0.0%	0.7%	-0.2%	0.6%	0.9%	0.3%	0.7%	0.6%	

The Evening Star Pattern

The evening star pattern is a 3 day reversal pattern that is supposed to signify the top of an uptrend. It is the exact opposite setup to the morning star pattern.

The evening star pattern rules re-cap

- Price has been in an up-trend.
- The first day of the pattern is a large up day.
- The second day of the pattern gaps up from the first day and creates a candle that doesn't close lower than the first day close.
- The second day is also an indecision day as signified by a small real body.
- The third day of the pattern is a large down day that closes lower than the half-way point of the first day.

The evening star pattern code

To define an uptrend when trading the evening star pattern we will stipulate that the first day of the pattern must also make a 2 day high.

A 'large up day' is defined by a day that closes 1.5% higher than it opened.

A 'small real body' of the second day is defined by stating that the difference between the open and close is less than 0.3%.

A 'large down day' is defined by a day that closes 1.5% lower than it opened.

The Amibroker formula for defining each of the aforementioned rules is as follows:

//

```
Big = abs((Close - Open)/Open) > 0.015;
BlackBody = C < O;
WhiteBody = C > O;
rng = abs((C-O)/O);
SmallRealBody = rng < 0.003 AND rng >0;
RealBodyGapUp = Min(O,C) > Max(Ref(O,-1),Ref(C,-1));
isPrevLargeWhite = Ref(big,-1) AND Ref(whitebody,-1);
```

Uptrend = **H** > Ref(HHV(**H**,2),-1);
isPrevUpTrend = Ref(uptrend,-1);
GapUpFromWhite = realBodyGapUp **AND** isPrevLargeWhite **AND** isPrevUptrend;
StarUp = smallRealBody **AND** gapUpFromWhite;

EveningStar = Ref(starUp,-1) **AND** blackbody **AND** big
AND C < Ref((**O** + **C**)/2,-2);

//

The evening star pattern test results (5 day holding period)
If we were to trade all of the evening star patterns during our test period that met the above rules and hold each open position for 5 days, we get the following equity curve:

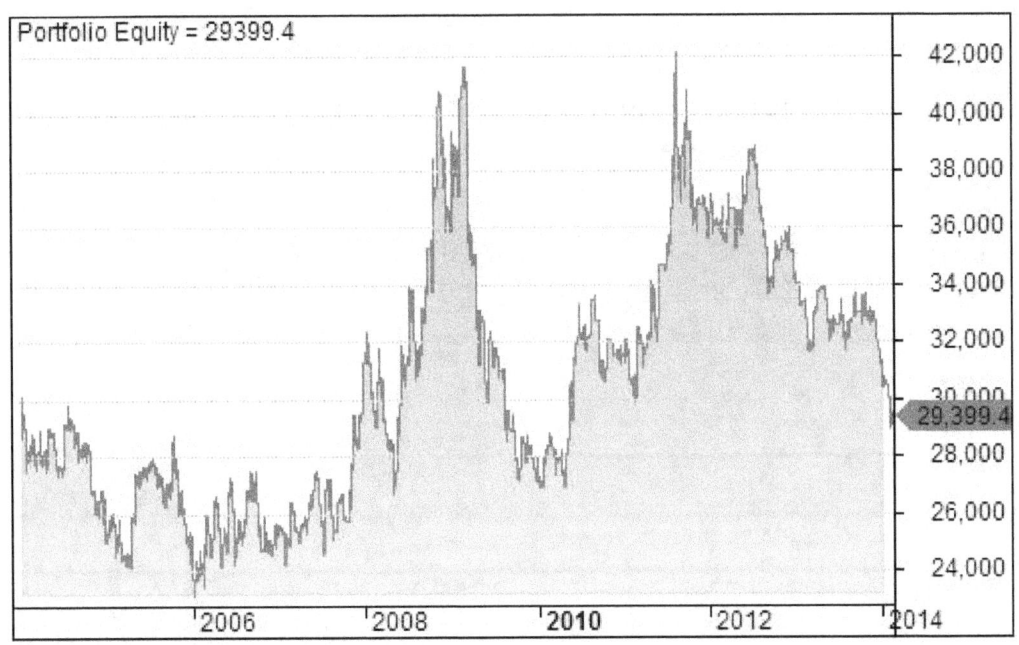

Notable **metrics include a 49.39% win-rate and an average 5 day return of -0.01%.**

The next chart will illustrate a typical trade. Note that I have also shown a pattern that occurs at a resistance zone. Trading the pattern at resistance didn't improve the outcome of the trade.

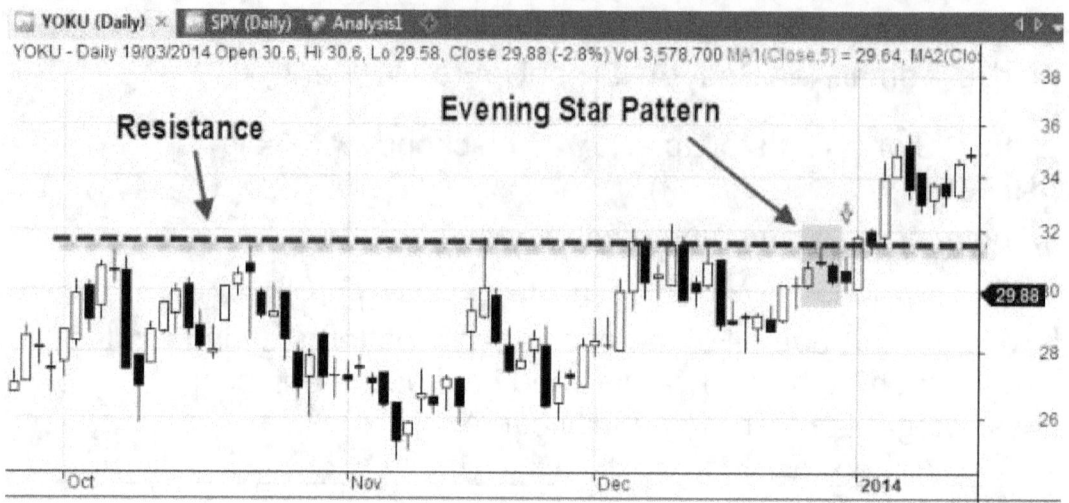

What is the best market condition for trading the evening star pattern?
Tests of the pattern in each of the various market conditions find that the performance of the evening star pattern can be improved if it is only traded when the **SPY is in a Strong uptrend.**

To remind you, this is now defined by the SPY having a 5 day MA above a 15 day MA and an RSI (3) above 70.

TILE - Daily 24/12/2013 Open 21.04, Hi 21.25, Lo 20.97, Close 20.99 (0.0%)

Evening
Star
Pattern.

SPY (Daily) × UA (Weekly) Analysis1

SPY - = 175.95, MA(spy,15) = 171.58, MA1(spy,5) = 175.10

SPY in strong
Uptrend on same
day as signal

SPY - = 81.70

WeeklyBOStops WeeklyCT EnergyPlain CRSI InsideBar IBshort RelStr Donchian

The results of only trading the evening star pattern when the SPY is in a strong up-trend are as follows:

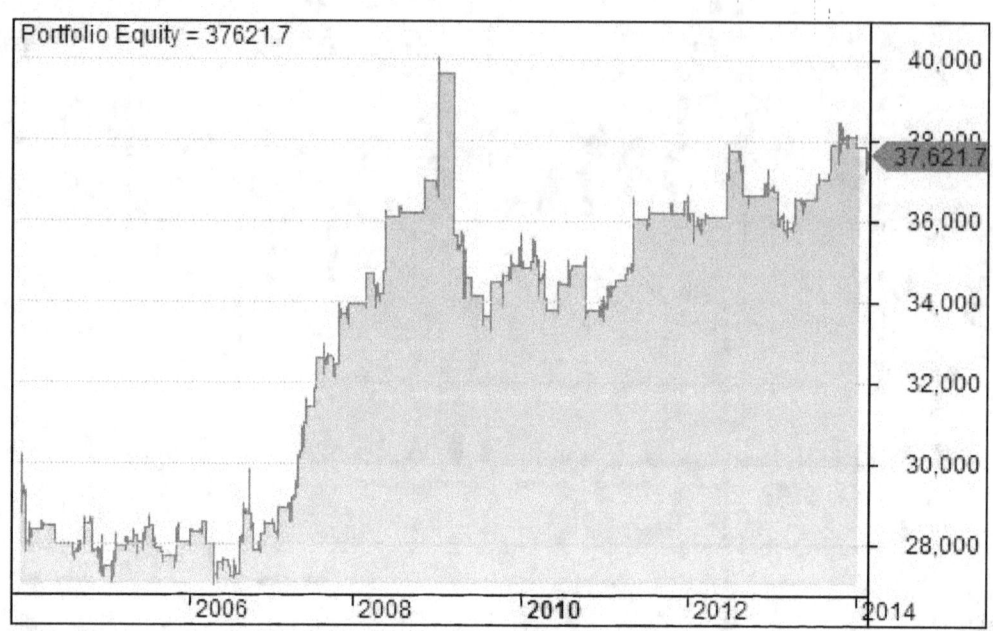

Notable performance metrics include a 55.39% win-rate and an average 5 day return per trade of 0.38%.

Remaining tests will include a rule which states that the SPY must be in a strong up-trend on the 3rd day of the evening star pattern.

Applying indicator filters to the evening star pattern

Every test that I have so far carried out in the book has included many filters that I haven't actually written about. That's because they are so ineffective that I didn't think the results were worth sharing.

However, just to give you a reminder of the type of filters that I have been testing I will present the results to the evening star pattern if using a filter that is often suggested by trading educators and system vendors as a way to increase the win-rate of a pattern.

The filter in question is often referred to as 'dynamic' support or resistance, (which makes it sound snazzy, but in reality it is just a moving average).

The suggestion often made is that candlestick patterns have a higher win-rate if they occur at these 'dynamic S/R zones'.

I have applied the following rule to every pattern in this book; 'Only trade the pattern if it is within 1% of the dynamic support or resistance zone'.

If I was trying to convince you that this was a high win-rate strategy, I would post the following charts while proudly proclaiming "Notice how well the patterns work at the 20 day MA!"

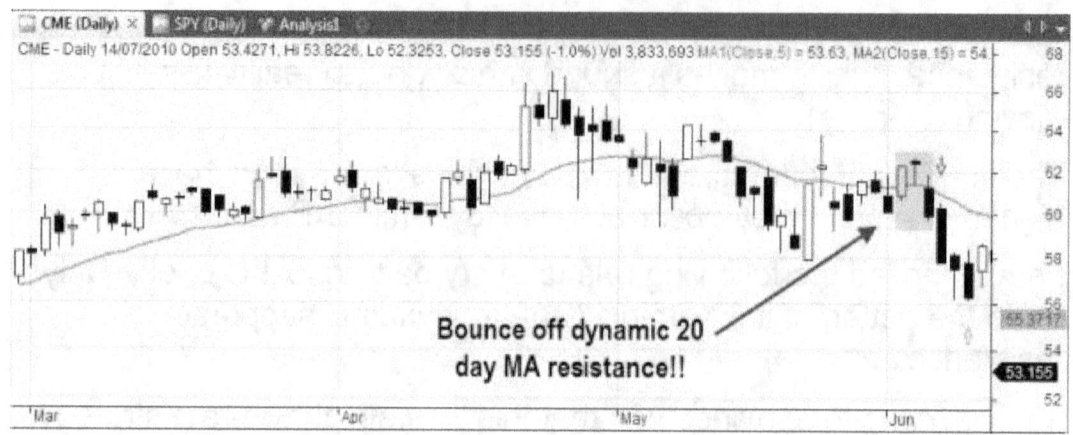

Bounce off dynamic 20
day MA resistance!!

Alas, the change to a patterns win-rate after applying many of the most popular filters are so insignificant that you have to seriously question where these ideas come from.

In reality, if we only trade the evening star pattern when they happen at a moving average, we get the following results:

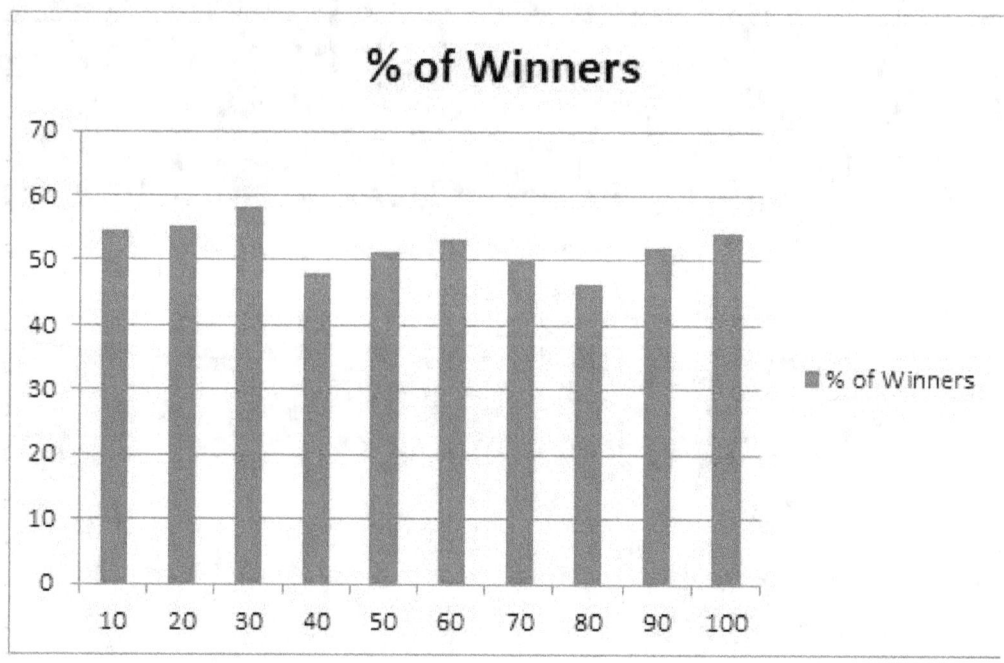

The *x* axis plots the moving average used in the test. Notice that none of the moving averages help to improve the win-rate of the standard strategy by more than 1 or 2 %. In some cases, such as the very popular 50 day MA, the win-rate is actually worse!

This is another example of why it pays to back-test any idea that you have read about before considering risking your hard earned money on it.

Do not get me wrong, some patterns do have a historical tendency to perform better if occurring at a particular moving average or if in the overbought or oversold condition, but only by testing the patterns can we know which are improved and more importantly whether the parameters used in the filter are robust and not simply curve-fit to the historical data.

Having cautioned the above, **a filter that was found to significantly improve the performance of an evening star pattern was a short term RSI spike.**

The short-term RSI spike filter states that an evening star pattern can only be traded if there is a RSI(2) reading above 90 on the second day of the pattern..

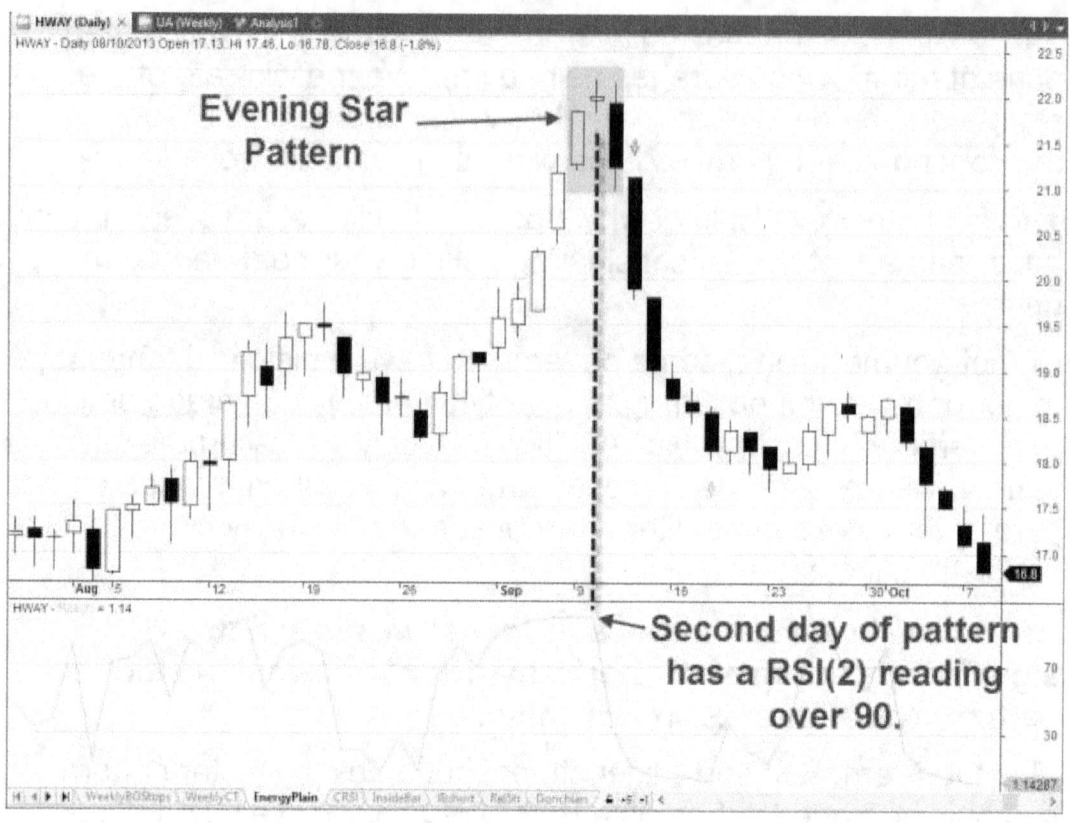

As the above chart illustrates, a high RSI(2) reading during the evening star pattern can precede a significant market collapse.

Applying stop-losses and profit targets to the evening star pattern

The first test that I did was to determine whether waiting for confirmation that the stock was weak on the day following the pattern would improve results. It didn't.

Placing a stop-loss above the high of the pattern also degraded the performance of the strategy.

Finally I tested the stop-losses and profit targets using a percent above or below our entry price. Remember too that all open positions are also closed after 10 days.

The optimum values found were 6% and 2% respectively.

- **The price must be above $20.00.**
- **The 20 day volume average must be above 250,000.**
- **The high of the first day in the pattern must be the highest high in the past 2 days.**
- **The SPY must have a 5 day MA above a 15 day MA and an RSI(3) above 70 on the day that the evening star pattern completes.**
- **The second day of the evening star pattern must have a RSI(2) reading above 90.**
- **Upon getting a valid signal, orders are placed to short the open of the following day.**
- **Apply a 6% stop-loss.**
- **Apply a 2% profit-target.**
- **Close all open positions after 10 days.**
- **Once a position is closed, 3 days must pass before we are allowed to trade a signal in the same stock.**

To code the strategy in Amibroker we can use the following formula:

//

```
SetTradeDelays(0,0,0,0);
SetOption("initialequity",30000);
SetOption ("MaxOpenPositions" , 5);
SetOption ("allowsamebarexit",false);
SetPositionSize(6000,spsValue);
SetBacktestMode(backtestregular);

NonAdjVol = (V * C)/OI ;

Index = Foreign ("SPY","C",True);
Indexfastma = MA (Index, 5);
Indexslowma = MA (Index, 15);
```

```
STU = indexfastma > indexslowma AND RSIa(index,3) > 70;

Big = abs((Close - Open)/Open) > 0.015;
BlackBody = C < O;
WhiteBody = C > O;
rng = abs((C-O)/O);
SmallRealBody = rng < 0.003 AND rng >0;
RealBodyGapUp = Min(O,C) > Max(Ref(O,-1),Ref(C,-1));
isPrevLargeWhite = Ref(big,-1) AND Ref(whitebody,-1);
Uptrend = H > Ref(HHV(H,2),-1);
isPrevUpTrend = Ref(uptrend,-1);
GapUpFromWhite = realBodyGapUp AND isPrevLargeWhite AND
isPrevUptrend;
StarUp = smallRealBody AND gapUpFromWhite;

EveningStar = Ref(starUp,-1) AND blackbody AND big
AND C < Ref((O + C)/2,-2);
Shortsetup = EveningStar
AND oi > 20
AND stu
AND Ref(RSI(2),-1) > 90
AND MA(nonadjvol,20) > 250000;

Cover =0;

shortPrice = Open;

Short = Ref(shortsetup,-1);

coverPrice = Close;

PT = Optimize("pt%",2,1,10,1);
SL = Optimize("SL%",6,1,10,1);
```

```
ApplyStop (stopTypeProfit,stopModePercent,pt,1,False,3);
ApplyStop (stopTypeloss,stopModepercent,sl,1,False,3);
ApplyStop (stopTypeNBar,stopModeBars,9,0,False,3);

PositionScore = 100 + Ref(nonadjvol,-1);
/////////////////////////////////////////////////////////////////////////////
```

To remind you, our initial test of the evening star pattern produced returns that were negative.

The win-rate of the pattern (when holding positions for 5 days) was 49.39% and the average gain per trade was -0.01%.

By applying further filters to the pattern, we have found that the performance can be improved.

The final strategy has the following key performance metrics: a 76.55% win-rate, an average gain per trade of 0.73% and a CAR/MDD of 0.59.

The following charts and tables show us the complete performance metrics of our final evening star pattern trading strategy:

	All trades	Long trades	Short trades
Initial capital	30000.00	30000.00	30000.00
Ending capital	39825.07	30000.00	39825.07
Net Profit	9825.07	0.00	9825.07
Net Profit %	32.75 %	0.00 %	32.75 %
Exposure %	4.66 %	0.00 %	4.66 %
Net Risk Adjusted Return %	702.41 %	N/A	702.41 %
Annual Return %	2.83 %	0.00 %	2.83 %
Risk Adjusted Return %	60.62 %	N/A	60.62 %
Total transaction costs	1084.42	0.00	1084.42
All trades	226	0 (0.00 %)	226 (100.00 %)
Avg. Profit/Loss	43.47	N/A	43.47
Avg. Profit/Loss %	0.73 %	N/A	0.73 %
Avg. Bars Held	3.97	N/A	3.97
Winners	173 (76.55 %)	0 (0.00 %)	173 (76.55 %)
Total Profit	25053.86	0.00	25053.86
Avg. Profit	144.82	N/A	144.82
Avg. Profit %	2.42 %	N/A	2.42 %
Avg. Bars Held	3.33	N/A	3.33
Max. Consecutive	13	0	13
Largest win	1310.88	0.00	1310.88
# bars in largest win	2	0	2
Losers	53 (23.45 %)	0 (0.00 %)	53 (23.45 %)
Total Loss	-15228.79	0.00	-15228.79
Avg. Loss	-287.34	N/A	-287.34
Avg. Loss %	-4.81 %	N/A	-4.81 %
Avg. Bars Held	6.06	N/A	6.06
Max. Consecutive	4	0	4
Largest loss	-778.10	0.00	-778.10
# bars in largest loss	2	0	2
Max. trade drawdown	-865.48	0.00	-865.48
Max. trade % drawdown	-14.37 %	0.00 %	-14.37 %
Max. system drawdown	-1713.99	0.00	-1713.99
Max. system % drawdown	-4.76 %	0.00 %	-4.76 %
Recovery Factor	5.73	N/A	5.73
CAR/MaxDD	0.59	N/A	0.59
RAR/MaxDD	12.73	N/A	12.73
Profit Factor	1.65	N/A	1.65
Payoff Ratio	0.50	N/A	0.50

1. Portfolio Equity

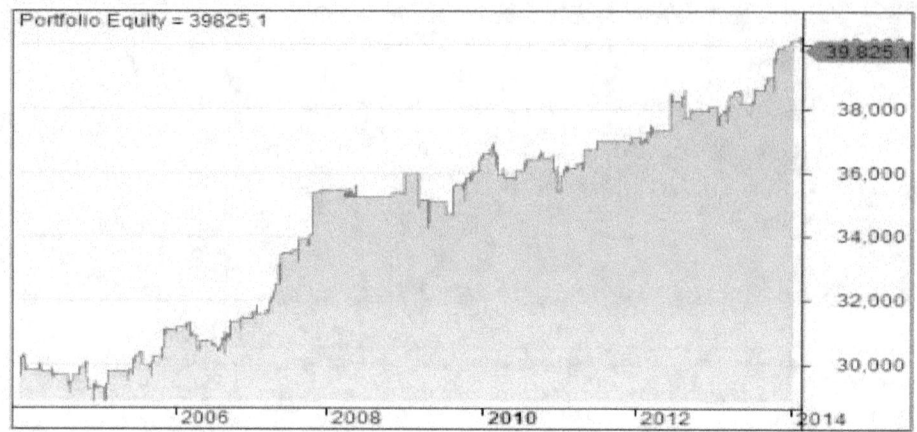

2. Underwater Equity

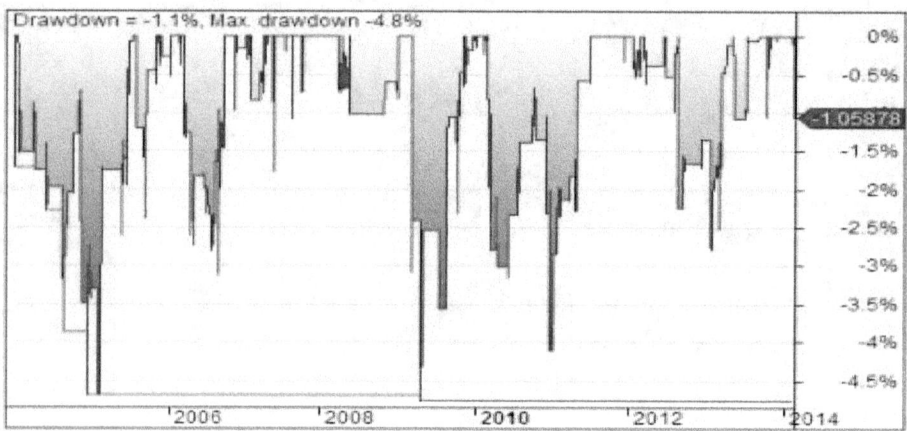

3. Profit Table

Year	Jan	Feb	Mar	Apr	May	Jun	Jul	Aug	Sep	Oct	Nov	Dec	Yr%
2004	-0.6%	-0.5%	0.0%	-0.2%	-0.1%	-0.2%	0.0%	-0.8%	0.8%	0.8%	-2.2%	0.2%	-2.9%
2005	0.0%	1.6%	0.0%	0.0%	-0.1%	1.8%	0.4%	-1.2%	0.8%	0.0%	2.7%	0.0%	6.1%
2006	0.4%	0.1%	-1.0%	-1.2%	0.6%	0.0%	-0.4%	0.6%	1.1%	0.8%	0.4%	-0.2%	1.2%
2007	0.7%	-0.4%	0.4%	1.8%	1.5%	2.3%	0.3%	1.0%	0.0%	0.3%	3.8%	0.3%	12.8%
2008	0.0%	0.0%	0.0%	-0.4%	-0.3%	0.0%	0.0%	0.0%	0.0%	0.0%	0.4%	0.0%	-0.2%
2009	1.7%	0.0%	-2.4%	0.0%	-0.1%	0.0%	-1.0%	2.1%	0.4%	0.6%	0.5%	1.3%	3.1%
2010	0.3%	0.6%	-2.5%	-0.2%	0.0%	0.7%	0.6%	0.3%	0.0%	0.0%	0.0%	-2.8%	-2.9%
2011	1.9%	0.2%	0.0%	0.2%	1.4%	0.0%	0.7%	0.0%	0.0%	0.0%	0.0%	0.3%	4.7%
2012	-0.3%	0.7%	0.3%	0.0%	0.0%	2.4%	0.0%	-1.4%	0.5%	0.1%	0.0%	0.3%	2.6%
2013	-0.9%	0.6%	1.2%	0.4%	-0.9%	0.0%	1.1%	0.0%	1.0%	2.2%	0.2%	0.3%	5.2%
2014	0.2%	-0.8%	N/A	N/A	N/A	N/A	N/A	N/A	N/A	N/A	N/A	N/A	-0.5%
Avg	0.3%	0.2%	-0.4%	0.0%	0.2%	0.7%	0.2%	0.1%	0.5%	0.5%	0.6%	-0.0%	

The Dark Cloud Cover Pattern

The dark cloud cover pattern is a 2 day pattern that occurs during an up-trend. As with each of our bearish candlestick patterns, the dark cloud cover pattern is supposed to signify that a change in investor sentiment has occurred and a reversal of the existing up-trend is imminent.

Also note that the dark cloud cover has the same rules as the piercing pattern, but in reverse. I should too point out that if the second day of the dark cloud cover pattern closes lower than the open of the first day, it becomes a bearish engulfing pattern.

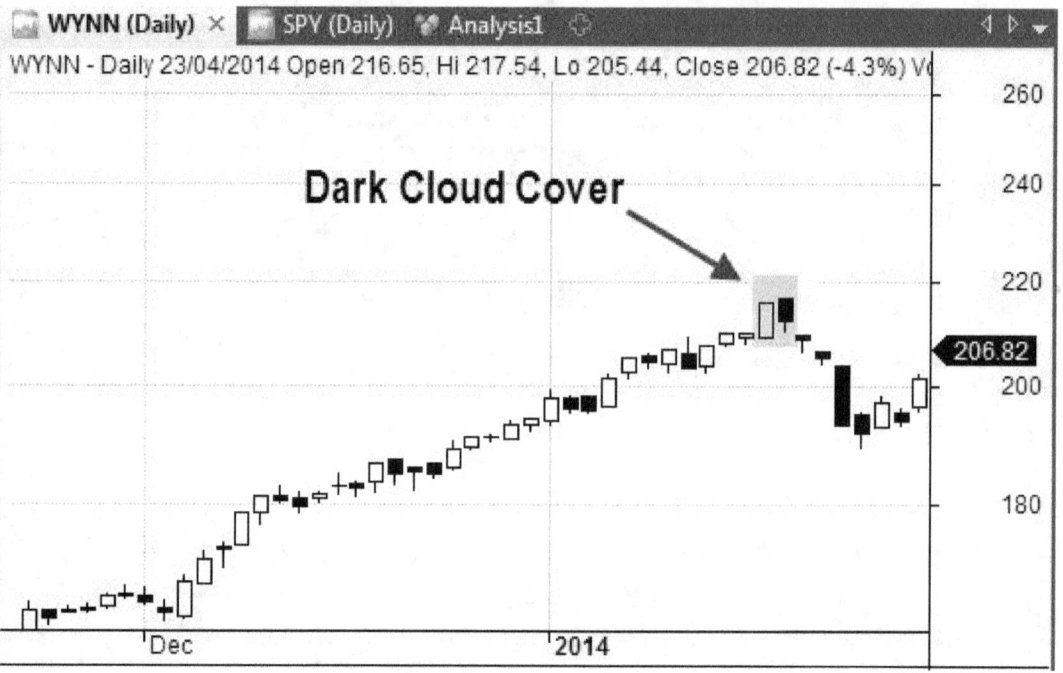

The dark cloud cover rules re-cap

- Price has been in an up-trend.
- The first day of the pattern is a strong and large up day.

- The second day of the pattern opens higher than the first day.
- The second day closes at least halfway into the real body of the first day.

The above rules leave a few areas of interpretation. We therefore need to more clearly define a prior 'uptrend' and a "strong and large up day".

Testing various x day highs that must be made by the first day in the dark cloud cover pattern discovers that the patterns which make a 20 day high perform adequately better than those that don't.

A strong and large up day is defined by stating that the first day of the pattern closes at least 1.5% higher than it opened and that the close minus the open is 2 times greater than the high minus the low.

By using the above rule we are only going to identify dark cloud cover patterns whereby the first day has relatively small shadows compared to the real body. This rule ensures that the 1.5% gains between the open and close are not part of a day that also had lots of intraday sellers.

For example:

ZMH - Daily 23/04/2014 Open 91.5, Hi 91.94, Lo 91.1, Close 91.45 (-0.3%) Vol 1,301,995 M

The first day has very little shadows in comparison to the large (white) real body.

The dark cloud cover pattern code

The Amibroker formula for defining the dark cloud cover pattern that makes a 20 day high is as follows:

//

Uptrend = **H** > Ref(HHV(**H**,20),-1);
BigWhite = (**Close - Open**)/**Open** > 0.015 **AND** (**Close - Open**) * 2 > **High - Low**;
BlackBody = **C** < **O**;

DarkCloudCover = Ref(bigwhite,-1) **AND** blackbody **AND O** > Ref(**H**,-1)
AND C <= Ref((**O+C**)/2,-1) **AND C** > Ref(**O**,-1) **AND** Ref(uptrend,-1);

//

The dark cloud cover pattern test results (5 day holding period)

When going short on the open that follows a dark cloud cover pattern at a 20 day high, the following equity curve was produced during the sample period:

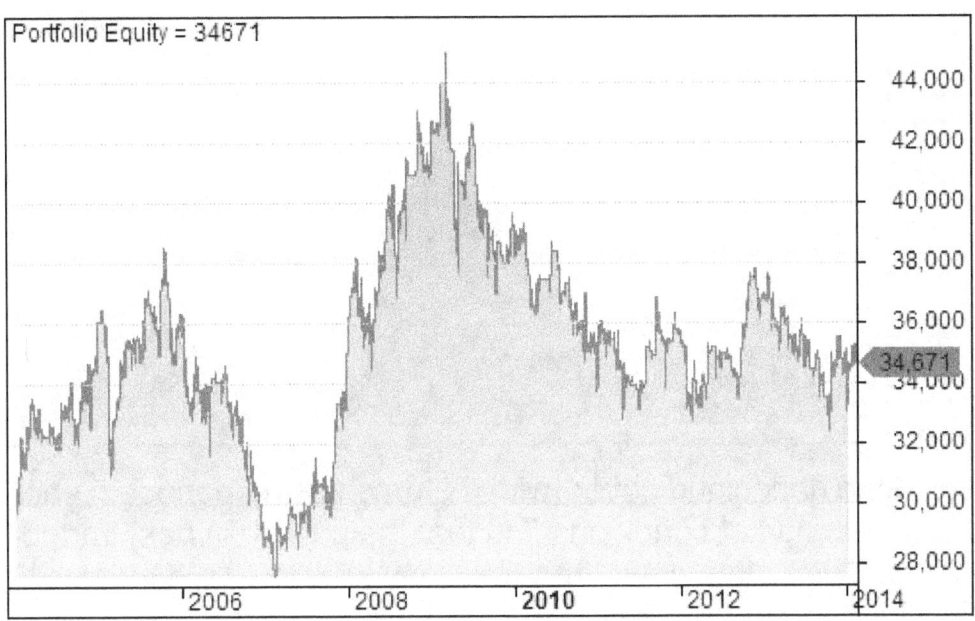

Seeing that the dark cloud cover pattern is so similar to the bearish engulfing pattern, it should come as no surprise that trading the pattern and holding open positions for 5 days is also a poorly performing strategy.

Notable performance metrics include a 49.74% win-rate and an average 5 day return per trade of 0.06%.

The following chart is typical of more than 50% of trades, 5 days later the price is higher than it was on the day of our entry. Note too how the multi-month resistance was no help in turning the market.

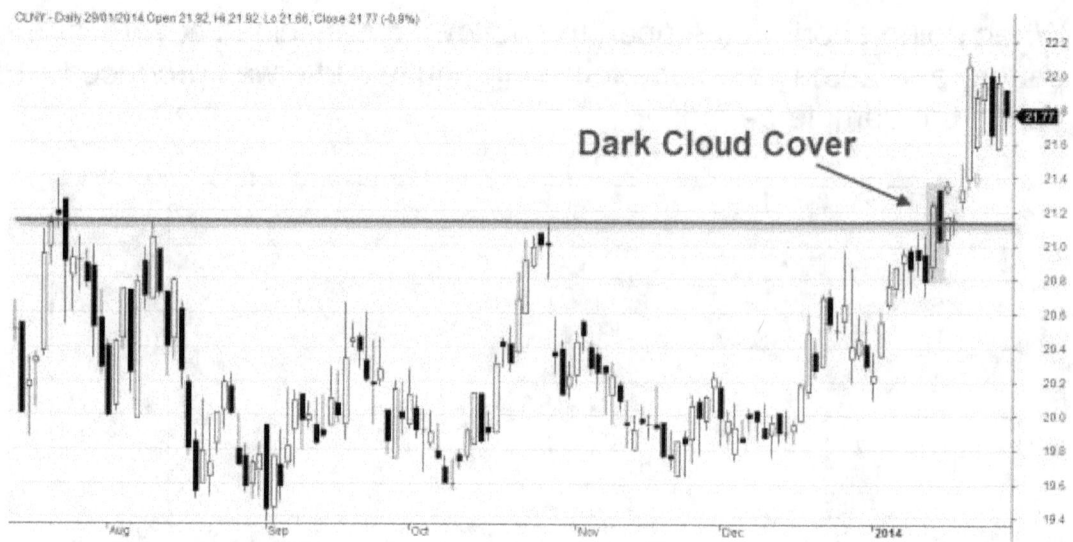

Dark Cloud Cover

What is the best market environment for trading the dark cloud cover pattern?

Tests of the dark cloud cover (with a 5 day holding period) in each of the different market conditions find that the pattern is best traded when the SPY is in a down-trend.

When applying the above rule, notable performance metrics include **a 50.23% win-rate and an average 5 day return per trade of 0.17%.**

Applying indicator filters to the dark cloud cover pattern

None of the conventional indicators (such as stochastics overbought, Bollinger bands, etc) were able to improve the performance of the dark cloud cover pattern.

However, there were two less conventional filters that did significantly improve the win-rate and CAR/MDD, the one caveat being that after applying the filters, we only had a trade sample size of roughly 150.

This is adequate enough for statistical significance, but more would have been better.

The two filters that I found to greatly improve the performance of the pattern were either based on the ATR or the Advance/Decline ratio of the NYSE.

The ATR filter was based on the theory that if the second day of the pattern has a larger range than the first day of the pattern, we know that the struggle between bulls and bears was fierce during the day but by the end of the day the bears have taken control.

The following test results indicate that the greater the range of the second day is compared to the first day's range, the better the 5 day performance becomes:

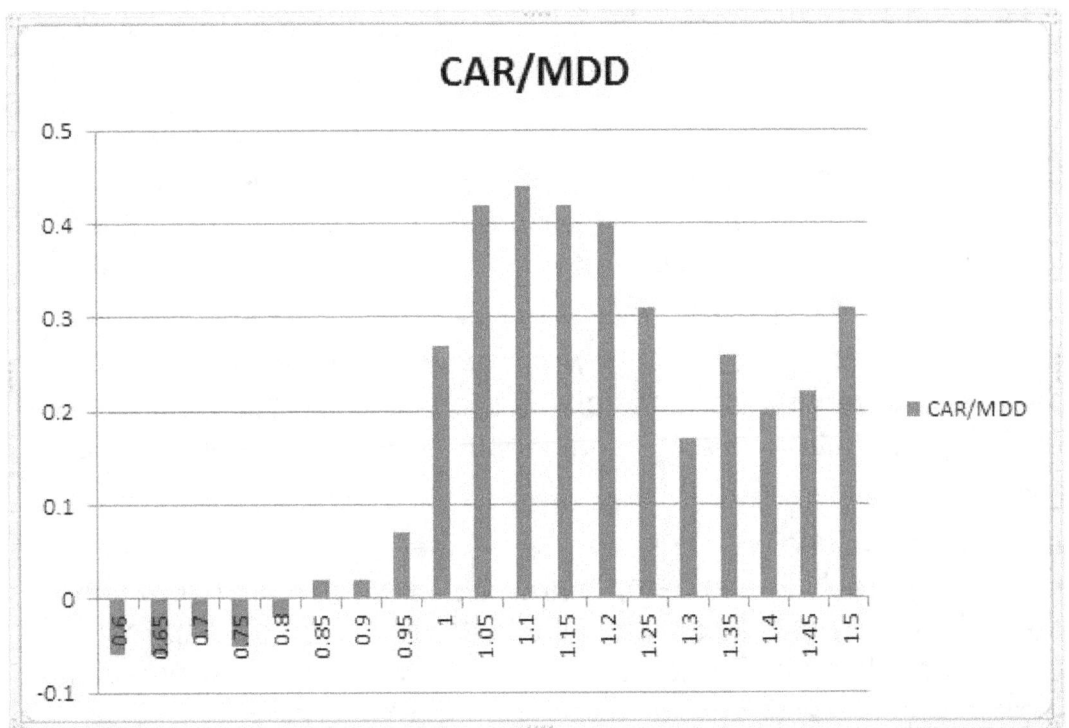

In the above chart, the multiplication factor of the first day range is plotted on the x axis. As you can see, when the range of the second day is smaller than 1 * the first day's range, the returns are flat to negative. But as we increase the size of the second day range, we see that the CAR/MDD improves significantly.

Perhaps a chart will explain it better.

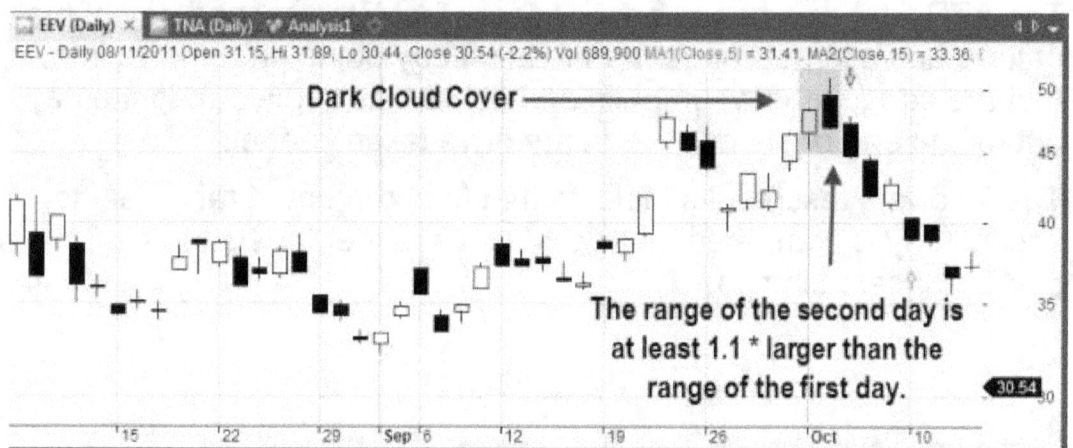

The next filter that improved our results was based on the theory that if the first day of the pattern occurred on the same day as a weak market, the second day sell-off would have more significance as a market turning point.

The NYSE A/D ratio tells us how many stocks have closed higher or lower during a particular session. Remember that the first day of the evening star pattern is a day that closes at least 1.5% higher than it opened.

If that higher close was *in spite* of a weaker broader market (as defined by the A/D ratio being below 1), it seems logical that when the second day of the pattern is weak, there will be more people caught offside by the sudden weakness in what was just one day earlier, one of the strongest stocks on the exchange.

Applying a range of A/D ratio levels to act as a filter gave us the following results (the A/D ratio on the first day of the pattern is plotted on the *x* axis):

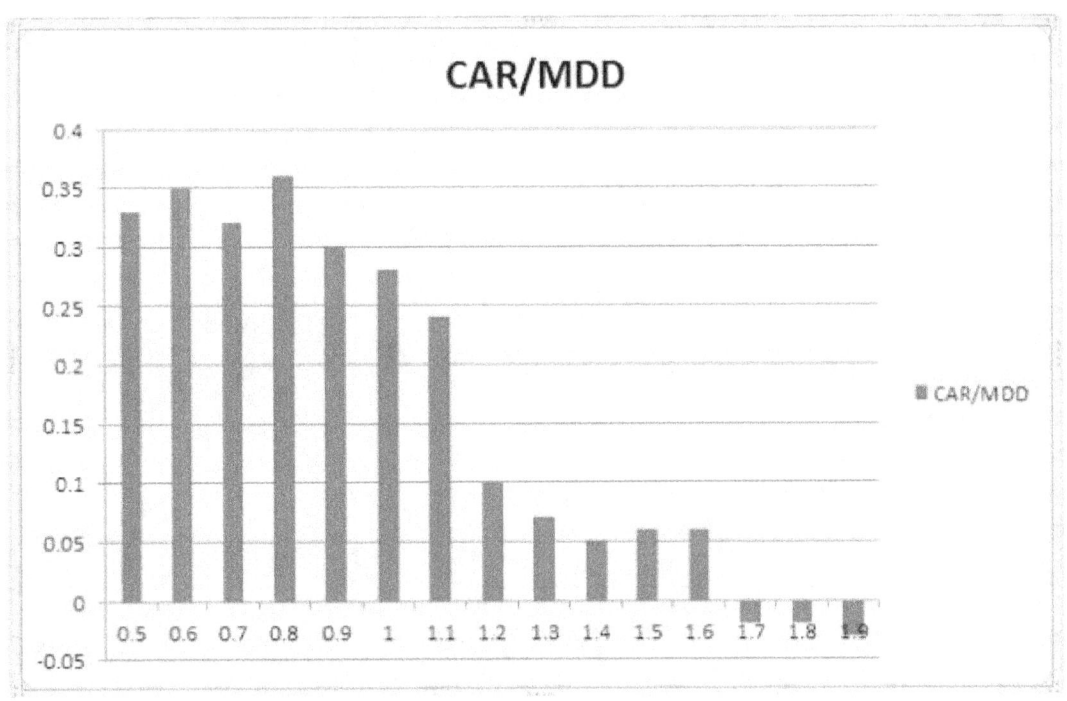

The above chart clearly shows that the weaker the broader market is on the first day of the pattern, the stronger the performance of the pattern becomes.

When combing both the ATR and A/D ratio filters, the win-rate of the evening star pattern becomes a very respectable 68.00%. The problem is that we only have a sample size of 50 trades. As this is on the small size, we won't combine the filters in the final strategy.

Instead, we will state that the evening star pattern can only be traded if the second day of the pattern has a daily range that is at least 5% greater than the range of the first day.

Applying stop-losses and profit targets to the dark cloud cover pattern
Before testing whether stop-losses or profit targets improve the strategy, I first wanted to know whether waiting for confirmation that a stock is weak *on the day following a dark cloud cover pattern* would improve the returns.

EPAM (Daily) ✕ TNA (Daily) 🦋 Analysis1 ◇   ◁ ▷ ▾

EPAM - Daily 15/08/2013 Open 31.67, Hi 31.83, Lo 30.27, Close 30.46 (-4.4%) Vol 348,700 MA1(Clos

Dark Cloud Cover

**Only sell if the price drops
below the low of the second
day's low.**

Instead of simply selling the open that follows the completion of a dark cloud cover pattern, the above rule would only permit us to go short if the price traded lower than the low of the pattern. Adding this rule seriously degraded the performance of the strategy.

The next tests were to determine whether a stop-loss that was placed above the high of the pattern would improve the strategy.

It didn't.

I also tested the strategy without a time based stop-loss but instead a stop-loss above the high of the pattern and a number of risk/reward multiple profit targets.

None of these test runs produced returns any better than were found by simply holding all open positions for 5 days.

The final tests were to determine the optimum values to use for a stop-loss and profit target. As with each of the strategies in this book, these stop-losses and profit targets are placed in the market to be executed intra-day.

The optimum values found were 8% and 5% for the stop-loss and profit target respectively. The following 3D optimization graph plots the values used as well as the corresponding CAR/MDD.

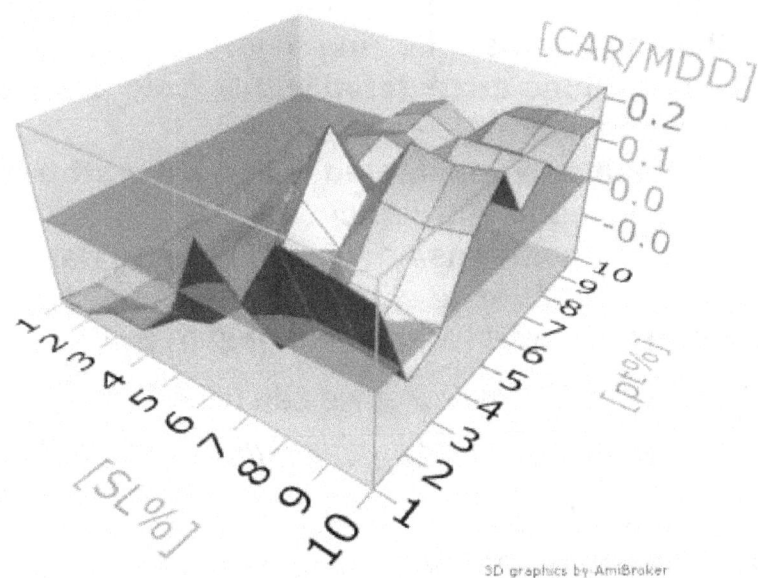

3D graphics by AmiBroker

It is again worth me pointing out that tight stop-losses are no good for a mean-reverting strategy such as this.

The final strategy will include a rule which states that all positions have a fixed profit target that is 5% below the entry price and a fixed stop-loss that is 8% above the entry price.

If the profit target is not executed within 10 days of holding a position, simply exit the position on the close of the 10th day.

- **The price must be above $20.00.**
- **The 20 day volume average must be above 250,000.**
- **The high of the first day in the pattern must be the highest high in the past 20 days.**
- **The SPY must have a 5 day MA beneath a 15 day MA on the day that the dark cloud cover pattern completes.**
- **The range of the second day in the pattern must be at least 5% greater than the range of the first day.**
- **Upon getting a valid signal, orders are placed to short the open of the following day.**
- **All positions are entered with a fixed profit target that is 5% beneath the entry price.**
- **All positions are entered with a fixed stop-loss that is 8% above the entry price.**
- **All open positions are closed after 10 days.**
- **Once a position is closed, 3 days must pass before we are allowed to trade a signal in the same stock.**

To code the strategy in Amibroker we can use the following formula:

//

```
SetTradeDelays(0,0,0,0);
SetOption("initialequity",30000);
SetOption ("MaxOpenPositions" , 5);
SetOption ("allowsamebarexit",false);
SetPositionSize(6000,spsValue);
SetBacktestMode(backtestregular);

Uptrend = H > Ref(HHV(H,20),-1);
BigWhite = (Close - Open)/Open > 0.015 AND (Close - Open) * 2 >
High - Low;
```

```
BlackBody = C < O;

DarkCloudCover = Ref(bigwhite,-1) AND blackbody AND O >
Ref(H,-1)
AND C <= Ref((O+C)/2,-1) AND C > Ref(O,-1) AND Ref(uptrend,-1);

Index = Foreign ("SPY","C",True);
Indexfastma = MA (Index, 5);
Indexslowma = MA (Index, 15);

DT = indexfastma < indexslowma;

Shortsetup = darkcloudcover
AND oi > 20
AND dt
AND MA(nonadjvol,20) > 250000
AND ATR(1) > 1.05 * Ref(ATR(1),-1);

Cover = 0;

shortPrice = Open;

Short = Ref(shortsetup,-1);
coverPrice = Close;

PT = Optimize("pt%",5,1,10,1);
SL = Optimize("SL%",8,1,10,1);

ApplyStop (stopTypeProfit,stopModePercent,pt,1,False,3);
ApplyStop (stopTypeloss,stopModepercent,sl,1,False,3);
ApplyStop(stopTypeNBar,stopModeBars,9,0,False,3);

PositionScore = 100 + Ref(nonadjvol,-1);
///////////////////////////////////////////////////////////////////////////////////////////
```

Test results for the dark cloud cover pattern

The following tables and charts show us the performance metrics of the dark cloud cover pattern when applying the above rules. **Notable metrics include a 64.85% win-rate, an average return per trade of 0.69% and a CAR/MDD of 0.17.**

	All trades	Long trades	Short trades
Initial capital	30000.00	30000.00	30000.00
Ending capital	36905.41	30000.00	36905.41
Net Profit	6905.41	0.00	6905.41
Net Profit %	23.02 %	0.00 %	23.02 %
Exposure %	6.32 %	0.00 %	6.32 %
Net Risk Adjusted Return %	364.24 %	N/A	364.24 %
Annual Return %	2.06 %	0.00 %	2.06 %
Risk Adjusted Return %	32.58 %	N/A	32.58 %
Total transaction costs	796.02	0.00	796.02
All trades	165	0 (0.00 %)	165 (100.00 %)
Avg. Profit/Loss	41.85	N/A	41.85
Avg. Profit/Loss %	0.69 %	N/A	0.69 %
Avg. Bars Held	6.23	N/A	6.23
Winners	107 (64.85 %)	0 (0.00 %)	107 (64.85 %)
Total Profit	28036.89	0.00	28036.89
Avg. Profit	262.03	N/A	262.03
Avg. Profit %	4.38 %	N/A	4.38 %
Avg. Bars Held	5.65	N/A	5.65
Max. Consecutive	9	0	9
Largest win	590.72	0.00	590.72
# bars in largest win	4	0	4
Losers	58 (35.15 %)	0 (0.00 %)	58 (35.15 %)
Total Loss	-21131.48	0.00	-21131.48
Avg. Loss	-364.34	N/A	-364.34
Avg. Loss %	-6.11 %	N/A	-6.11 %
Avg. Bars Held	7.29	N/A	7.29
Max. Consecutive	3	0	3
Largest loss	-674.95	0.00	-674.95
# bars in largest loss	5	0	5
Max. trade drawdown	-674.95	0.00	-674.95
Max. trade % drawdown	-11.27 %	0.00 %	-11.27 %
Max. system drawdown	-3792.42	0.00	-3792.42
Max. system % drawdown	-12.31 %	0.00 %	-12.31 %
Recovery Factor	1.82	N/A	1.82
CAR/MaxDD	0.17	N/A	0.17
RAR/MaxDD	2.65	N/A	2.65
Profit Factor	1.33	N/A	1.33
Payoff Ratio	0.72	N/A	0.72

1. Portfolio Equity

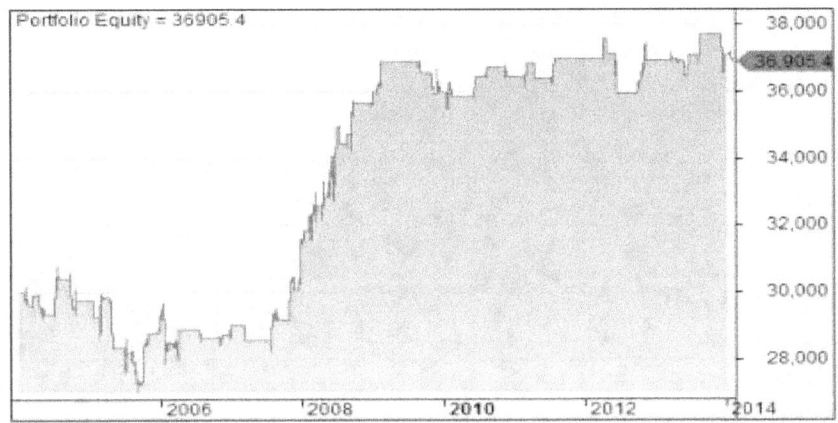

2. Underwater Equity

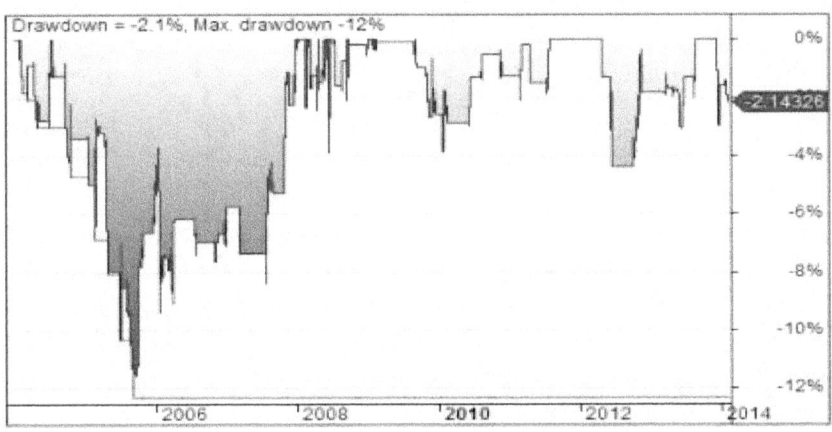

3. Profit Table

Year	Jan	Feb	Mar	Apr	May	Jun	Jul	Aug	Sep	Oct	Nov	Dec	Yr%
2004	0.0%	-1.2%	1.0%	-1.6%	-0.3%	0.0%	4.0%	-0.3%	-0.0%	-2.1%	0.0%	0.0%	-0.8%
2005	-1.0%	-0.6%	1.9%	-2.1%	-2.9%	0.0%	-0.6%	-2.1%	-1.1%	4.7%	0.7%	1.0%	-2.4%
2006	-3.9%	2.1%	-0.1%	1.5%	0.0%	0.0%	-0.3%	-0.5%	0.0%	0.0%	0.3%	0.5%	-0.5%
2007	0.5%	0.0%	-1.7%	0.0%	0.0%	0.0%	0.0%	2.4%	-0.2%	1.3%	1.8%	3.0%	7.3%
2008	2.8%	1.5%	0.8%	2.3%	-1.4%	3.6%	1.2%	0.9%	2.3%	0.5%	0.0%	0.0%	15.1%
2009	1.1%	2.3%	0.0%	0.0%	0.0%	0.0%	0.0%	0.0%	-0.9%	0.0%	-1.7%	0.1%	0.9%
2010	-0.1%	0.3%	-0.5%	0.0%	0.0%	1.6%	0.0%	0.8%	0.0%	0.0%	-0.3%	-0.5%	1.3%
2011	0.0%	0.0%	1.1%	-1.3%	0.0%	0.0%	0.8%	0.8%	0.0%	0.0%	0.0%	0.0%	1.4%
2012	0.0%	0.0%	0.0%	0.4%	0.0%	-3.1%	0.0%	0.0%	0.0%	1.7%	1.0%	0.0%	-0.1%
2013	0.0%	0.0%	0.3%	-0.2%	-0.0%	-0.5%	0.9%	1.6%	0.0%	0.0%	0.0%	-3.0%	-0.9%
2014	1.4%	-0.6%	N/A	N/A	N/A	N/A	N/A	N/A	N/A	N/A	N/A	N/A	0.9%
Avg	0.1%	0.3%	0.3%	-0.1%	-0.5%	0.2%	0.6%	0.3%	0.0%	0.6%	0.2%	0.1%	

208

The Hanging Man Pattern

The hanging man is a 1 day reversal pattern that occurs during an up-trend. It is the exact same setup as the hammer, but because it is supposed to signify a reversal of an up-trend and not a downtrend it has a different name.

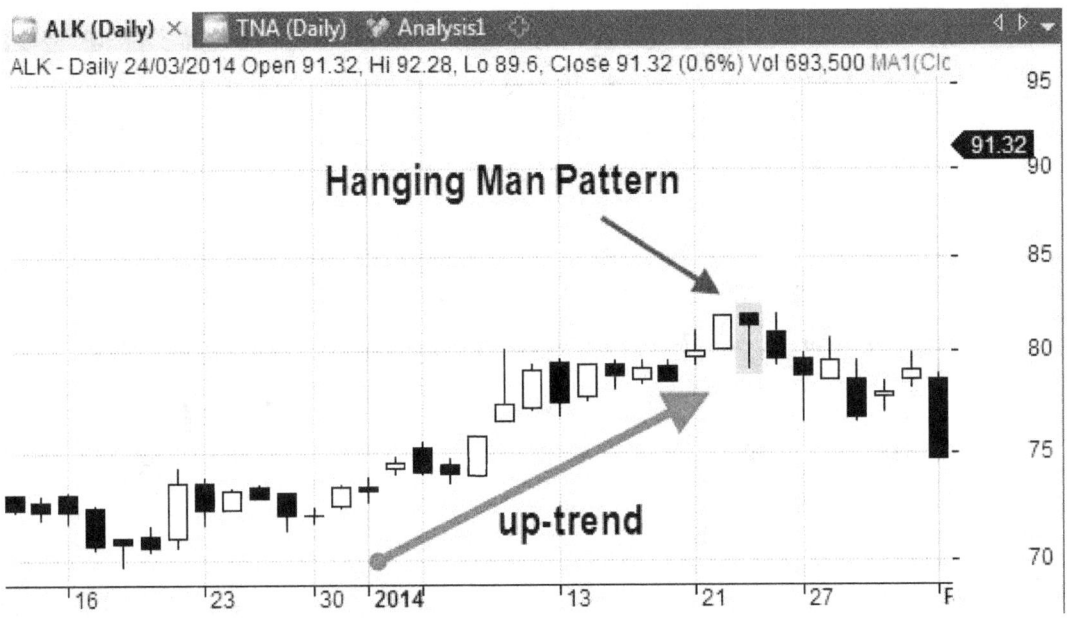

The hanging man pattern rules re-cap

- Price must be in an up-trend.
- The hanging man day must have a lower shadow at least 2 times longer than the real body.
- The upper shadow must be 10% less than the entire day range.
- The real body must close in the upper half of the entire day range.

The hanging man pattern code

Regarding the definition of the prior up-trend...tests show that the hanging man pattern performs well when the day before the pattern has made a 5 day high.

Remaining tests will include a rule which states that the hanging man pattern must be preceded by a candle that has made a 5 day high.

The Amibroker formula for defining each of the aforementioned rules is as follows:

//

Uptrend = **H** > Ref(HHV(**H**,5),-1);
rngx = abs(**H** - **L**);
body = abs(**O**-**C**);
lowerShadow = Min(**O**,**C**) - **L**;
uppershadow = **H** - Max(**O**,**C**);

UmbrellaLine = uppershadow < rngx*0.1 **AND** lowershadow > body*2;

HangingMan = umbrellaline **AND** Ref(uptrend,-1);

///

The hanging man pattern test results (5 day holding period)

Shorting all of the hanging man patterns during our test period that met the above rules and holding each open position for 5 days produced the following equity curve:

Although the returns are negative, the above chart illustrates quite clearly that having a strategy which shorts the market can at times be very beneficial to the overall returns of a portfolio.

If you had only been shorting hanging man patterns during 2008, you would have doubled your money while your next door neighbour would have probably lost 50% off the value of their portfolio.

Notable metrics over the entire sample period include a 46.86% win-rate and an average 5 day return per trade of -0.04%.

During 2008, we had multiple set-ups similar to those seen in the following chart of RRC:

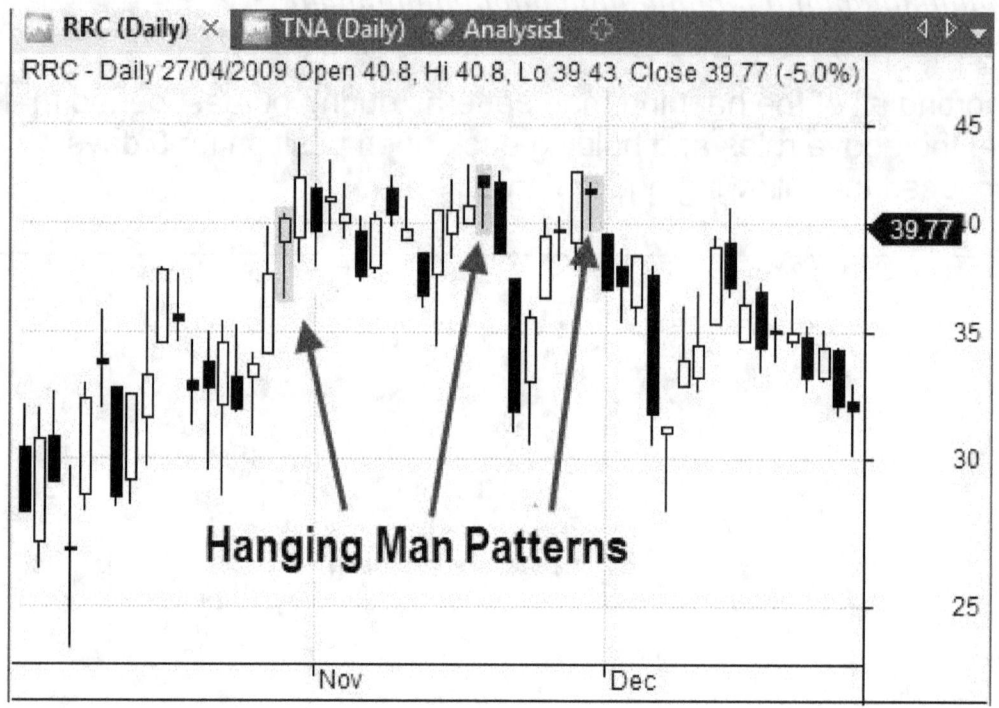

What is the best market environment for trading the hanging man pattern?

Tests suggest that the hanging man pattern performs well as a short-term reversal signal when the broader market is in a down-trend rally. To remind you, this is defined by the SPY having a 5 day MA below a 15 day MA and the RSI (3) above 70.

When applying the above SPY filter to the hanging man pattern the following equity curve was produced during our sample period:

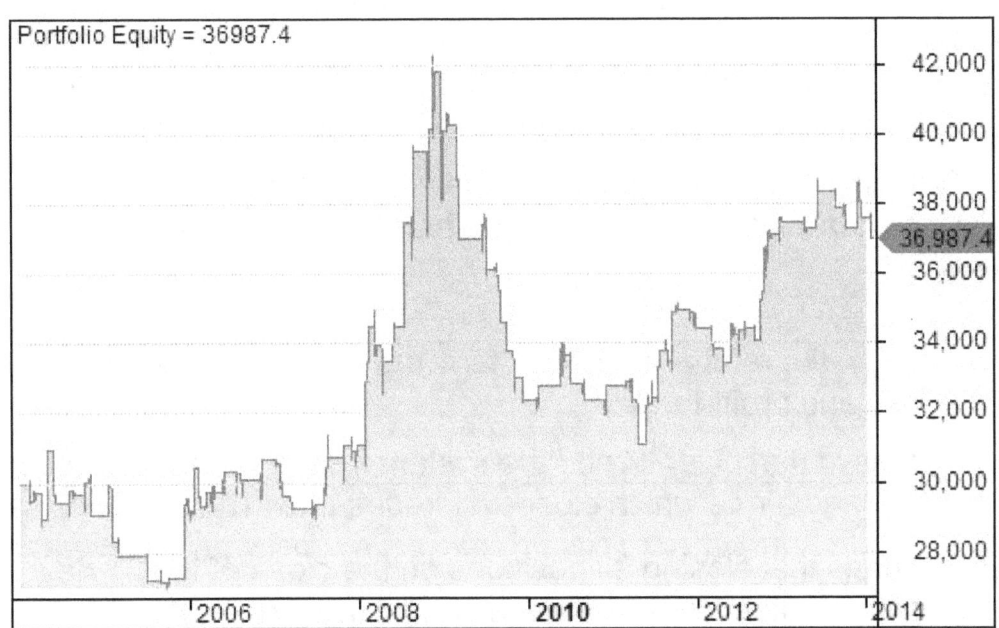

Notable performance metrics include a 47.36% win-rate and an average 5 day return per trade of 0.28%.

Remaining tests will include a filter that only allows going short hanging man patterns if the SPY is in a down-trend rally.

Applying indicator filters to the hanging man pattern

I'm probably beginning to sound like a broken record, but tests have again found little evidence that standard technical indictor filters are able to improve the performance of the pattern.

However, applying a more specific market environment filter to our strategy provides evidence that the hanging man pattern is more likely to precede a 5 day reversal if it occurs when the broader market has been weak during the previous 4 weeks.

To gauge such a market environment we can use a ROC filter that will plot the 1 month performance of the SPY.

The SPY ROC(20) threshold filter that produced the best CAR/MDD was **0%**. That is to say, we are only permitted to short a stock which has made a hanging man pattern if the pattern was made on the same day that the 20 day ROC of the SPY was less than 0%.

Our final strategy will include a rule which states that the hanging man pattern must occur when the SPY ROC(20) is below 0%.

Applying stop-losses and profit targets to the hanging man pattern

Interestingly, the returns of the strategy are degraded when applying a stop-loss and profit-target.

Stop-losses in particular turned the system from a winner to a loser, as did applying a rule which closes all trades after 10 days.

It so happens that closing all positions on the close of the 5th day provides the best returns during the sample period.

The final rules of the hanging man pattern trading strategy

- **The price must be above $20.00.**
- **The 20 day volume average must be above 250,000.**
- **The high of the day that precedes the hanging man pattern must be the highest high in the past 5 days.**
- **The SPY must have a 5 day MA beneath a 15 day MA on the day that the hanging man pattern completes.**
- **The SPY must have an RSI (3) reading above 70 on the day that the pattern completes.**
- **The SPY must have a 20 day ROC below 0% on the day that the pattern completes.**
- **Upon getting a valid signal, orders are placed to short the open of the following day.**
- **All open positions are closed after 5 days.**
- **Once a position is closed, 3 days must pass before we are allowed to trade a signal in the same stock.**

To code the strategy in Amibroker we can use the following formula:

//

```
SetTradeDelays(0,0,0,0);
SetOption("initialequity",30000);
SetOption ("MaxOpenPositions" , 5);
SetOption ("allowsamebarexit",false);
SetPositionSize(6000,spsValue);
SetBacktestMode(backtestregular);

Uptrend = H > Ref(HHV(H,5),-1);
rngx = abs(H - L);
body = abs(O-C);
lowerShadow = Min(O,C) - L;
uppershadow = H - Max(O,C);
UmbrellaLine = uppershadow < rngx*0.1 AND lowershadow >
body*2;

HangingMan = umbrellaline AND Ref(uptrend,-1);

NonAdjVol = (V * C)/OI ;

Index = Foreign ("SPY","C",True);
Indexfastma = MA (Index, 5);
Indexslowma = MA (Index, 15);

WTD = indexfastma < indexslowma AND RSIa(index,3) > 70;

Shortsetup = Hangingman
AND oi > 20
AND wtd
AND MA(nonadjvol,20) > 250000
AND ROC(index,20) < 0;
```

```
Short = Ref(shortsetup,-1);

Cover = OnSecondLastBarOfDelistedSecurity;

shortPrice = Open;

coverPrice = Close;

ApplyStop(stopTypeNBar,stopModeBars,4,0,False,3);

PositionScore = 100 + Ref(nonadjvol,-1);
///////////////////////////////////////////////////////////////////////////////
```

Test results for the hanging man pattern trading strategy

The following tables and charts show us the performance metrics of the hanging man pattern when applying the above rules. **Notable metrics include a 44.62% win-rate, an average gain per trade of 0.40% and a very low CAR/MDD of 0.08.**

	All trades	Long trades	Short trades
Initial capital	30000.00	30000.00	30000.00
Ending capital	34639.02	30000.00	34639.02
Net Profit	4639.02	0.00	4639.02
Net Profit %	15.46 %	0.00 %	15.46 %
Exposure %	6.00 %	0.00 %	6.00 %
Net Risk Adjusted Return %	257.83 %	N/A	257.83 %
Annual Return %	1.42 %	0.00 %	1.42 %
Risk Adjusted Return %	23.75 %	N/A	23.75 %
Total transaction costs	903.89	0.00	903.89
All trades	195	0 (0.00 %)	195 (100.00 %)
Avg. Profit/Loss	23.79	N/A	23.79
Avg. Profit/Loss %	0.40 %	N/A	0.40 %
Avg. Bars Held	5.00	N/A	5.00
Winners	87 (44.62 %)	0 (0.00 %)	87 (44.62 %)
Total Profit	23581.71	0.00	23581.71
Avg. Profit	271.05	N/A	271.05
Avg. Profit %	4.53 %	N/A	4.53 %
Avg. Bars Held	5.00	N/A	5.00
Max. Consecutive	9	0	9
Largest win	1109.79	0.00	1109.79
# bars in largest win	5	0	5
Losers	108 (55.38 %)	0 (0.00 %)	108 (55.38 %)
Total Loss	-18942.69	0.00	-18942.69
Avg. Loss	-175.40	N/A	-175.40
Avg. Loss %	-2.93 %	N/A	-2.93 %
Avg. Bars Held	5.00	N/A	5.00
Max. Consecutive	9	0	9
Largest loss	-1270.08	0.00	-1270.08
# bars in largest loss	5	0	5
Max. trade drawdown	-1270.08	0.00	-1270.08
Max. trade % drawdown	-21.17 %	0.00 %	-21.17 %
Max. system drawdown	-5188.82	0.00	-5188.82
Max. system % drawdown	-17.25 %	0.00 %	-17.25 %
Recovery Factor	0.89	N/A	0.89
CAR/MaxDD	0.08	N/A	0.08
RAR/MaxDD	1.38	N/A	1.38
Profit Factor	1.24	N/A	1.24
Payoff Ratio	1.55	N/A	1.55

1. Portfolio Equity

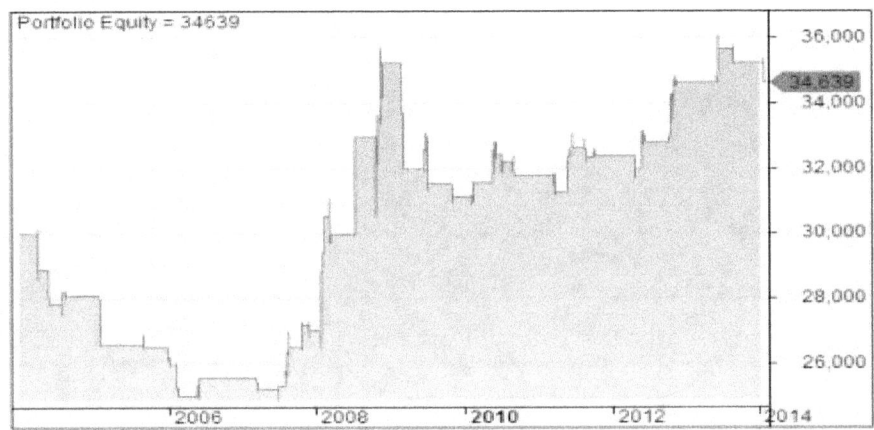

2. Underwater Equity

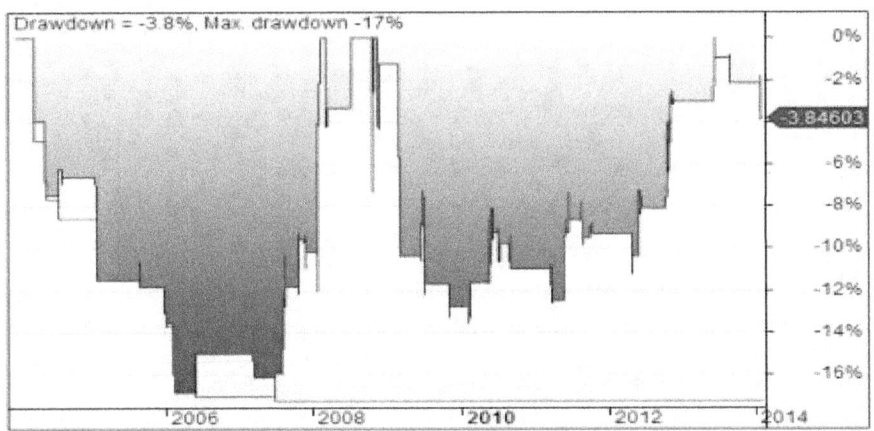

3. Profit Table

Year	Jan	Feb	Mar	Apr	May	Jun	Jul	Aug	Sep	Oct	Nov	Dec	Yr%
2004	0.0%	0.0%	0.3%	-3.9%	-3.9%	0.3%	-0.3%	1.1%	0.0%	0.0%	0.0%	0.0%	-6.4%
2005	0.0%	-5.3%	0.0%	0.0%	0.0%	0.0%	0.0%	0.0%	-0.4%	0.0%	0.0%	0.0%	-5.6%
2006	-1.9%	-3.8%	0.0%	0.0%	1.4%	0.9%	0.0%	0.0%	0.0%	0.0%	0.0%	0.0%	-3.6%
2007	0.0%	0.0%	-1.4%	0.0%	0.0%	0.0%	0.3%	4.9%	0.0%	-0.4%	1.5%	0.8%	5.6%
2008	0.0%	13.0%	-1.7%	0.0%	0.0%	0.0%	9.9%	0.0%	0.0%	-5.1%	6.7%	5.6%	30.5%
2009	0.0%	0.0%	-9.2%	0.0%	0.0%	-0.2%	-1.2%	0.0%	0.0%	0.0%	-1.2%	0.0%	-11.6%
2010	0.0%	1.2%	0.0%	0.0%	0.8%	2.0%	-0.6%	0.0%	-1.4%	0.0%	0.0%	0.0%	2.0%
2011	0.0%	0.0%	-1.7%	0.0%	0.0%	4.4%	0.0%	-0.9%	0.0%	0.2%	0.0%	0.0%	1.9%
2012	0.0%	0.0%	0.0%	-1.3%	1.7%	0.9%	0.0%	0.0%	0.0%	4.4%	1.1%	0.0%	6.9%
2013	0.0%	0.0%	0.0%	0.0%	0.0%	3.0%	0.0%	0.0%	-1.2%	0.0%	0.0%	0.0%	1.8%
2014	0.0%	-1.7%	N/A	N/A	N/A	N/A	N/A	N/A	N/A	N/A	N/A	N/A	-1.7%
Avg	-0.2%	0.3%	-1.4%	-0.5%	-0.0%	1.1%	0.8%	0.5%	-0.3%	-0.1%	0.8%	0.6%	

The Bearish Kicker Pattern

The bearish kicker pattern is a 2 day pattern that is supposed to signify a significant change of investor sentiment and precede a bearish move of the market.

The bearish kicker rules re-cap

- Price has been in an up-trend.
- The first day is an up day.
- The second day opens equal to or lower than the first day's low.
- The second day high is lower than the first day low.

Except for the definition of a prior uptrend, the basic rules which characterise the bearish kicker pattern leave no room for interpretation.

Regarding an 'up-trend', initial tests indicate that the bearish kicker pattern **is not improved** by specifying that the first day of the pattern has made an X day high.

However, the bearish kicker pattern can be improved if we specify that the first day and second day of the pattern both have at least 1% between their respective open and close.

For example:

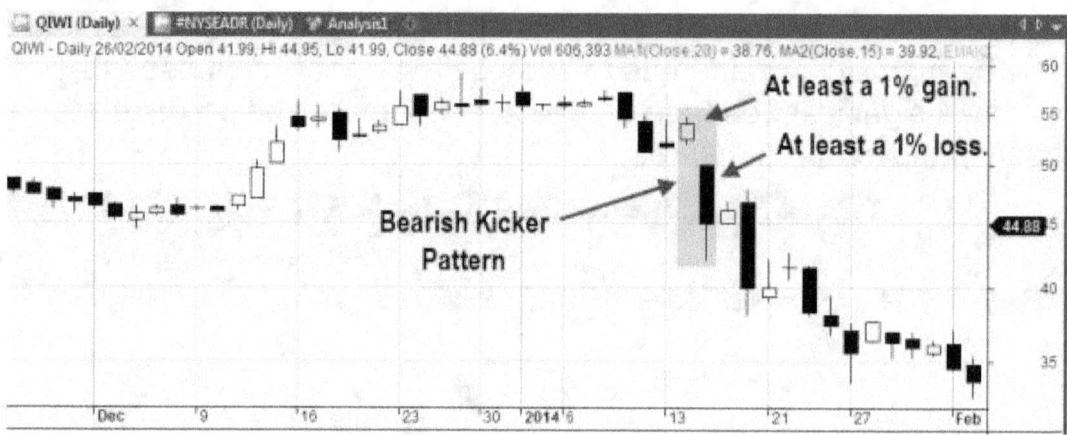

At least a 1% gain.

At least a 1% loss.

Bearish Kicker Pattern

The bearish kicker pattern code

Using Amibroker you can write the bearish kicker as follows:

//

BigWhite = (**Close - Open**)/**Open** > 0.01;
BigBlack = (**Open - Close**)/**Open** > 0.01;

BearishKick = Ref(**O**,-1) < Ref(**C**,-1) **AND O** <= Ref(**O**,-1)
AND C <= **O AND H** < Ref(**L**,-1) **AND** bigblack **AND**
Ref(bigwhite,-1);
//

The bearish kicker pattern test results (5 day holding period)

When going short on the open following a bearish kicker, and holding open positions for 5 days, we produced the following equity curve during our sample period.

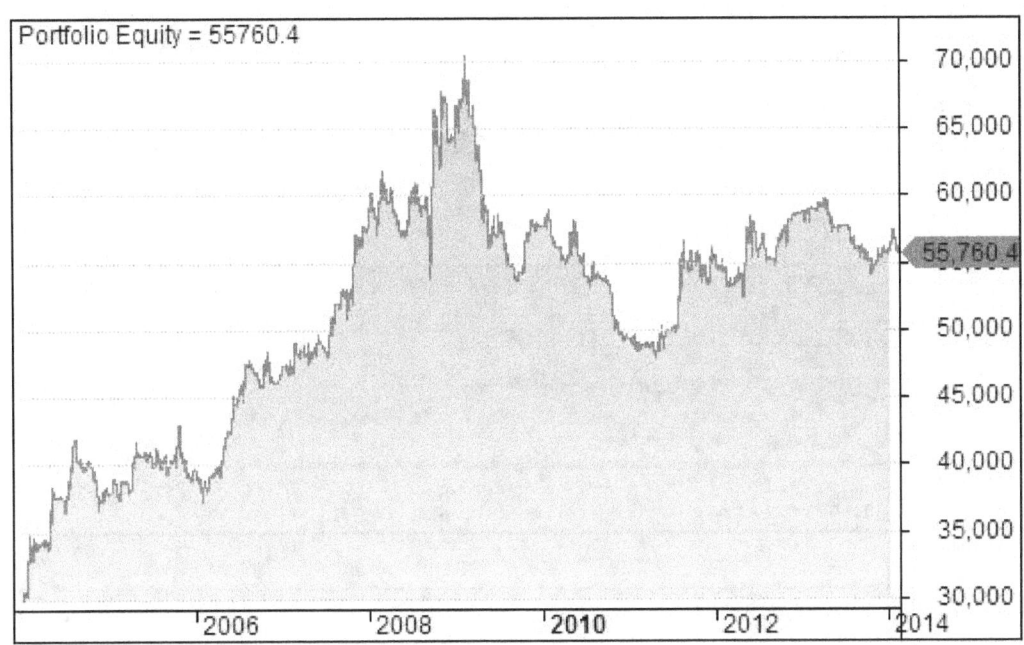

Portfolio Equity = 55760.4

Notable performance metrics when holding positions for 5 days include a 50.75% win-rate and an average 5 day return per trade of 0.34%.

What is the best market environment for trading the bearish kicker pattern?

Tests of the bearish kicker pattern during our sample period find that the pattern can be improved if only traded when the broader market is in a down-trend.

This is defined by the 5 day MA of the SPY being beneath the 15 day MA of the SPY.

Remaining tests will include a rule which states that the bearish kicker pattern can only be traded if it occurs when the 5 day MA of the SPY is below the 15 day MA of the SPY.

Applying indicator filters to the bearish kicker pattern

Tests of the bearish kicker signal with a variety of technical filters produced some interesting results.

The best CAR/MDD was far and away found when applying a Bollinger band filter. When applying a rule which stated that we could only trade the bearish kicker pattern if the first day of the pattern closed higher than the upper Bollinger band, **the test run produced a 57.14% win-rate and an average return per trade of 0.75% .**

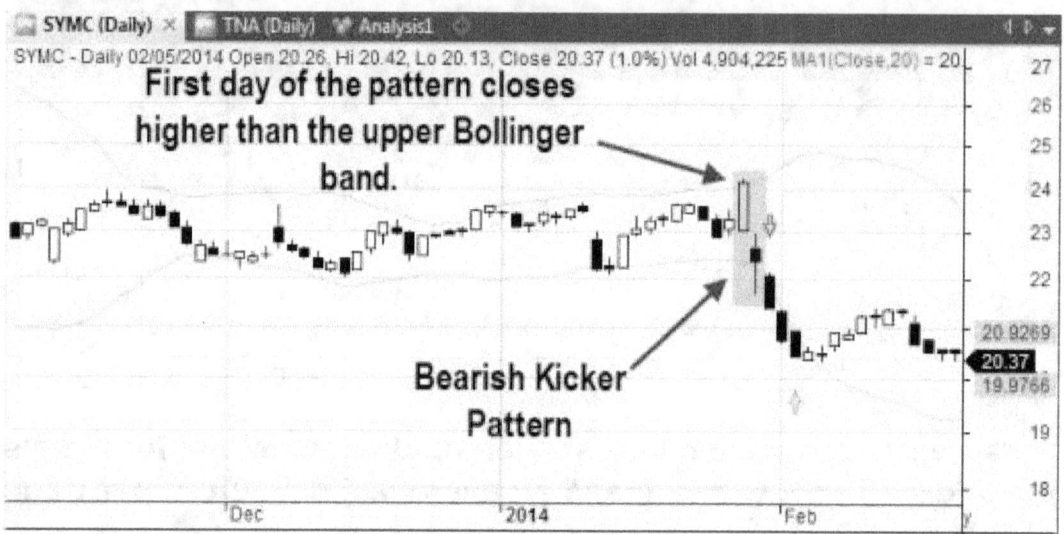

The one caveat to the above rule is that after applying it, the total amount of trades made during the sample period was only 56. This is too low for me to want to carry forward to any out of sample testing.

A filter which also produced good results, while also providing many more trading opportunities, was based on the 10 day ROC.

My theory was that the stronger a stock had been over the previous couple of weeks, the more likely that it would make a significant short-term pullback when preceded by the gap-down which characterises the bearish kicker pattern.

As with the AD filter referred to in the previous chapter, my idea is that if more people get caught offside by a sudden move lower, subsequent falls should be pronounced.

The following table plots the 10 day ROC % on the *x* axis and the corresponding average 5 day return if shorting all stocks that have just made a bearish kicker pattern.

Note that the stronger the stock has performed during the previous 10 days, the more that it falls after a bearish kicker pattern.

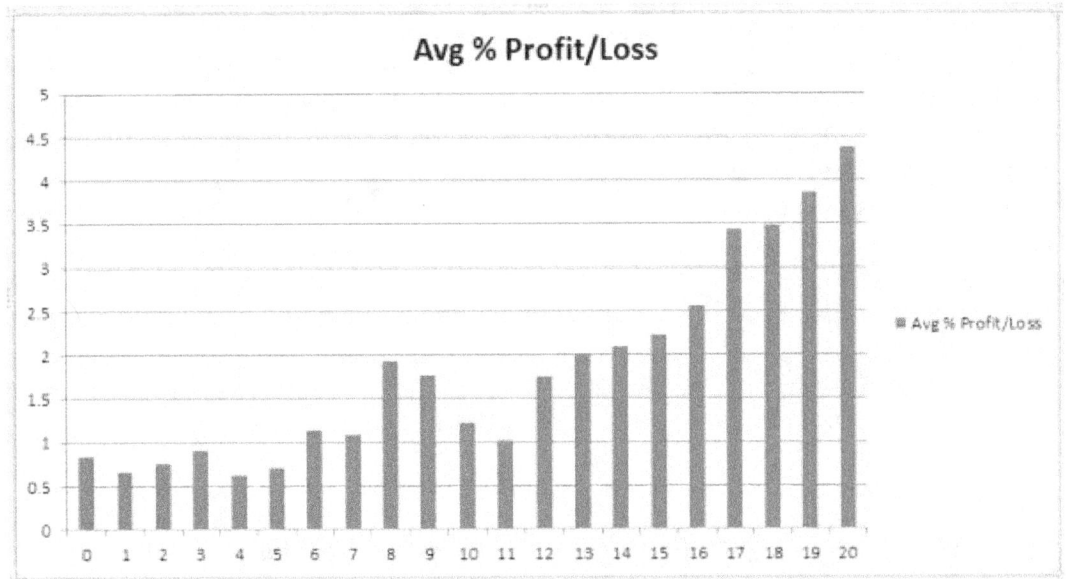

While it may seem as though the best course of action would be to include a ROC filter that only permitted trading bearish kicker patterns if the 10 day ROC was 15% or more, we again find that such a filter is too restrictive and we are left with too few trades.

As ever, we will simply take the rule which provided the highest number for our objective function.

The best CAR/MDD is found when using a 10 day ROC threshold of 0. That is to say, we are only permitted to short the bearish kicker pattern if the stock has a positive 10 day performance over the past 10 days as calculated on the close of the first day of the pattern.

A chart should make it clearer:

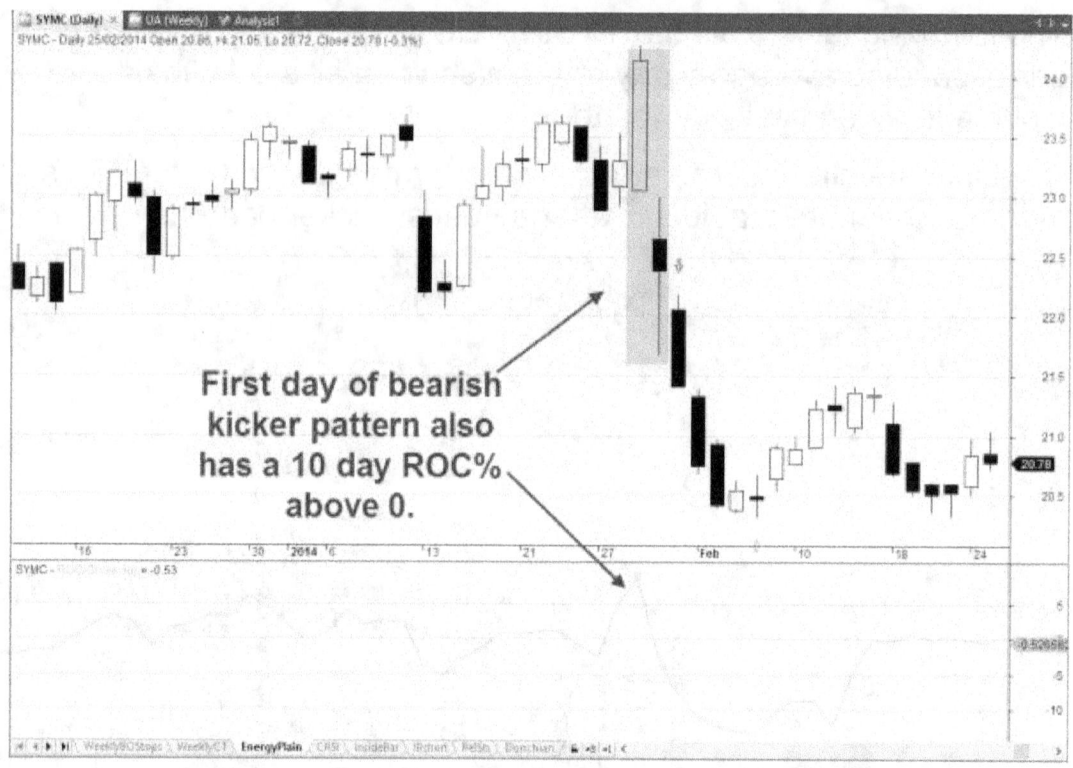

First day of bearish
kicker pattern also
has a 10 day ROC%
above 0.

Our final strategy will include a rule which states that we can only short a stock on the day following a bearish kicker pattern if the 10 day ROC was above 0% on the first day of the pattern.

Applying stop-losses and profit targets to the bearish kicker pattern
Tests found no evidence that waiting for further confirmation that the market was weak following the signal would improve the returns.

Simply entering on the open of the day following the signal is the best course of action.

Tests of the strategy with a variety of different stop-losses and profit targets find that the optimum values during the sample period were 8% and 3% respectively. All of the values used are plotted in the following 3D optimization graph.

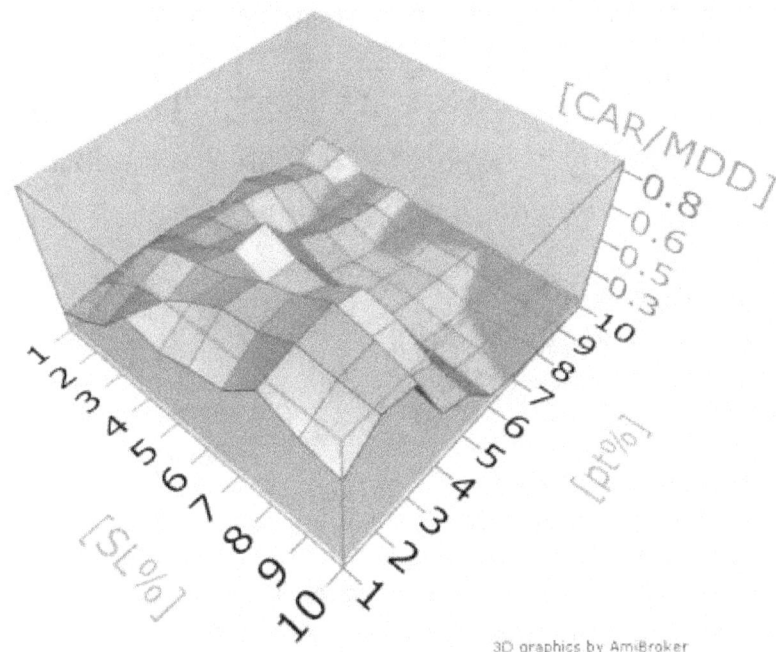

3D graphics by AmiBroker

As with the majority of other short only systems, the best returns are found if applying a tight profit target and a wide stop-loss.

The final strategy will include a rule which states that all open positions have a fixed 3% profit target beneath the entry price and a fixed 8% stop-loss above the entry price.

The final rules of the bearish kicker pattern trading strategy

- **The price must be above $20.00.**
- **The 20 day volume average must be above 250,000.**
- **The SPY must have a 5 day MA beneath a 15 day MA on the day that the bearish kicker pattern completes.**
- **The 10 day ROC of the individual stock must be above 0% on the first day of the pattern.**
- **Upon getting a valid signal, orders are placed to short the open of the following day.**
- **Apply a 8% stop-loss.**
- **Apply a 3% profit-target.**

- **All positions are closed after 10 days.**
- **Once a position is closed, 3 days must pass before we are allowed to trade a signal in the same stock.**

To code the strategy in Amibroker we can use the following formula:

///

```
SetTradeDelays(0,0,0,0);
SetOption("initialequity",30000);
SetOption ("MaxOpenPositions" , 5);
SetOption ("allowsamebarexit",false);
SetPositionSize(6000,spsValue);
SetBacktestMode(backtestregular);

BigWhite = (Close - Open)/Open > 0.01;
BigBlack = (Open - Close)/Open > 0.01;

BearishKick = Ref(O,-1) < Ref(C,-1) AND O <= Ref(O,-1) AND C <=
O
AND H < Ref(L,-1) AND bigblack AND Ref(bigwhite,-1);

NonAdjVol = (V * C)/OI ;

Index = Foreign ("SPY","C",True);
Indexfastma = MA (Index, 5);
Indexslowma = MA (Index, 15);

DT = indexfastma < indexslowma;


ROCUp = ROC(C,10) > 0;

Shortsetup = Bearishkick
AND oi > 20
AND MA(nonadjvol,20) > 250000
```

```
AND dt
AND Ref(ROCUp,-1);

Short = Ref(shortsetup,-1);

Cover = 0;

shortPrice = Open;

coverPrice = Close;

PT = Optimize("pt%",3,1,10,1);
SL = Optimize("SL%",8,1,10,1);

ApplyStop (stopTypeProfit,stopModePercent,pt,1,False,3);
ApplyStop (stopTypeloss,stopModepercent,sl,1,False,3);
ApplyStop(stopTypeNBar,stopModeBars,9,0,False,3);

PositionScore = 100 + Ref(nonadjvol,-1);
///////////////////////////////////////////////////////////////////////////
```

Test results for the bearish kicker pattern trading strategy

The following tables and charts show us the performance metrics of the bearish kicker pattern when applying the above rules. **Notable metrics include a 73.60% win-rate, an average return per trade of 1.26% and a CAR/MDD of 0.86.**

	All trades	Long trades	Short trades
Initial capital	30000.00	30000.00	30000.00
Ending capital	52793.28	30000.00	52793.28
Net Profit	22793.28	0.00	22793.28
Net Profit %	75.98 %	0.00 %	75.98 %
Exposure %	6.01 %	0.00 %	6.01 %
Net Risk Adjusted Return %	1264.53 %	N/A	1264.53 %
Annual Return %	5.72 %	0.00 %	5.72 %
Risk Adjusted Return %	95.17 %	N/A	95.17 %
Total transaction costs	1444.08	0.00	1444.08
All trades	303	0 (0.00 %)	303 (100.00 %)
Avg. Profit/Loss	75.23	N/A	75.23
Avg. Profit/Loss %	1.26 %	N/A	1.26 %
Avg. Bars Held	4.44	N/A	4.44
Winners	223 (73.60 %)	0 (0.00 %)	223 (73.60 %)
Total Profit	51351.32	0.00	51351.32
Avg. Profit	230.27	N/A	230.27
Avg. Profit %	3.85 %	N/A	3.85 %
Avg. Bars Held	3.55	N/A	3.55
Max. Consecutive	21	0	21
Largest win	1752.28	0.00	1752.28
# bars in largest win	2	0	2
Losers	80 (26.40 %)	0 (0.00 %)	80 (26.40 %)
Total Loss	-28558.04	0.00	-28558.04
Avg. Loss	-356.98	N/A	-356.98
Avg. Loss %	-5.97 %	N/A	-5.97 %
Avg. Bars Held	6.94	N/A	6.94
Max. Consecutive	8	0	8
Largest loss	-862.79	0.00	-862.79
# bars in largest loss	2	0	2
Max. trade drawdown	-1085.06	0.00	-1085.06
Max. trade % drawdown	-18.13 %	0.00 %	-18.13 %
Max. system drawdown	-3119.29	0.00	-3119.29
Max. system % drawdown	-6.69 %	0.00 %	-6.69 %
Recovery Factor	7.31	N/A	7.31
CAR/MaxDD	0.86	N/A	0.86
RAR/MaxDD	14.23	N/A	14.23
Profit Factor	1.80	N/A	1.80
Payoff Ratio	0.65	N/A	0.65

1. Portfolio Equity

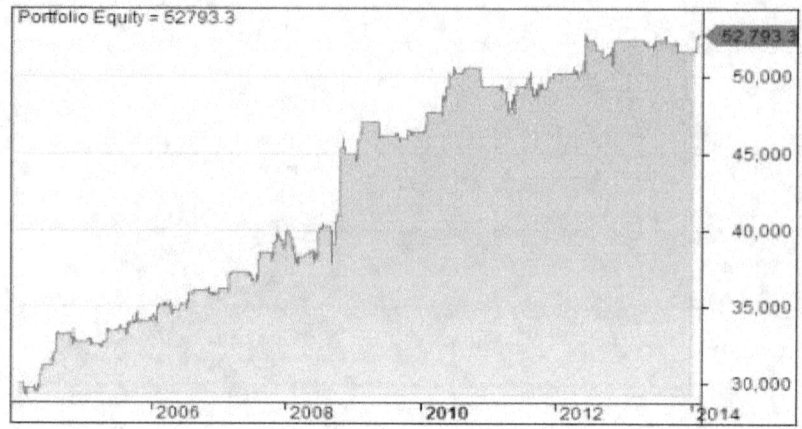

2. Underwater Equity

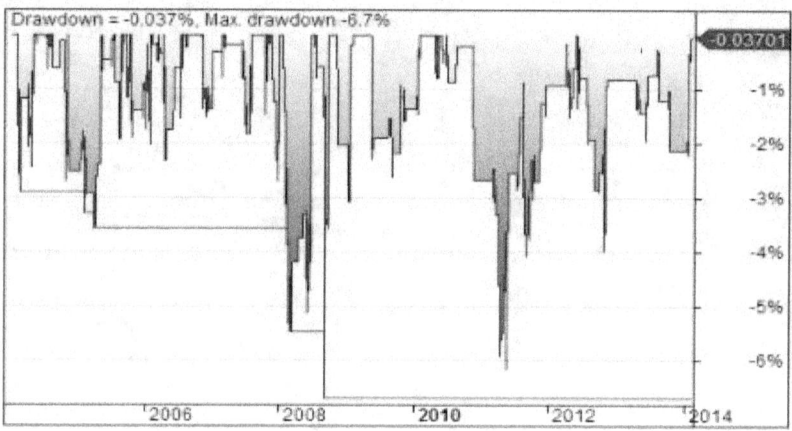

3. Profit Table

Year	Jan	Feb	Mar	Apr	May	Jun	Jul	Aug	Sep	Oct	Nov	Dec	Yr%
2004	0.0%	-0.9%	-0.2%	3.1%	1.8%	0.0%	3.3%	3.0%	0.5%	-0.2%	-1.6%	0.0%	9.0%
2005	0.8%	-1.2%	-0.7%	3.1%	0.2%	-0.1%	0.4%	1.3%	0.2%	0.3%	0.0%	0.5%	4.9%
2006	-0.2%	2.6%	-0.0%	-1.6%	0.6%	1.2%	2.1%	0.5%	0.0%	0.0%	-0.5%	-0.3%	4.3%
2007	1.1%	-0.5%	3.5%	0.0%	0.0%	-0.6%	-0.6%	4.7%	0.0%	-0.7%	2.8%	-1.4%	8.4%
2008	2.4%	-3.2%	-0.4%	0.5%	0.5%	0.1%	3.9%	0.0%	-3.0%	16.1%	-0.7%	0.0%	16.1%
2009	0.7%	3.7%	0.0%	0.0%	-2.2%	0.3%	0.0%	0.4%	-0.7%	1.1%	-0.2%	0.0%	3.1%
2010	0.6%	2.1%	0.0%	0.0%	3.6%	2.1%	-0.2%	0.7%	0.0%	0.0%	-1.6%	-0.9%	6.4%
2011	0.0%	0.0%	-0.4%	-3.0%	-0.3%	3.9%	-0.0%	-1.1%	0.8%	0.2%	1.5%	0.3%	1.8%
2012	0.0%	0.0%	0.0%	-0.6%	1.0%	3.8%	-0.4%	-0.8%	-0.9%	0.8%	1.3%	0.0%	4.2%
2013	0.0%	0.0%	0.0%	-0.3%	-0.3%	0.7%	0.0%	-0.5%	0.0%	-0.9%	0.0%	0.0%	-1.3%
2014	0.2%	1.9%	N/A	N/A	N/A	N/A	N/A	N/A	N/A	N/A	N/A	N/A	2.1%
Avg	0.5%	0.4%	0.2%	0.1%	0.5%	1.1%	0.9%	0.8%	-0.3%	1.7%	0.1%	-0.2%	

233

The Bearish Harami Pattern

The bearish harami pattern is commonly known in the west as a bearish inside day. It is a 2 day pattern where the first day is a continuation of an up-trend and creates a large up day.

The second day creates a smaller body and the open and closing price are contained within the open and closing price of the first day. The bearish harami is exactly the same pattern as a bullish harami pattern, except that it occurs during an up-trend.

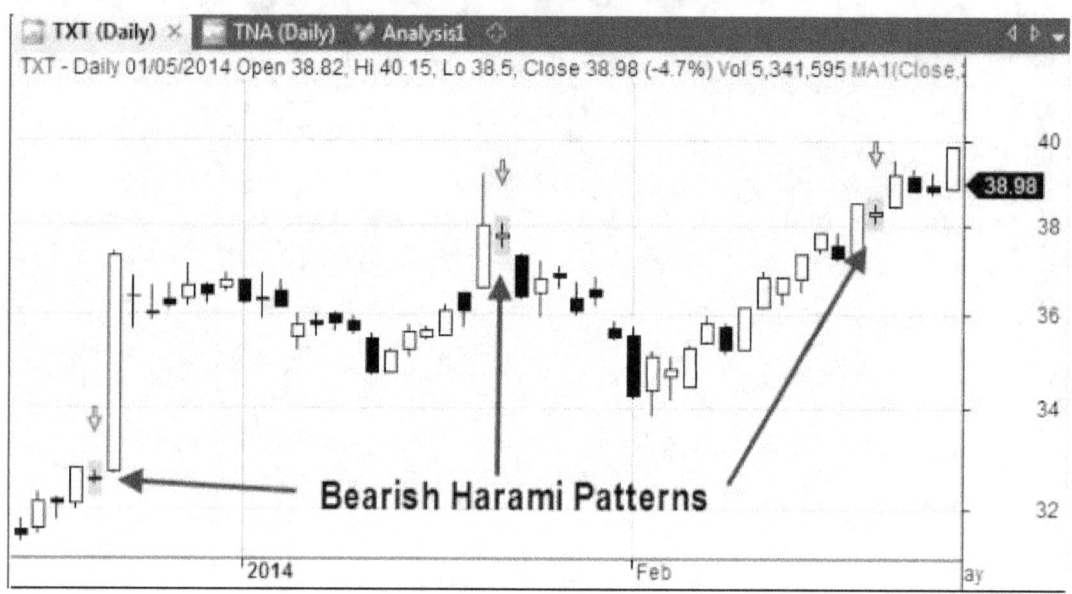

Bearish Harami Patterns

The bearish harami pattern rules re-cap

- The price must be in an up-trend.
- The first day is a large up day.
- The second day opens lower than the first days close and closes higher than the first days open.
- The second day can either be an up day or a down day. (I shall test both rules to determine whether one is better than the other.)

- Some people require that the high and low of the second day are within the first day range as well. (As I did with the bullish harami pattern, I will also test that rule too.)

The first test that I carried out was to best define an uptrend. I found that if **we are only allowed to trade bearish harami patterns when they're preceded by a day that makes a 20 day high**, we can improve the performance of the pattern.

I also tested the bearish harami pattern as an up day or a down day, to my surprise **the pattern performed better when the second day of the pattern closed higher than the open.**

Lastly, I tested the pattern with a further rule which stated that the low and high of the second day must be within the range of the first day. This rule produced no improvement in the performance of the pattern.

The only other areas of ambiguity that remain are the definition of a 'large up day' and a 'small real body'.

As with the other patterns tested so far, I will **define a 'large up day' as a day which closes at least 1.5% higher than the open** and a 'small real body' will be defined as a day that has less than 0.3% between the open and close.

The bearish harami pattern code

```
/////////////////////////////////////////////////
UpTrend = H > Ref(HHV(H,20),-1);
rng = abs((C-O)/O);
WhiteBody = C > O;
SmallRealBody = rng < 0.003 AND rng > 0;
Big = abs((Close - Open)/Open) > 0.015;

BearishHarami = Ref(big AND whitebody,-1) AND smallRealBody
```

AND Min(**O,C**) > Ref(**O,**-1) **AND** Max(**O,C**) < Ref(**C,**-1) **AND** Ref(uptrend,-1)
AND O < C;
///

The bearish harami pattern test results (5 day holding period)
When shorting all stocks that met the above rules and holding open positions for 5 days, the following equity curve was produced during our sample period:

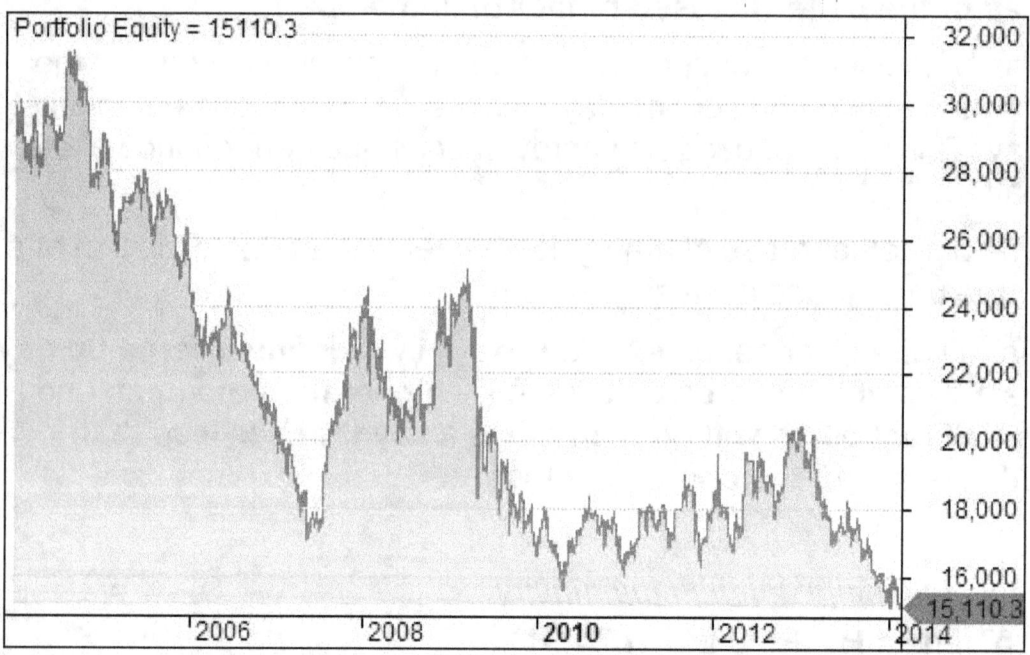

Notable performance metrics include a 47.69% win-rate and an average 5 day return per trade of -0.20%.

What is the best market environment for trading the bearish harami pattern?
Tests of the bearish harami pattern with a variety of market environment filters produced some surprising results.

237

Whereas the rest of the bearish patterns tested have so far been improved if the SPY is in a down-trend, the bearish harami pattern is improved by only trading it when the SPY is in an **strong uptrend** (defined by the SPY 5 day MA being above the SPY 15 day MA and the RSI (3) of the SPY being above 70).

Remaining tests will apply a filter to the bearish harami pattern that only permits a trade if the pattern is completed on the same day that the SPY is in a strong uptrend.

When applying the above market environment filter to our test sample, we produce the following equity curve:

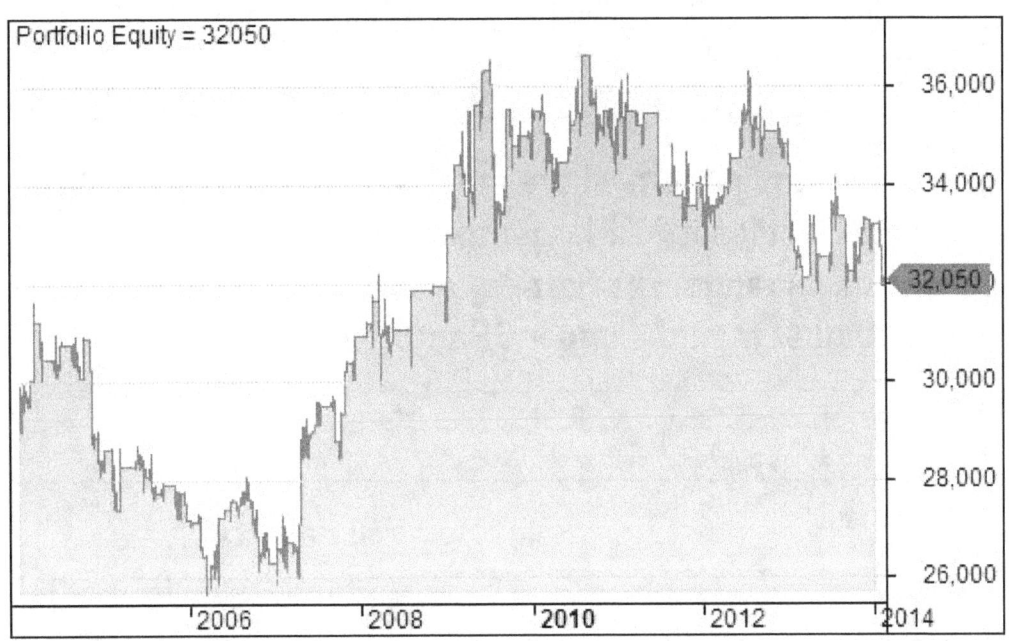

Notable performance metrics include a 49.69% win-rate and an average 5 day return per trade of 0.04%.

Applying indicator filters to the bearish harami pattern

A number of additional filters were able to significantly improve the performance of the bearish harami pattern during the test period.

The first improvement was found when applying a filter that only allowed the bearish harami to be a valid signal if the first day of the pattern had a range that was at least 20% larger than the range of the second day of the pattern.

The second improvement was found when applying a filter that only allowed the bearish harami to be a valid signal if the first day of the pattern closed higher than the upper Bollinger band.

Finally, tests found that the bearish harami pattern was a better reversal signal when produced by a stock that had risen at least 30% over the most recent quarter (60 days).

The following illustration highlights what your charts will look like after applying the above filters:

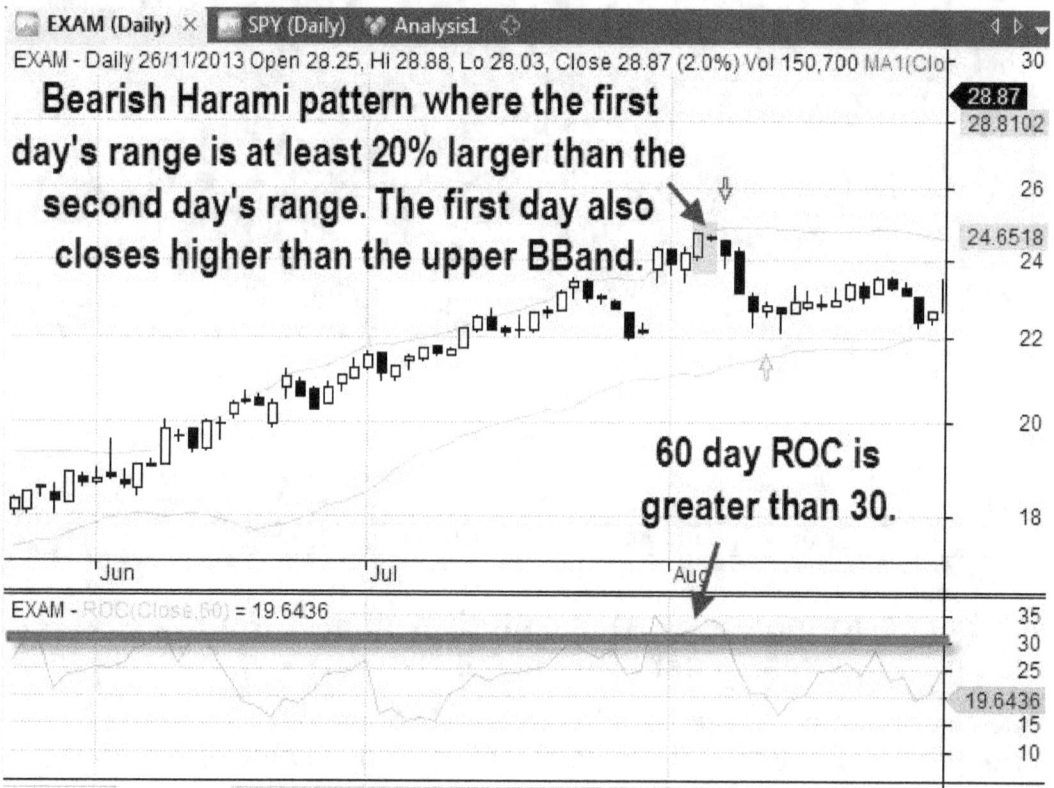

The final strategy will include each of the 3 filters that are mentioned above.

Applying stop-losses and profit targets to the bearish harami pattern

The final strategy will include a fixed profit target that is placed 4% below the entry price and a fixed stop-loss that is 10% above the entry price. All open positions are closed after 10 days.

The final rules of the bearish harami pattern trading strategy

- **The price must be above $20.00.**
- **The 20 day volume average must be above 250,000.**
- **The first day of the bearish harami pattern must make a 20 day high.**
- **The SPY must have a 5 day MA above a 15 day MA on the day that the bearish harami completes.**
- **The SPY must have a RSI (3) reading above 70 on the day that the bearish harami completes.**
- **The first day of the pattern must have a range that is more than 20% greater than the range of the second day of the pattern.**
- **The first day of the pattern must close above the upper Bollinger band.**
- **The stock must have a 60 day ROC above 30% on the first day of the pattern.**
- **Upon getting a valid signal, orders are placed to short the open of the following day.**
- **All positions have a fixed profit target that is 4% below the entry price.**
- **Stop-loss are 10% above the entry price.**
- **All positions are closed after 10 days.**
- **Once a position is closed, 3 days must pass before we are allowed to trade a signal in the same stock.**

To code the strategy in Amibroker we can use the following formula:

```
/////////////////////////////////////////////////////////

SetTradeDelays(0,0,0,0);
SetOption("initialequity",30000);
SetOption ("MaxOpenPositions" , 5);
SetOption ("allowsamebarexit",false);
SetPositionSize(6000,spsValue);
SetBacktestMode(backtestregular);

UpTrend = H > Ref(HHV(H,20),-1);
rng = abs((C-O)/O);
WhiteBody = C > O;
SmallRealBody = rng < 0.003 AND rng > 0;
Big = abs((Close - Open)/Open) > 0.015;

BearishHarami = Ref(big AND whitebody,-1) AND smallRealBody
AND Min(O,C) > Ref(O,-1) AND Max(O,C) < Ref(C,-1) AND
Ref(uptrend,-1)
AND O < C;

NonAdjVol = (V * C)/OI ;

Index = Foreign ("SPY","C",True);
Indexfastma = MA (Index, 5);
Indexslowma = MA (Index, 15);

STU = indexfastma > indexslowma AND RSIa(index,3) > 70;

Shortsetup = BearishHarami
AND oi > 20
AND stu
AND Ref(C,-1) > Ref (BBandTop( C, 20, 2 ),-1)
AND MA(nonadjvol,20) > 250000
AND Ref(ROC(C,60),-1) > 30
```

```
AND Ref(ATR(1),-1) > 1.20 * ATR(1);

Short = Ref(shortsetup,-1);

Cover = 0;

shortPrice = Open;

coverPrice = Close;

PT = Optimize("pt%",4,1,10,1);
SL = Optimize("SL%",10,1,10,1);

ApplyStop (stopTypeProfit,stopModePercent,pt,1,False,3);
ApplyStop (stopTypeloss,stopModepercent,sl,1,False,3);
ApplyStop(stopTypeNBar,stopModeBars,9,0,False,3);

PositionScore = 100 + Ref(nonadjvol,-1);
/////////////////////////////////////////////////////////////////////
```

Test results for the bearish harami pattern trading strategy
The following tables and charts show us the performance metrics of
the bearish harami pattern when applying the above rules.

**Notable metrics include a 64.17% win-rate, an average gain per
trade of 0.90% and a CAR/MDD of 0.42.**

	All trades	Long trades	Short trades
Initial capital	30000.00	30000.00	30000.00
Ending capital	36426.66	30000.00	36426.66
Net Profit	6426.66	0.00	6426.66
Net Profit %	21.42 %	0.00 %	21.42 %
Exposure %	4.34 %	0.00 %	4.34 %
Net Risk Adjusted Return %	493.96 %	N/A	493.96 %
Annual Return %	1.93 %	0.00 %	1.93 %
Risk Adjusted Return %	44.46 %	N/A	44.46 %
Total transaction costs	581.40	0.00	581.40
All trades	120	0 (0.00 %)	120 (100.00 %)
Avg. Profit/Loss	53.56	N/A	53.56
Avg. Profit/Loss %	0.90 %	N/A	0.90 %
Avg. Bars Held	6.15	N/A	6.15
Winners	77 (64.17 %)	0 (0.00 %)	77 (64.17 %)
Total Profit	18072.28	0.00	18072.28
Avg. Profit	234.70	N/A	234.70
Avg. Profit %	3.92 %	N/A	3.92 %
Avg. Bars Held	4.32	N/A	4.32
Max. Consecutive	14	0	14
Largest win	652.08	0.00	652.08
# bars in largest win	2	0	2
Losers	43 (35.83 %)	0 (0.00 %)	43 (35.83 %)
Total Loss	-11645.61	0.00	-11645.61
Avg. Loss	-270.83	N/A	-270.83
Avg. Loss %	-4.53 %	N/A	-4.53 %
Avg. Bars Held	9.42	N/A	9.42
Max. Consecutive	7	0	7
Largest loss	-696.37	0.00	-696.37
# bars in largest loss	5	0	5
Max. trade drawdown	-758.31	0.00	-758.31
Max. trade % drawdown	-12.52 %	0.00 %	-12.52 %
Max. system drawdown	-1533.31	0.00	-1533.31
Max. system % drawdown	-4.57 %	0.00 %	-4.57 %
Recovery Factor	4.19	N/A	4.19
CAR/MaxDD	0.42	N/A	0.42
RAR/MaxDD	9.73	N/A	9.73
Profit Factor	1.55	N/A	1.55
Payoff Ratio	0.87	N/A	0.87

1. Portfolio Equity

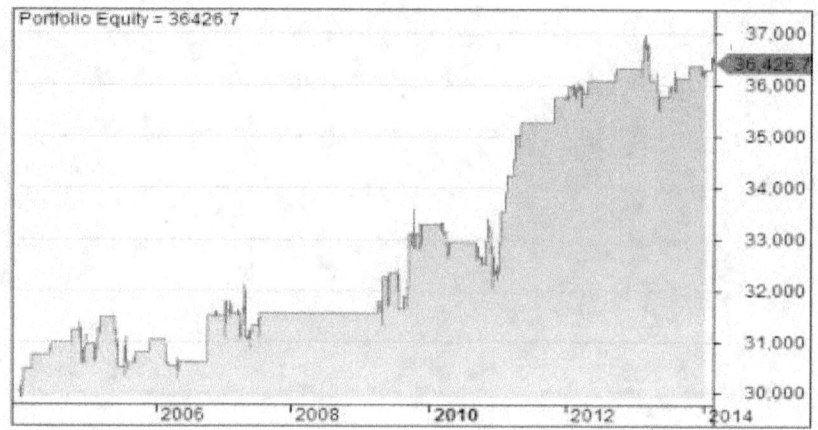

2. Underwater Equity

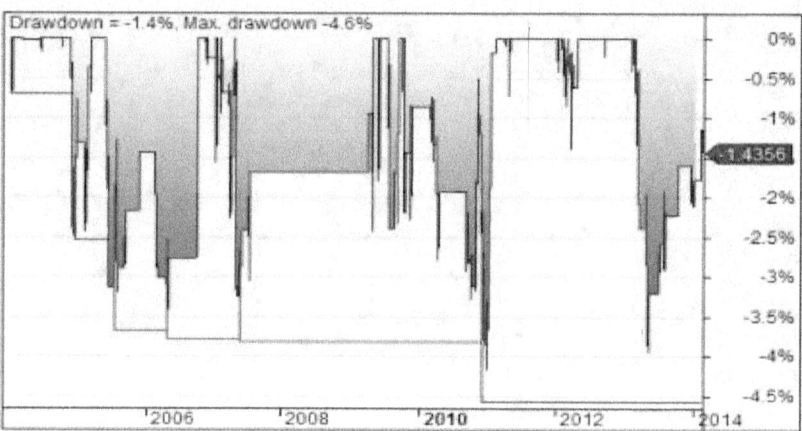

3. Profit Table

Year	Jan	Feb	Mar	Apr	May	Jun	Jul	Aug	Sep	Oct	Nov	Dec	Yr%
2004	1.6%	0.0%	0.9%	0.0%	0.0%	0.8%	0.0%	0.0%	0.0%	0.8%	-1.9%	1.1%	3.2%
2005	0.0%	1.0%	0.8%	0.0%	-0.8%	-2.4%	0.1%	0.1%	0.7%	0.0%	0.8%	0.0%	0.3%
2006	0.0%	-0.0%	-1.6%	-0.2%	0.4%	0.0%	0.0%	0.0%	0.0%	2.9%	0.0%	0.0%	1.5%
2007	0.3%	-0.2%	-0.4%	2.0%	-3.1%	0.7%	0.8%	0.0%	0.0%	0.0%	0.0%	0.0%	0.1%
2008	0.0%	0.0%	0.0%	0.0%	0.0%	0.0%	0.0%	0.0%	0.0%	0.0%	0.0%	0.0%	0.0%
2009	0.0%	0.0%	0.0%	0.7%	1.5%	0.3%	-0.1%	-1.3%	3.8%	-0.0%	0.1%	0.5%	5.5%
2010	0.0%	0.0%	-0.5%	-0.6%	0.0%	0.0%	0.0%	0.0%	-0.9%	-0.3%	2.0%	-2.6%	-2.9%
2011	3.7%	2.1%	0.0%	1.9%	1.1%	0.0%	0.0%	0.0%	0.0%	0.6%	0.8%	0.0%	10.7%
2012	0.6%	-0.2%	-0.1%	0.4%	0.2%	0.0%	0.0%	0.0%	0.7%	0.0%	0.0%	0.0%	1.5%
2013	0.0%	1.5%	-2.1%	-0.0%	-0.8%	0.0%	0.7%	0.4%	0.0%	0.7%	0.0%	-0.5%	-0.3%
2014	0.3%	0.3%	N/A	N/A	N/A	N/A	N/A	N/A	N/A	N/A	N/A	N/A	0.6%
Avg	0.6%	0.4%	-0.3%	0.4%	-0.1%	-0.1%	0.1%	-0.1%	0.4%	0.5%	0.2%	-0.2%	

The Shooting Star Pattern

The shooting star pattern is a 1 day pattern that is the same as the inverted hammer except that it occurs during an up-trend.

The shooting star shows indecision because even though buying has occurred during the day, the bears have taken control of the market to close the price in the lower half of the day's range.

The shooting star pattern rules re-cap

- Price has been in an up-trend.
- The upper shadow must be at least 2 times larger than the real body.
- The lower shadow must be less than 10% of the entire day range.
- The real body must be in the lower half of the entire day range.
- The shooting star can be an up day or a down day. But it is often written that the shooting star as a down day has more bearish implications. (Our tests will tell us of that is true.)

Tests indicate that the shooting star pattern can be improved if the day that precedes the pattern has also made a 20 day high.

Tests of the pattern as an up day or a down day found that although the pattern performed better if it was a down day, there were far fewer occurrences of the pattern (314 trades during the sample period).

However, due to the better performance **I will tentatively apply a rule which states that the shooting star pattern must be a down day.**

The shooting star pattern code

//

```
UpTrend = H > Ref(HHV(H,20),-1);
rng = abs((C-O)/O);
SmallRealBody = rng < 0.003 AND rng > 0;
LongUpperShadow = H - Max(O,C) > (H - L) *0.67;
RealBodyGapUp = Min(O,C) > Max(Ref(O,-1),Ref(C,-1));
lowerShadow = Min(O,C) - L;
rngy = H-L;
shaven = lowerShadow < rngy*0.1;
```

ShootingStar = smallRealBody **AND** shaven **AND** realBodyGapUp **AND** longuppershadow **AND** Ref(uptrend,-1) **AND C < O**;

//

The shooting star pattern test results (5 day holding period)
During the test period, applying the above rules and holding all open positions for 5 days produced the following equity curve:

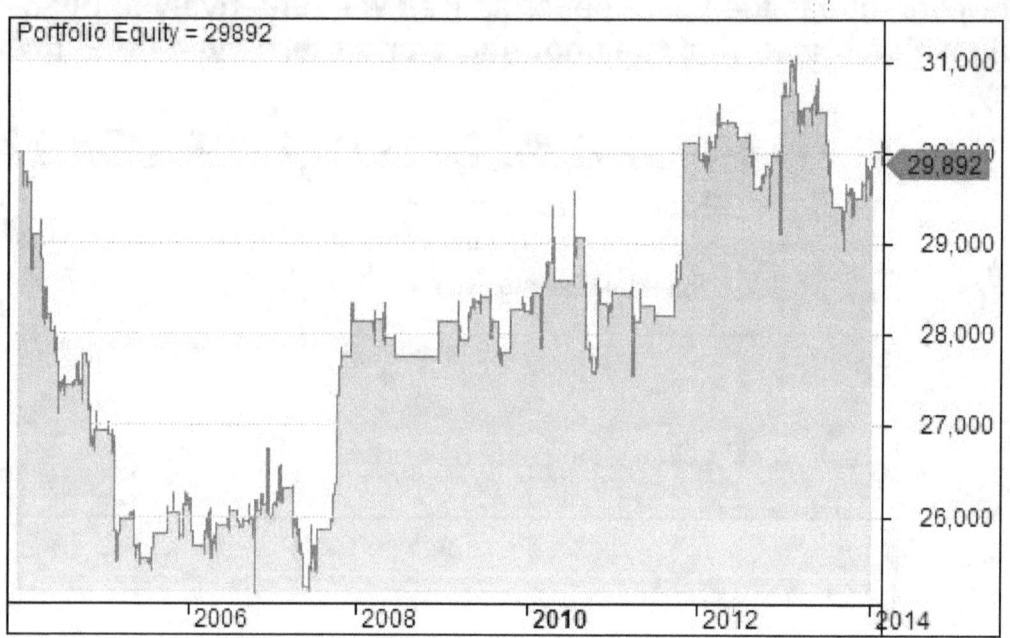

Notable performance metrics include a 49.62% win-rate and an average 5 day return per trade of -0.01%.

Even after optimizing the definition of an uptrend and only allowing the pattern if it is a down day, the results are still very poor.

What is the best market condition for trading the shooting star pattern?
A problem with having so few trades made during the sample period is that the changes to the performance of the strategy when filtering by the market environment have less statistical significance.

For example, if we are only allowed to trade the shooting star pattern when the SPY is in a downtrend that is currently correcting, the win-rate of the pattern becomes 54%, but there is only 26 trades executed over the entire 10 years.

With the above said, **remaining tests will not filter the shooting star pattern by market environment.**

Applying indicator filters to the shooting star pattern
After applying a multitude of technical indicator filters to the shooting star pattern, I found little evidence that the pattern can be incorporated into a worthwhile trading strategy.

The best results were found if applying a filter that only allowed going short after a shooting star pattern if the day before the pattern had a CSRI reading that was above 85.

However, after applying the CSRI filter the number of trades made during the sample period was only 70.

As so few trades are made, I will forgo testing the pattern with different stop-losses and profit targets and instead present the results of the pattern (with the CSRI > 85 filter) if simply holding open positions for 5 days.

The final rules of the shooting star pattern trading strategy

- **The price must be above $20.00.**
- **The 20 day volume average must be above 250,000.**
- **The shooting star pattern must close lower than it opens.**
- **The shooting star pattern must be preceded by a day that has a CSRI reading that is above 85.**

- **All positions are held exited at the close of the 5th day.**
- **Once a position is closed, 3 days must pass before we are allowed to trade a signal in the same stock.**

In Amibroker these rules can be written as:

//

```
SetTradeDelays(0,0,0,0);
SetOption("initialequity",30000);
SetOption ("MaxOpenPositions" , 5);
SetOption ("allowsamebarexit",false);
SetPositionSize(6000,spsValue);
SetBacktestMode(backtestregular);

#include <Connerrsi.afl>;

UpTrend = H > Ref(HHV(H,20),-1);
rng = abs((C-O)/O);
SmallRealBody = rng < 0.003 AND rng >0;
LongUpperShadow = H - Max(O,C) > (H - L)*0.67;
RealBodyGapUp = Min(O,C) > Max(Ref(O,-1),Ref(C,-1));
lowerShadow = Min(O,C) - L;
rngy = H-L;
shaven = lowerShadow < rngy*0.1;

NonAdjVol = (V * C)/OI ;

Index = Foreign ("SPY","C",True);
Indexfastma = MA (Index, 5);
Indexslowma = MA (Index, 15);


ShootingStar = smallRealBody AND shaven AND realBodyGapUp
AND longuppershadow AND Ref(uptrend,-1) AND O > C;

Shortsetup = shootingstar
AND oi > 20
AND Ref (Connorsrsi(2,3,100),-1) > 85
```

```
AND MA(nonadjvol,20) > 250000;
Short = Ref(shortsetup,-1);
Cover = 0;

shortPrice = Open;
coverPrice = Close;

ApplyStop(stopTypeNBar,stopModeBars,4,0,False,3);

PositionScore = 100 + Ref(nonadjvol,-1);
/////////////////////////////////////////////////////////////////////////////////
```

Test results for the shooting star pattern trading strategy

The following tables and charts show us the performance metrics of the shooting star pattern when applying the above rules. **Notable metrics include a 61.43% win-rate, an average 5 day return of 1.20% per trade and a CAR/MDD of 0.48.**

	All trades	Long trades	Short trades
Initial capital	30000.00	30000.00	30000.00
Ending capital	35036.81	30000.00	35036.81
Net Profit	5036.81	0.00	5036.81
Net Profit %	16.79 %	0.00 %	16.79 %
Exposure %	2.09 %	0.00 %	2.09 %
Net Risk Adjusted Return %	804.54 %	N/A	804.54 %
Annual Return %	1.54 %	0.00 %	1.54 %
Risk Adjusted Return %	73.73 %	N/A	73.73 %
Total transaction costs	338.46	0.00	338.46
All trades	70	0 (0.00 %)	70 (100.00 %)
Avg. Profit/Loss	71.95	N/A	71.95
Avg. Profit/Loss %	1.20 %	N/A	1.20 %
Avg. Bars Held	5.00	N/A	5.00
Winners	43 (61.43 %)	0 (0.00 %)	43 (61.43 %)
Total Profit	8552.07	0.00	8552.07
Avg. Profit	198.89	N/A	198.89
Avg. Profit %	3.32 %	N/A	3.32 %
Avg. Bars Held	5.00	N/A	5.00
Max. Consecutive	6	0	6
Largest win	1269.00	0.00	1269.00
# bars in largest win	5	0	5
Losers	27 (38.57 %)	0 (0.00 %)	27 (38.57 %)
Total Loss	-3515.25	0.00	-3515.25
Avg. Loss	-130.19	N/A	-130.19
Avg. Loss %	-2.18 %	N/A	-2.18 %
Avg. Bars Held	5.00	N/A	5.00
Max. Consecutive	3	0	3
Largest loss	-496.18	0.00	-496.18
# bars in largest loss	5	0	5
Max. trade drawdown	-631.80	0.00	-631.80
Max. trade % drawdown	-9.08 %	0.00 %	-9.08 %
Max. system drawdown	-961.49	0.00	-961.49
Max. system % drawdown	-3.20 %	0.00 %	-3.20 %
Recovery Factor	5.24	N/A	5.24
CAR/MaxDD	0.48	N/A	0.48
RAR/MaxDD	23.00	N/A	23.00
Profit Factor	2.43	N/A	2.43
Payoff Ratio	1.53	N/A	1.53

1. Portfolio Equity

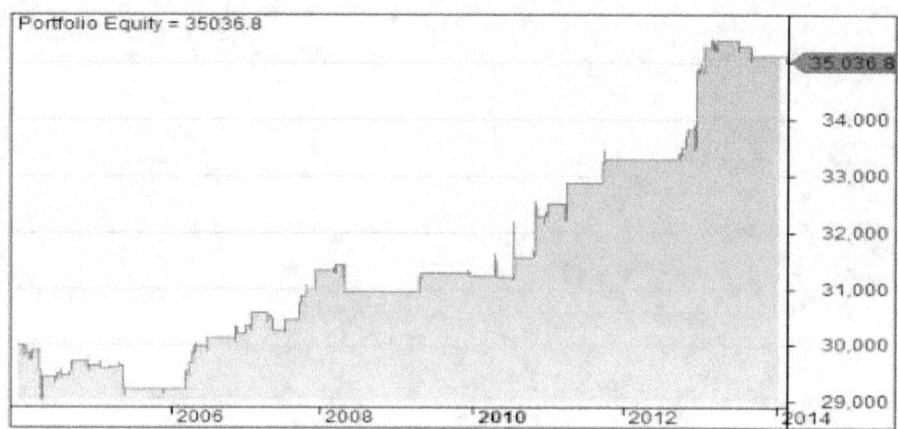

2. Underwater Equity

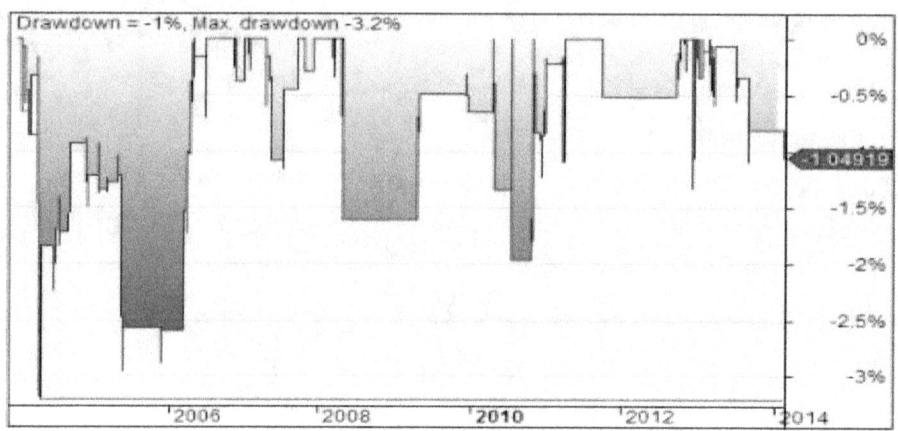

3. Profit Table

Year	Jan	Feb	Mar	Apr	May	Jun	Jul	Aug	Sep	Oct	Nov	Dec	Yr%
2004	-0.1%	-0.4%	0.1%	-1.5%	0.0%	-0.4%	0.5%	0.0%	0.8%	0.0%	0.1%	-0.3%	-1.2%
2005	-0.1%	0.0%	0.1%	0.1%	-1.4%	0.0%	0.0%	0.0%	0.0%	0.0%	-0.1%	0.1%	-1.4%
2006	0.0%	0.0%	1.1%	1.0%	0.5%	0.0%	0.5%	0.0%	0.0%	0.0%	0.2%	0.0%	3.4%
2007	0.5%	0.8%	0.0%	-0.2%	-0.9%	0.0%	0.6%	0.0%	0.6%	1.3%	-0.2%	1.1%	3.7%
2008	0.0%	0.0%	0.3%	0.0%	-1.6%	0.0%	0.0%	0.0%	0.0%	0.0%	0.0%	0.0%	-1.2%
2009	0.0%	0.0%	0.0%	0.0%	1.1%	0.0%	0.0%	0.0%	0.0%	0.0%	0.0%	-0.2%	1.0%
2010	0.0%	0.0%	0.0%	0.9%	-1.0%	0.0%	2.0%	-0.8%	0.0%	0.4%	2.0%	-0.0%	3.4%
2011	0.6%	0.0%	-0.0%	1.2%	0.0%	0.0%	0.0%	0.0%	1.1%	0.2%	0.0%	0.0%	3.1%
2012	0.0%	0.0%	0.0%	0.0%	0.0%	0.0%	0.0%	0.0%	0.3%	0.4%	1.0%	2.9%	4.6%
2013	1.4%	-0.1%	-0.1%	0.5%	0.0%	0.0%	-0.3%	0.0%	-0.5%	0.0%	0.0%	0.0%	0.9%
2014	0.0%	-0.2%	N/A	N/A	N/A	N/A	N/A	N/A	N/A	N/A	N/A	N/A	-0.2%
Avg	0.2%	-0.0%	0.1%	0.2%	-0.3%	-0.0%	0.3%	-0.1%	0.2%	0.2%	0.3%	0.4%	

www.ingramcontent.com/pod-product-compliance
Lightning Source LLC
Chambersburg PA
CBHW082208290526
45794CB00009B/3474